26

FOTO**TORST**

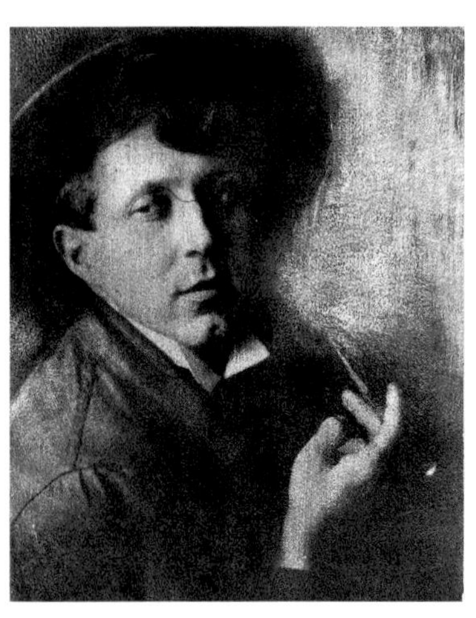

The publisher expresses his sincere thanks to the National Archives, Prague.
The author expresses his sincere thanks to Emilie Benešová, Annalisa Bini, Stanislav Doležal, Anna Fárová,
Sylvie Henguely, Kateřina Klaricová, Dagmar Mazancová, Jan Mlčoch, Eva Poláčková, Hana Ročňáková,
Pavel Scheufler, Kateřina Scheuflerová, Ivana Skálová, Naďa Slezáková, Taťána Součková, Jitka Štětková,
and Dušan Veselý.

Vydáno ve spolupráci s Národním archivem v Praze.

ISBN 978-80-7215-301-5

JOSEF MOUCHA

František **Drtikol**

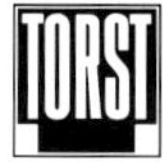

František Drtikol, Portraits

> "The center of the universe is everywhere."[1]
> František Drtikol

The facade of the Drtikol family home on Wenceslas Square in the venerable silver-mining town of Příbram attracts attention owing to a commemorative plaque that says: "In 1907–10, the world-renowned photographer and artist František Drtikol (1883–1961), a native of Příbram, had his first studio in this house."

Drtikol has long been a fixed star on the international art market and his work is much sought after by museum curators the world over. But that was not always the case. It all started when the collector Rudolf Skopec showed works by Drtikol at the 1967 Interkamera trade fair in the U Hybernů building, Prague. Acting on information from Skopec, the art historian Anna Fárová picked up Drtikol's bequest from a farm in the village of Uholičky, central Bohemia, where it had been unceremoniously deposited after having been removed from the collections of the Museum of Decorative Arts, Prague, in 1961. This absurd rejection of Drtikol's donation, which was given to the Museum gradually up to the year 1942 (the third year of the Second World War and the German occupation), has been attributed to the "times when the Museum of Decorative Arts, as part of the National Gallery, lacked a sufficiently defined program of its own."[2]

Fárová transferred Drtikol's photographs from the National Museum of Technology back to the Museum of Decorative Arts in 1970, and organized a substantial exhibition devoted entirely to Drtikol. From that point on she repeatedly returned to his work. In the mid-1980s she wrote the first large monograph about Drtikol, and in 1998 she made a selection of his metaphysical photographs for the Galerie Rudolfinum, Prague. Stanislav Doležal, the initiator of this retrospective, also offered a cross-section of Drtikol's own paintings. At the same time, a portfolio called *František Drtikol Photographer, Painter, Mystic*, was published, which goes beyond the universally acclaimed period of the first three decades of Drtikol's creative photography. The first time the paintings were returned to the public eye in any considerable way was with a traveling exhibition organized by the art historian Hana Rousová in the late 1980s. Called "Line/Color/Form," the exhibition was accompanied by a catalogue.

The cross-sections of Drtikol's work, which were compiled by the historian of photography Vladimír Birgus and were published in Czech and English with a good deal of biographical information in its historical context together with a detailed biographical chronology, established a comprehensive background to subsequent, more specialized articles and volumes about Drtikol's life and works.

Jan Mlčoch, Curator of the Photography Collection at the Museum of Decorative Arts, Prague, remarked in the press release about the exhibition, *Photographs from 1901–14 and the Album From Large and Little Courtyards of Old Prague*: "The artistic legacy of the Czech photographer František Drtikol, comprising several thousand works, has frequently been commemorated in exhibitions. The main focus has always been on the 1920s, when he was dazzling the public with his Art Deco nudes. [...] What has yet to receive greater attention, however, is the period of his sojourn in Munich, his first studio in Příbram, and the early work in Prague, when he made unique works in the spirit of Art Nouveau pictorialism, in the form of 'photograph-paintings'." Somewhat surprisingly, this enumeration of his works can be expanded to include the broadest field of Drtikol's photography, portraits. Though most portfolios have included some samples, this Fototorst volume is the first work to be devoted solely to Drtikol's portraiture.

It was his father who presented Drtikol with the prospect of going into the photography business. The young Drtikol would have chosen to train as a painter at an academy, but that idea met with no support at home. He was the third child in the family of a merchant who was faced with providing dowries for his two daughters.

The future artist spent three unfruitful years as an apprentice with the Příbram photographer Antonín Mattas (1898–1901). In his studio Drtikol found most inspiration in the monthly *Das Atelier des Photographen*. It published works by the portraitists Nicola Perscheid, Rudolph Dührkoop, Hugo Erfurth, Erwin Raupp, the brothers Theodor and Oskar Hofmeister, all of whom, the photographer and theorist Jiří Jeníček writes in the introduction to his interview with Drtikol, were "staunch advocates of the views and ideas formulated at the first international photography exhibition, held at Hamburg, 1893. Back then Wilhelmine Germany saw the pillars of its reactionary, commercial, amateur photography fall to the pickaxes of the progressively oriented new generation of photographers, which proudly proclaimed: 'Photography is art!'"[3]

Dührkoop used to urge his colleagues to think beyond the stereotype of lighting portraits from above and in front, which was determined by the structure of the studio. The building let daylight into the studio through glassed-in parts of the roof and one of the walls. Dührkoop pointed out that the main source of light could come from other directions – horizontally, and even from below. The aim was to supplement time-honored approaches. In the year Drtikol was born, Dührkoop opened a portrait studio in Hamburg and gradually demonstrated in practice that photography could be used to express oneself independently of other fields of the visual arts. He tried to achieve the special quality of distinctly photographic portraits and also the "truth" of the material. From there, the way led to Purism and pure photogeneity.

The periodical *Das Atelier des Photographen* set Drtikol on the road to innovation. The journey began with a period of study abroad. In Munich, the capital of Bavaria, pulsating with the German version of Art Nouveau, Jugendstil, Drtikol trained at the Lehr- und Versuchsanstalt für Photographie, from 1901 to 1903, receiving, for its day, first-class training, including instruction in drawing and art history, as well as chemistry and accounting. In the interview with Jeníček, Drtikol complained that "lighting the head, the figure, and any object at all was still done in the old way back then, using Daguerre's principle: front lighting and overhead lighting."[4] From his first days in Munich Drtikol didn't hesitate to experiment with electric light, and did so with success, even though he had only a small table lamp. At the same time, however, he did not forget to mention that the school made the students study the works of Rembrandt, Dürer, Cranach the Elder, Holbein, van Dyck, and Velázquez, with an emphasis on the portrait. It cultivated, for example, a feeling for the variety of the oval shapes of the face, the variety of looks from the same eyes at different times, and the effect of various positions of the hand or inclinations of the head. Photographers were meant to develop a feel for art by looking at etchings, drawings, and paintings in galleries.

It was in Munich that Drtikol adopted the view that there is in essence only one kind of art, though it has a thousand forms: "Ars una, species mille." His years at the school were followed by travels to gain experience in portrait studios in Karlsruhe, Germany, and Chur, Switzerland, V. E. Grán's studio in Turnov, northern Bohemia, and then with Josef Faix, Prague. His efforts to stay and work in Munich and Paris didn't turn out as he had hoped. During this *wan-derjahr* Drtikol realized he could not work for an employer whose outlook was narrower than what he had just acquired. He had the self-confidence of the con-summate artist: "Just out of school I got a job in Karlsruhe," he wrote years later in his autobiography (which goes up to 1948): "I was there for only a little while, because my boss [Theodor Schuhmann], though a photographer at a princely court, was photographically behind the times."[5]

Drtikol began his career after completing his three-year service in the Austro-Hungarian Army. In 1907, with his father's assistance, he opened up a portrait studio in Příbram. It was located behind the house that the Drtikols had owned since 1880. His alleged inability to make a profit from the studio (which is repeated in one work about Drtikol after another) in this frequently visited place of pilgrimage may have been due to his proclivity for nudes. After all, Drtikol's studio (as I was kindly informed by Hana Ročňáková, curator of the Drtikol Gallery, Příbram) was taken over by Václav Petřík, a portraitist, and in 1948 the business was run by Petřík's son Miroslav.

The permanent exhibition of Drtikol's works is in the residence of the archbishops of Prague, which was built by the first of them, Arnošt z Pardubic, in the fourteenth century. An adviser to Emperor Charles IV, Arnošt z Pardubic owned Příbram and the area around it from 1348 onwards, and helped the town to compete with the Bohemian cult center by giving a statute of the Mother of God to the Svatá Hora chapel. This royal mining town became the center of education in mining engineering. It is dominated by the Castle of Mary, which, in Drtikol's youth, long processions of pilgrims used to climb 365 steps to get to. Pilgrims naturally returned home from here with souvenirs, including photo-graphs. The studio was at the very foot of this sacred acropolis. One entered it across the courtyard of a house on a luxurious part of Wenceslas Square, and it was also illuminated with daylight from above.

On some Art Nouveau postcards the renowned cultural center of Příbram rises up from the radioactive uranium-rich ground of the industrial suburb, across the arc of a steel bridge, and over railroad tracks and the church of Svatá Hora (Holy Mountain). Above the mountain arches a rainbow: in pastel bands it sparkles from a rosy haze to a golden color and through the spectrum from green to azure. This is the symbolism of the astral spheres, Creation, the Lord's covenant with man, and the idea of reconciliation on Judgment Day. In his youth, Drtikol had these continuous reminders before his eyes everyday, and his vivid imagination never ceased to contemplate the elemental forces of Earth and the dimensions of the biblical image "And the Word was made flesh."

Drtikol's days in Příbram, as Fárová has noted, did not mean a period of artistic stagnation: "From these years we have excerpts from literature – poems, fiction, and philosophers' thoughts – written in a beautiful hand, almost like calligraphy. The selection is intelligent, testifying to his being well read, having a breadth of views and literary taste. Drtikol wasted no time. In these years he was educating himself and working on his art, and he made a number of photographs of the mines of Příbram (1908–09), which were published by Štenc, Prague, as postcards at the beginning of his definitive entry to Prague."[6] Drtikol later gave the negatives of the Příbram silver miners, together with the photos of coal mining in Kladno, to the Czech Press Agency. Originally he made them using the manipulatable method of the oil-pigment print. The information they provide is more important than their picturesque quality.[7]

Hardly anything is known about the Příbram portraits. Mlčoch notes in the press release for the exhibition: "few documents have been saved. The exquisite beauty of woman was depicted in a soft haze, whose decorative effect was further underscored with sensitive work employing the chromatic shades of the prints."[8]

With the spread of daguerreotypes in the late 1830s and early 1840s, photography began to represent a special case of the division between industrial production and hand-crafted work. Machine-made goods long tried to satisfy the demand for a decorative form, at least on the surface. Daguerreotypes came to resemble painted miniatures in the way they were mounted and sometimes tinted too. When Drtikol was coming up, however, the medium of photography, owing to the technology involved, lacked the status of being considered unique. That was reserved solely to works blessed by the touch of the artist's hand.

Drtikol was trained in the tradition of European motifs and symbols in art. He was able to intensify this tradition by stylizing his photographs, including the demanded decorativeness of the outer form. "The better, longer-lasting prints, such as carbon, platinum, oil-pigment, and gum-bichromate prints, are to be mounted and framed," writes the photographer V. J. Bufka in his 1913 book on the rudiments of photography, "if possible, to give the impression of being a lithograph or engraving rather than an ordinary photograph. Handmade paper, Japans, and the like are very suitable for that purpose."[9]

Art Nouveau art photography remained dependent on its handmade precursors, even though amateur photography done as a hobby was spreading like an avalanche. In 1888 Kodak produced a camera that was easy to operate and required no tripod. In February 1900 it managed to push down the cost of making one to a dollar, and during the year it sold 100,000 of them. Drtikol, by contrast, always set great store by his artistic talent, which appeared back when he was in primary school. Fárová has drawn attention to one work of his from when he was ten, which she describes as a "small high-quality watercolor landscape from 1893."[10] For Drtikol, then, the pictorial effect was not a superficial matter or mere decorativeness. Rather, it developed from an initial idea to a final artifact.

Although Prague is close to Příbram, it pulsates with a different rhythm. That was probably the chief reason Drtikol moved from his home town to the heart of the Bohemian Kingdom in 1911.

Forward-looking groups of people added further dynamism to the arts in Prague in the 1910s. "Those who didn't catch the main current and turn their backs on the old instruction manuals in time," writes the art historian Josef Kroutvor, "were pushed to the sidelines, to secondary branches of the river. It was not their fault, nor did their work lose its intrinsic value, but things were moving more quickly, in the sense of Rimbaud's demand for absolute modernity."[11] Guests from abroad were invited to the exhibitions of local groups or less-formal associations. The works of Fauvists, Expressionists, Futurists, and Cubists used to appear together in Prague. Nevertheless, in 1910–12 even Sursum, an association of the second generation of Symbolists, was active. Drtikol had much in common with its members, both in the orientation of their works and personally, and he made portraits of the Sursum artists Josef Váchal in 1913, Jan Zrzavý in 1919, and Jan Konůpek in 1928. It is generally true that Symbolism did not constitute a style, but in Bohemia and Moravia, unlike Paris, it left its mark on the content of the work of many artists, including Cubists. "The art of photography," Kroutvor notes, "merged in the Modern period with esoteric science and the mystery of the world as a means of inner self-expression and as a depiction of the external world too."[12]

Drtikol's work is interesting for more than just historical reasons. After all, his creations were returned from oblivion and were able to fascinate new viewers. According to the art historian Petr Wittlich, "the subject matter actually goes beyond the bounds of the medium, which even today presents a challenge to artists' predominant way of thinking."[13]

The more or less unchanging studio in Vodičkova ulice, Prague – which completely disregarded overhead daylight – brought Drtikol commissions, prestige, and space to make his art. In the same street, however, was his greatest competition, the studio of Jan Langhans, which was nicknamed "the photography factory."[14]

Drtikol sought to attract customers with the words: "In an instant, a bright ray of light controlled by the artist's sensibility faithfully creates a unique keepsake for you and your loved ones for ever."[15] The client would take the lift up to the fourth floor of Hulicius House. From the entrance hall, a friendly woman assistant would take him or her to the vestibule of the apartment studio. For a while, that was the job of the photographer Gertruda Fischerová, future wife of Drtikol's colleague Jaroslav Rössler (1902–1990). If one client had just been seated in the studio, which consisted of two communicating rooms, the one who arrived next could leaf through illustrated periodicals or photography magazines. Drtikol used to try and form an opinion of his clients immediately in the fancily furnished reception room decorated with samples of his art. He wanted to see each client before he or she began to act affectedly. As he remarked in the interview with Jeníček: "the portraitist should be acquainted with the sitter. He has to be able to read the different shades of the sitter's psyche from the face, from the movement of the eyes. He has to know whom he has in front of him. He has to give priority to what is essential in the face, considering the unessential to be only distracting, and to tilt the head or body back, forward, or sideways accordingly, while also determining what lighting to use."[16]

The interview Jeníček conducted also reveals what lenses Drtikol used: "I had two portrait lenses: one no-name f = 60 cm with a depth of field, such that when I focused on the nose, then the ears, eyes, and chin were in focus at a distance of three meters. The second was shallower, a Darlot f = 40 cm. Whether working in the 30 × 40 cm format or the *carte-de-visite*, I never went below this focal length."[17]

Drtikol did not let anyone but himself look after famous clients. Consequently, the authorship of the portraits that have been preserved only as negatives and were given to the Czech Press Agency is guaranteed.[18] Drtikol liked to make portraits using the daylight that poured through the bay window and corner windows. A series of thirteen photos of the actress Anna Sedláčková from 1912, in negatives that are now in the National Archives, Prague, preserves the intimacy of the milieu and even the lived-in atmosphere of the studio. Describing Drtikol's new Prague studio, Karel Anderle, the president of the Czech Amateur Photographic Society, called Drtikol's approach to portraiture even before the First World War expressly artistic. Says Anderle: "It shows that in modern portrait photography, artists were moving away from earlier stereotypical studios with overhead light, turning their attention, thanks to the optics and machine-tool industry, to making portraits and printing in natural light, just as each individual person lives in his or her own home, without any tasteless artificial decoration or background. Using a live model Drtikol showed us in practice all possible kinds of lighting, without any reflecting screens, floodlights, and blinds, by merely moving the sitter about the room."[19]

Drtikol gradually developed various ways of lighting. In the Jeníček interview he describes the whole process as follows: "I decided what kind of lighting to use case by case. Above the head of the sitter I placed a 500-watt lamp, and directly below that, behind his back, another 500-watt bulb, so that his body and head were in the space and not stuck on the backdrop. On the left and the right I had two carbon arc Jupiter lamps of 2,000 watts each, and

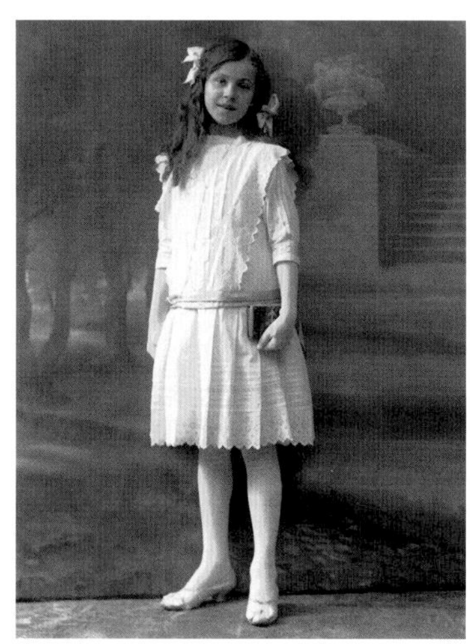

Untitled / Bez názvu, c. 1909
(ČTK FO 00117686)

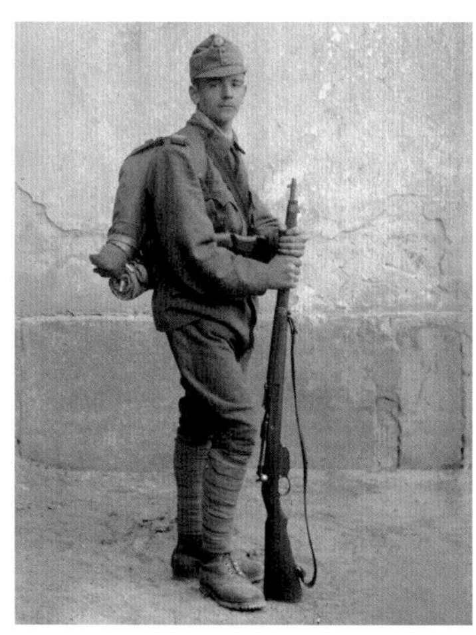

Untitled / Bez názvu, 1914
(ČTK FO 00117679)

sometimes, in addition, a third one to get the maximum glow of the hair. In addition, I also had a carbon arc lamp with a 6,000 watt condenser, which I would set up myself when necessary. With it I achieved a balance, got rid of distracting inessentials. With artificial light and daylight I tried to capture what life had inscribed in the face and figure."[20]

Clearly, Drtikol's interest in expanding the light spectrum was more than just technical. By precise lighting he also changed the definiteness of the portraits. Not only in number but also in meaning, individualized portraits prevailed over the sweetly hazy outlines of the early pictures with mere suggestions of faces.

Drtikol's approach to establishing a set of portraits of important politicians and artists was like that of his ambitious contemporaries and even predecessors.[21] He intended part of the set to be a Czech Parnassus. Most of the series was made in the studio, but he also added to it with works made elsewhere. He photographed the great sculptor Stanislav Sucharda in 1913, for example, at his own photo studio but also where Sucharda happened to be working at the time. The apparently bizarre portraits with chest bared were made as models for other works. Sucharda, for example, commissioned photographs of the actors Eduard Vojan (1913) and Marie Hübnerová (1915), and the sculptor Jan Štursa ordered a portrait of the model Růžena Kopecká (1919).[22]

The modest furniture of the studio was dominated by two comfortable, though unphotogenic armchairs that had served an extraordinarily long time. The pattern of the upholstery went well with the lozenge print of the wallpaper. The basic furnishings included a black screen, which facilitated drawing on the glass plates of the negatives. In the 1910s sometimes blurred exposures (owing to motion), rather than snapshots, became the basis of Drtikol's work, which he creatively continued to build on. The greater the creative manipulation in turning the negative into a print, the greater the gap between bare facts and original artistic interpretation, which appears in the earliest glass negatives. This is particularly striking in the refined *Portrait of Anna Sedláčková* (1913; negative 1912) with the painted-in background like a pre-Giotto landscape. Similarly, in his work in the interwar period Drtikol, using carbon-pigment transfer, added unreal mirror images. Simply the collection of the Museum of Decorative Arts, Prague, provides a clear idea of the diversity of his ways of printing. Nevertheless the printing of portraits directly from negatives is standard. Drtikol himself used it when he made "Bromograf" prints for collectors.

Moreover, he predetermined the way the photographs would be published, for example, in the Fototorst series, by choosing the portraits of eminent people with regard to their potential interest for future generations and in the fact that he gave negatives, rather than prints, to the Czech Press Agency after closing down his business.

The nostalgia for various Revival styles remained at variance with the prerequisites of the mass production of photographs until the approaches connected with arts and crafts became antiquated. The conflict between the periods came to a head with Art Nouveau and the subsequent supplanting of that style. It then became unnecessary to conceal the properties peculiar to the medium of photography. The situation is aptly illustrated in a letter of 9 January 1916 from the writer-priest Jakub Deml, in which he requests Drtikol's colleagues to make a new print from an old negative: "I would ask, however, that you change, or leave out, the background behind the head."[23]

Kroutvor has enriched the description of Drtikol's development by including Modern photography, signs of which "appear even before 1910, followed by the most fertile years, interrupted by the war, and the long period till the mid-1920s, before finally fading away."[24]

"Drtikol a spol." (Drtikol & Co.) continued to operate even during the Great War while the master was away. When he returned to Prague four years later, he was making drawings reflecting the vogue for mythology in art. Because he wanted his business to generate some revenue relatively fast, Drtikol made many prints from old negatives. He was used to labeling the prints not by the year of the negative, but by the year the print itself was made, a system he adhered to throughout his productive years. This has contributed to a further blurring of the boundaries between the individual stages of his art photographs, and makes it difficult to date the portraits with certainty.

Testimony about the unchanging nature of these practices, which were bolstered by the requirements of running a business, is provided by Rössler, Drtikol's onetime employee. He revealed to Martin Stein, a student of photography and his first biographer, the changes Drtikol made to the portrait of Filippo Tommaso Marinetti, founder of the Futurist movement. Stein describes how Rössler got Drtikol's interest with his bromoil print, the *Imaginary Portrait of Ore Tarraco* (1922): "several times he came to look at it. Eventually, he apparently said: 'but make it for me as a carbon print', which is technically impossible. It was as if he wanted to assure himself of the futility of such efforts."[25] In the following year, 1923, however, Drtikol defamiliarized the portrait *Filippo Tommaso Marinetti* in a way that could be reproduced: "He used the same technique as before," Stein notes, "when he added landscape backgrounds and so forth to his nudes. On a glass-plate negative coated with a matt finish he applied paint with a brush."[26] In a letter of 6 February 1987, to the art historian Kateřina Klaricová, who was preparing a book about Drtikol, Rössler provides details of this approach. Drtikol, he writes, was truly surprised at Rössler's *Imaginary Portrait of Ore Tarraco*, and later tried to conjure up a similar effect by, as Rössler says, manipulations "on an 18 × 24 cm plate, covered with a matt lacquer, and, using a spatula, granular black powdered paint. It was impossible in this way to give it a Cubist appearance. The result was blurry streaks in the print. Two other members of M[arinetti]'s entourage also worked in this way. I don't see why he wanted to use this method to suggest a Cubist portrait."[27] An example of a background that was later made Cubist-like is connected with the portrait of the writer and opera singer Marie Calma (née Veselá) (dating from 1922). But the nearly 85-year-old Rössler was bothered more by the attempt to make a nude into a Cubist work by adding Cubist-like elements afterwards. (Reproduced in the present publication, this photo is in the collection of the Museum of Decorative Arts, Prague.) Although Marinetti's portrait remains unknown, Stein managed to find a record of it. On a file card of the Museum, dating from 1942, it appears under no. 62, titled "Set of 81 photographic portraits from the studio of František Drtikol, Prague, from 1910–30." The collection of the Museum of Decorative Arts comprises hundreds of portraits by Drtikol, varying greatly in quality from art works to portraits of children. Stein explains that unlike bromoil, the carbon print, Drtikol's favorite, does not allow the artist to use a brush to make an imaginary portrait. Drtikol therefore considered work done in the carbon-pigment process to be pure photography.

And Rössler, who apprenticed in Drtikol's studio in 1917–20, first had to come to terms with bromoil prints, sometimes doing mostly manual work. It made him famous, however, as a pioneer of Avant-garde abstraction. The Avant-garde sought to break links with symbols and other subject matter that reached back to the very beginning of history. Although they have been ungratefully forgotten, the revolutionary intentions defined the generation that came up not only together with Drtikol, but also against him. Their spokesman in Prague was

Karel Teige. The apostles of the new visions tried to do away with the cultural legacy of bourgeois society, and with their excesses they sought to toll the bell for the unity of the many art forms done in the spirit of Drtikol. "The generation of Modern art was the last for whom the ideals of classical antiquity were still a living example," Kroutvor remarks.[28] It is simply wrong to see the evolutionary creativity of Drtikol as being in the same category as the iconoclasm of the Avant-garde. These were two opposing fronts in their day.

Although after the First World War Drtikol gradually stopped using malleable processes to try and suppress the qualities that make a photograph a photograph, he remained determined to imprint photography with his interpretation of the inner world. That corresponds well to the principles of Modern photography as defined by Kroutvor: "Modern photography thinks in poetic images, which is most strongly manifested in landscapes and symbolic scenes, but rarely appears in portraits. All Modern photographers wanted mainly to be, and in fact were, poets of the picture. Each of them had the perceptive, sensitive soul of the poet, with which he or she tried to come to terms with the modern world and its orientation to technology. [...] Hermeticists and visionaries, the first Modern photographers, poets and thinkers, in search of Modern beauty, they were not only original artists, but were also strong personalities. Their situation was truly unique: they now saw in the Modern way, that is, purely photographically, but were still thinking in the old way. They would not seem sufficiently Modern to the post-war generation, and the Avant-garde was pushing them off the scene. Modern photographers would end as loners, their work would be overlooked or forgotten, and some would return to painting."[29]

Drtikol's early works were in the Art Nouveau style, but he moved on to Modernism once he arrived in Prague. In the interwar period it changed into an individual style, which was later called by the term we know today, Art Deco.

In 1918, with the declaration of the Czechoslovak Republic in late October, Drtikol began again to complete the series of eminent Czechoslovaks. After the world war, like many other artists, he felt called upon to express his attitude to Czech statehood: "[Foreign] Minister [Edvard] Beneš is probably somewhere else altogether in his thoughts, in Geneva or Parliament. He is puffing out his face a bit, unconsciously of course; his eyes are darting back and forth; he's in a hurry. Here one suddenly has to say a word or two to bring him back to reality, and at the same moment take the picture."[30] The period is well described by words written on a bank in the city of Ostrava, Moravia, from 1923: "This building was erected in the fifth year of our new history, in support of work, when the country had cast off the foreign yoke, and faith in a bright future was being carried throughout the land."

All these people with clear features, which Drtikol's spotlight draws out of the twilight of early chiaroscuro and once softly idealized backdrops onto the stage of the new era, are no longer subjects of His Imperial and Royal Majesty, but are, instead, citizens of a new republic. And he devoted himself with equal attention to visitors from abroad. "Drtikol received the highest official recognition with a commission to make a portrait of the Czechoslovak president, Tomáš G. Masaryk," writes Fárová, and then quotes the following from the dust-jacket of a portfolio of five photographs published by Emporium: "Drtikol, whose workshop is the source of these photographs, is one of those few pioneers who for a number of years have been trying to free the portrait photograph from the stereotype. Two signs of good photography are evident in his works: the character of the person is captured in the facial expression and the attitude, and a sound knowledge of technique is visible without the empty mannerisms of the craftsman. Drtikol has made a large series of portraits of some of our leading scholars, artists, and writers. These works have an historic value, but they also bear witness to the keenness of his artistic eye and skill."[31]

Portrait photography from the years of the First Republic is characterized by continuing simplification. Drtikol was probably sincere whenever he declared that retouching a picture of a face was fundamentally wrong, and that in fact he never did it.[32] The collection of negatives in the National Archives demonstrate that occasional manipulation was done to make a decorative or symbolic background. Whereas before the First World War Drtikol executed regular orders straightforwardly, in the 1920s he was even portraying celebrities in simple settings. From 1922 onwards, he no longer did decorative painting-in of photos. Instead of ornaments and added geometric backgrounds he used drapes with floral or abstract prints or sometimes without any pattern at all. More often he showed the simply furnished studio. He didn't completely do away with illusive backgrounds, yet he made sure that using light to shape the space did not compete with the sitter.

The ideal was a well-disposed sitter in simple clothes. As Drtikol writes in his only published article: "If the sitter submits to the will of the photographer, that's half the game right there. The photographer will then best know how to portray the person, whether from the left or the right, *en face*, and so forth. At this point I would add that almost everyone is different from each side. Man really does have two faces: the face has two different appearances, which the profile divides, sometimes a person is good looking from one side, yet that's not typical of him, or vice versa."[33]

Drtikol used ingenious methods to boost the reputation of his company, and with the inventive use of the Art Deco style he earned a reputation as a suitable representative of the Czechoslovak Republic establishment. In 1925 he was asked to lend his photographs to be shown at the Paris Exhibition. The Czechoslovak state made it possible for him to exhibit independently, and he was rightly awarded a prize by the jury in the field of photography and cinematography.

In this period of his photography Drtikol was using geometric decors custom-made for him by the National Theatre workshops. He made attractive use of them in his arrangement of the actress Jarmila Horáková. Her portrait is an example of how his commercial work paralleled photographs Drtikol made strictly for himself. The nearly abstract purism of the late 1920s and early 1930s – the period of photographing carved cutouts – also has its counterpart in designs for decorative lamps.

Meticulous work with the negative remained close to Drtikol's heart even in his abstemious, yet all the more inventive, phase in the second half of the 1920s. "Plain and simple glossy photography is best," Drtikol reassuringly told the people attending his courses in the early 1930s.[34] Yet in addition to that strictly held view of silver bromide material, he also loved carbon prints. In a letter to the Royal Photographic Society, London, he recommended pigment processes as suitable for making photographs for collectors: "Such pictures would certainly fetch a good price, especially when only a specific number of signed prints were made from a single negative, say ten at most."[35]

The large number of preserved portraits from the 1920s is evidence of the popularity of Drtikol's business. As the photographer himself recalled with satisfaction, "The door was never shut."[36] But then came the crash on Wall Street in 1929. Whereas in Paris, the Mecca of Western art at the time, the publisher Antoine Calavas was offering collectors the first of an unfinished series of a limited-edition Drtikol publication, in Prague the Drtikol company was about to go under.

Drtikol's account books would be a superb source of information about the changes in the number of his studio commissions, but their whereabouts is unknown. What is known is that Drtikol's business partner for eight years (1913–21) was Augustin Škarda, a civil engineer who was active in the amateur photography movement. "In 1921, I decided to split with my partner owing to discrepancies in the management of the studio during the war and for three years afterwards," notes Drtikol in his autobiography. None the less, the "a spol." (& Co.) part of the company name did not disappear from the blindstamp of the studio, though Drtikol would no longer ever have any business partner. Evidence of that is in the documents of the Commercial Court, which are in the State Regional Archive, Prague. Thus, for example, the Regional Commercial Court in Prague sent a question to Prague City Hall, 11 May 1929, regarding the Drtikol studio, which suggests that Drtikol would remain the sole owner: "according to the register of companies no change had been made in the company since 1921."

After three dramatic sessions in court, in which he failed to defend himself against Drtikol's accusation, Škarda left the company in late May 1921. For a proper understanding of the suit the following passage of Škarda's statement to the Commercial Court, Prague, from 13 December 1920, is important: "The plaintiff long ago systematically worked on getting rid of me, as soon as he saw that the business had, mainly thanks to me, become a first-rate art business. He used every means to achieve this end; it was mainly the poor state of my nerves, which contributed to his making this old plan a reality. As a result of my intensive involvement [in the amateur photography movement] I began to suffer from bad nerves even before the war, and things got worse during my days in the army. This illness, in connection with the utter impossibility of getting a professional book-keeper during the war, was the sole reason the accounts were not kept by me in the manner listed under Section 28 of the Commercial Code, without, I would emphasize, any fraud having been determined."

Drtikol responded 16 December 1920 with a supplement to his own version of events, which had been presented 29 November of that year. In an attempt to end joint ownership of the business he wrote to the Commercial Court in Prague: "If in case no. C III 69/20 it has been determined by all three courts that my partner had cheated me of the sum of 13,696.53 crowns, it is completely irrelevant that he, the defendant, denies this fact. Concerning the sum of 38,540 crowns, the defendant expressly admitted during the trial at this court on 10 November 1920, that after being sued he withdrew a large sum of money in roughly this amount and that he had no intention of returning it. In any event, the undisputed sum of 13,696 crowns and 53 hellers, which this suit will have to recover from Mr. Škarda is clearly enough to justify a conflict, and there is no need now, if the defendant denies it, to be concerned with this second sum of money."

The court documents reveal that during the long drawn-out court battle Drtikol's wife, Ervina Kupferová, was an employee of Drtikol a spol.

A number of mysteries related to Drtikol remain, however. Apart from the large amount of work from Příbram, Jeníček's interview with Drtikol makes no mention of the first Prague clients. Among them there were apparently some secondary-school graduates, who had their photographs taken to be used in collages of sixteen classes.

How many times must Drtikol have had to make portraits of husbands and wives, particularly newlyweds? In the wartime selection of negatives for the Czech Press Agency, couples were no longer important. Not one of the 39 extant photos of Edvard Beneš and his wife Hana shows them together.

The negatives – usually always of individual people – bear the marks of neglect in the 1940s and 1950s. The National Archives now keeps them in rooms with properly controlled humidity and temperature. The set does not contain fine-art photography, of which there were relatively many works in the portrait genre, and it clearly differs from the commercial photographs. Nor are there any self-portraits of the photographer here.

We don't know which photographs of eminent people Drtikol published on postcards and which he published in various "Bromograf" series. In her book, Klaricová mentions that Drtikol published 24 nudes in the mid-1920s and as many as 120 in the early 1930s. The prints of nudes, bearing the emblem of the Karel Podlipný Bromografia company in Poděbrady on the front, are, however, more often seen on the market than Drtikol's portraits are, partly because they are more attractive to collectors. The question remains how many were made. The only evidence we have is the photographer Josef Ehm's later claim that "most were individually made prints in small numbers of copies, rather than the mass production of 'Bromografs.'"[37]

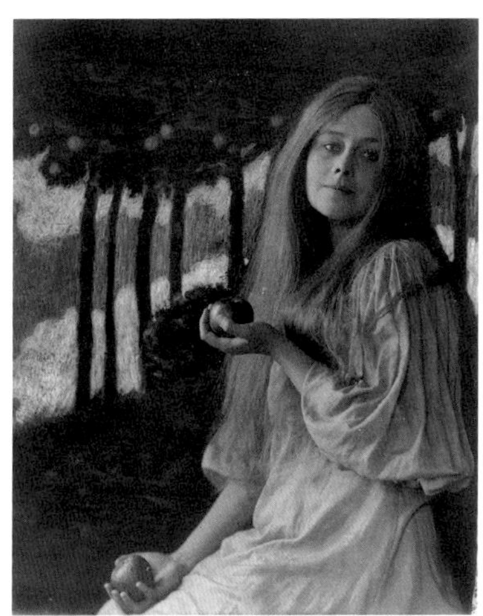

Anna Sedláčková, 1912 (NA 56666)

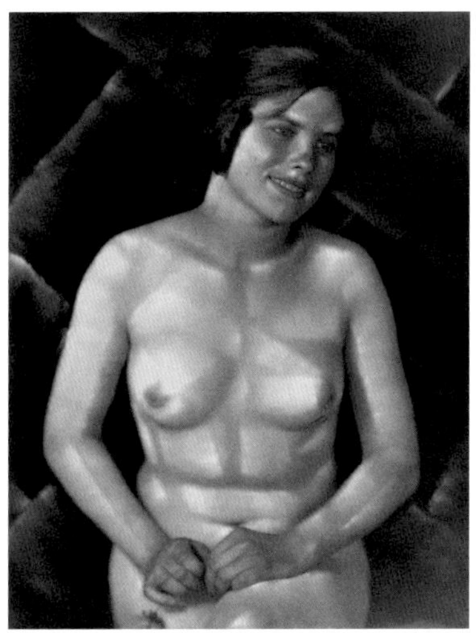

Untitled / Bez názvu, 1922
(GF UPM 39734)

Instead of the officious faces of the Austrian Emperor, which commonly appeared in photographs during Drtikol's youth, faces from silent film generally came into vogue. The actress Anny Ondra (real name, Anny Ondráková), for example, ordered from Drtikol a portfolio of portraits with a wide range of expressions and poses, from sports to glamour. Posing at a little table with a bowl of artificial fruit and skis before a white curtain, however, seemed anachronistic, though it was no secret she was role-playing. When "talkies" were on the rise and form was following function, it was no longer so easy in modern Prague to cling to old ideas of arranging a picture. And although, for example, in his Dresden period (which continued into 1934) the prominent portraitist Hugo Erfurth made due with his "old master style" on the lively arts scene of the small provincial capital, Drtikol needed to modernize his business in the 1930s if he was to remain at the top. But unlike, say, Edward Steichen (four years his senior), Drtikol didn't manage to adapt his studio. The future of photography was in the style of Functionalism and the snapshot, the opposite of studio Art Deco. The would-be aesthetic of the theatre, imitated for technical reasons in the easily controlled lighting of the studio, came to naught. As soon as young photojournalists appeared, taking photographs right in the theatre, the death knell was sounded for theatrical poses in the studio. Drtikol had to have seen this coming. In a 1924 issue of *Gentleman* magazine he even wrote: "As for me, I would portray a person, if possible, while he was at work. Then his face has a natural expression, his soul is embodied in the character of his head. That is what photography is about. Although it is no longer possible to make portraits like that, I would say that it would be good if that man came to the studio as if by chance, in his everyday clothes or the ones he likes to wear best, not all decked out. After all, it is not his outward appearance we want to immortalize!"[38]

But did Drtikol intend to accept the demands of the new times? When the Swiss magazine *Camera* asked him for some photographs, he included in the parcel a letter to Adolf Herz, the editor, dated 30 August 1930, in which he says: "Lots of photographers have got bogged down in the current trend of New Objectivity, and now don't know how to get out of it because they see no new star to follow."[39]

From today's perspective, Drtikol is clearly an artist, whether he was expressing himself with photography, drawing, or painting. For his contemporaries, however, that was not obvious. In his interview with Jeníček, Drtikol summed up his experience as follows: "Visitors came from the east, west, north and south, from overseas, from the whole world. Gold, silver, and bronze medals, first and second prizes, diplomas, recognition, honorary memberships – all of that is now in the archive of the Museum of Decorative Arts, Prague, to which I also donated negatives and pictures. There was also, however, quite a lot of bitterness, simply because in this country the photograph has always been considered a naturalistic transfer print of reality. When I think of all the conversations I had with leading figures on the Czech art scene! Almost everybody, except for the artist and art critic J. R. Marek, tried to persuade me that photography is a peripheral appendage of human cultural activity. Whatever the case, for me photography was always art, never a milch cow [...]."[40]

Of the uninhibited nature of Drtikol's art portraits, the photography historian Antonín Dufek has written appreciatively: "The opportunity to emphasize truth instead of beauty or personal charm provides more room for maneuver. Consequently, the Drtikol portraits that are most original in terms of form are those that depict women."[41]

It's clear, of course, that Drtikol used his extraordinary sensibility also while searching for the true character of his sitter. Jana Šmejkalová, an art historian, writes: "Drtikol's work forms a single, indivisible whole, because the photographic portrait (a visible manifestation), which Drtikol intensively devoted himself to, is the resultant force of the artist's unique inner experience."[42] Her view is well supported by Drtikol's own words: "The artist makes his work with so much love and understanding and puts his soul, his self, into it! That is what determines the work. Whether it is made this or that way [...] is of secondary importance."[43] Or, from his correspondence: "That is also why there are so few real artists, painters, sculptors. Their work is too rational, not emotional. They forget that art is a matter of feeling rather than reason, and that's why it doesn't matter whether I make a picture with a lens or a brush. The important thing is that the result corresponds to what my artistic sensibility tells me."[44]

Drtikol related his maxims to portraiture as well: "I never photographed the person," he recalled in an interview. "I was seeking to give an artistically and psychologically true account of him."[45] He wanted the ordinariness of the titles of the portraits he exhibited also to suggest that he was concerned with fine art: *Portrait* (1926), *Head* (1930), *Profile* (1930). They are written in his own hand on the back of the prints that he once gave to the Museum of Decorative Arts in Prague. The ideas contained in the commissioned photographs and the fine-art photographs overlap, so that Drtikol's words in many ways apply to both branches: "To photograph is to try repeatedly to capture from the external forms of man a suggestion, a hint, of his soul. For me it is a pleasure in itself, not only a means to achieve the photograph. [...] I try to capture the mere form only when I am making photographs of models for a sculptor or painter. To imbue the portrait with character – that is to say, understanding the character of the sitter – is their [the sculptor's and painter's] business. Otherwise I always try to make the thing in the face, in the figure – the immaterial, the character – material. [...] On principle, I use the least amount of props, decor, or aids to evoke mood. Objects that have the power to evoke because they are connected to a certain idea, because they are traditional symbols, lead to banal, hackneyed compositions. I myself have had bad experience, say, using a skull. [...] I might look, for example, only at a stone or the folds of fabric in various kinds of lighting, and before my eyes these things change under the subtle touch of Light. [...] Looking is in itself an art."[46]

Drtikol believed that every being carried the Divine Spark within itself.[47] And, if possible, he sought to help it to shine through. None the less, for practical reasons he could not turn down commissions asking for a superficial representation conforming to current tastes. As he said: "If the portrait is really meant to be only what one appears to be, you will understand what a hard job the photographer has to make something that not only you like but that he likes too."[48]

Unsurprisingly, in Drtikol's portraits a vertical orientation clearly predominates. The compositions are based on the alternation of half-length and full-length figures. Sometimes they are based on attributes, such as instruments for musicians, books for writers, or mere hints of the theatre for actors or ballet dancers. It is quite well known how Drtikol used to evoke the impression of movement in the static figures of his nudes: he achieved dynamics by having his models strike relaxed poses, and by composing along the diagonal. From his several dance series one senses the pulse of collaboration between the photographer and the ballet dancers as well as the mutual trust in the successful results of their own contributions. The changes in the arrangements of repeated portraits of the same sitter reveal a search for the most apposite expression of the sitter's inner self. Lighting the features and using a psychological approach to communicate with the sitters resulted, as Wittlich notes, in "a remarkable series of portraits of faces known and unknown, always capturing with great sensitivity the intellectual potential of the 1910s and 1920s."[49]

Some clients occasionally came back, and so their aging is observable from one portrait to the next. A good example is the art historian V. V. Štech. He, by the way, was known for considering photography mere documentation, denying it any artistic merit. Otakar Hostinský, Professor of Aesthetics at Prague, whose view of the photographic portrait was formed in the days of decorative Art Nouveau, though in a progressive spirit, said: "Using optics and chemistry, photography mercilessly records and irrevocably freezes everything and anything that is taking place during exposure. [...] If the moments are rare when man's nature fully appears in his face, like in a mirror, they are even rarer in the photographer's studio, and yet when such a fortuitous moment occurs, one can expect a truly successful photographic portrait."[50]

Three decades later, the art historian Hana Volavková claimed that artists had let the portrait genre go to seed: "The efforts to create new style exhausted the creative people of our century, leaving portraiture, where direct contact with the client plays such an important role, to artists who were rarely concerned with the present day and its spirit. Most of the portraits we find in families today, we can with a clear conscience categorize as conventional art."[51] She does not mention photography in the article, talking instead about painters, yet it is photography that provided a way out of the dilemma. "How can modern man have his portrait made in a form so old-fashioned, so out of date?" she asks.

"How can one let oneself be immortalized in a picture or a sculpture that already seems bizarre because of its insincerity and artificiality."[52]

Back when he was still running his business Drtikol wrote: "When photographing a hundred people some of them are bound to interest the photographer,"[53] thus admitting that working on commission had more than just its financial benefits. Although the preserved set of portraits also contains descriptive shots, Drtikol's efforts to avoid stereotypes were frequently successful. Decades later, however, his work remained largely hidden, not fully appreciated, yet it is thanks only to anonymous prints of Drtikol's photos that we know many faces of the elite of interwar Czechoslovakia.

Even though nudes, frowned upon by the Communist régime, do not predominate in his photography, the Drtikol portraits were wrongfully neglected in the past. After all, he was a photographer with a distinctive style, who was internationally recognized, and had been present at the birth of Czech art photography. As Fárová remarks: "The relationship between a painterly conception and features peculiar to photography, together with special subject matter, an emphasis on the relationship between Eros and Thanatos, and the myth of Woman, were something unique, opening up roads for this recent medium in our country and, as I see it today, throughout the world."[54]

His photographic nudes have, however, remained Drtikol's most sought-after works. These include in particular his carbon prints from the second half of the 1920s. His art work, however, continued on long after he himself had vanished from the public eye. Yet, adoration of the artistic potential of the medium of photography often ignores the fact that it was its commercial use, which led photographers in the nineteenth and twentieth centuries to take the social initiative in competition with fine artists. Ultimately, even the negatives of portraits by Drtikol have survived thanks to the information they contain rather than owing to the long forgotten artist.

Drtikol's work itself is based on harmony. It expresses the unity of mind and body, bridging the gulf between idealism and materialism. This volume of Drtikol portraits could have easily opened by saying that each of the published pictures links the high culture of form with the full expression of the Spirit, or, in Drtikol's own words, "If I admit that God is omnipresent, then he is closest to me within me, in myself."[55]

Notes

1   František Drtikol, *Duchovní cesta*, Prague: Svět, 2004, p. 36.

2   Anna Fárová, *Fotograf František Drtikol (tvorba z let 1903–35)*, Prague: Museum of Decorative Arts, 1972, p. 10. For more about Fárová and Drtikol, see Josef Moucha, "Dvě otázky pro Annu Fárovou," *Ateliér* 10 (1997), no. 24, p. 3.

3   Jiří Jeníček, "Na besedě u Františka Drtikola," *Československá fotografie* 6 (1955) no. 2, pp. 16–17.

4   Ibid, p. 17. Bohumil Markl noted: "since a properly lit portrait is inconceivable without diffused light, we must, if the roof of the studio is too short, turn to artificial means to get it." B. Markl, "Praktické upotřebení světla a stínu v atelieru," *Fotografický obzor* 8 (1900), no. 10, p. 152.

5   A copy of the undated memoirs is deposited in the Museum of Decorative Arts, Prague.

6   Fárová, *Fotograf František Drtikol (tvorba z let 1903–35)*, p. 19.

7   Drtikol expresses the artistic taste of the *Belle Époque* in an undated, untitled, 67-page essay on the gum-bichromate process, the draft versions of which are deposited in the Museum of Decorative Arts, Prague. "Retouching, particularly portraits," Drtikol writes," should be done as little as possible, and one should always think ahead whether one wants to draw out a certain stroke or completely retouch an area, whether that might change the whole characterization of a person. The lens, however, sees too many details. Wrinkles or spots, which have no influence on the appearance, can be retouched." Judging from the format of the pages this could be part of the large unpublished series "Nauky o fotografii" (On Photography), which is mentioned in Drtikol's point-form biography under the year 1918.

8   Jan Mlčoch, *Fotografie z let 1901–1914 a album Z dvorů a dvorečků staré Prahy*, Prague: Museum of Decorative Arts and Kant, 1999, pp. 17–18; by the same publisher in English as *Frantisek Drtikol: Photographs from the Period Between 1901–1914 and the Album from Large and Little Courtyards of Old Prague* and French *Frantisek Drtikol: Photographies des années 1901–1914 et L'Album Les cours et courettes du vieux Prague.*

9   Vladimír Jindřich Bufka, *Katechismus fotografie. Úvod do fotografie pro fotografy amateury*, Prague: Hejda & Tučck, 1913, p. 165.

10   Fárová, *Fotograf František Drtikol (tvorba z let 1903–35)*, p. 34. For illustrations, see Mlčoch, *František Drtikol*, p. 11.

11   Josef Kroutvor, *Česká fotografická moderna*, Prague: Museum of Decorative Arts, 1989, no page numbers.

12   Josef Kroutvor, "Česká fotografická moderna," *Revue Fotografie* 34 (1990), no. 3, p. 70.

13   Petr Wittlich, "Drtikolova mystika," *Ateliér* 11 (1998), no. 9, p. 16.

14   Pavel Scheufler, *Stará Praha Jana Langhanse*, Prague: Baset, 2000, p. 19; by the same publisher in German, *Das alte Prag des Jan Lanhans*, and English, *Old Prague from Jan Langhans.*

15   František Drtikol, "Moderní umělecká fotografie," Prague, advertising leaflet of Drtikol's company, (n.d.).

16   Jeníček, "Na besedě u Františka Drtikola," p. 18.

17   Ibid.

18   See also Martin Stein, "Jaroslav Rössler," Dissertation, the Photography Department, Academy of Performing Arts in Prague, 1984, pp. 10, 12.

19   K. A. (Karel Anderle), "Klub návštěvou v atelieru Drtikolově," *Fotografický obzor* 20 (1912), no. 3, pp. 71–72.

20   Jeníček, "Na besedě u Františka Drtikola," p. 18.

21   See also Pavel Scheufler, *Jindřich Eckert*, Prague: Odeon, 1985; P. Scheufler, *Jan Langhans*, trans. Derek Paton, Prague: Torst, 2005; Libor Jůn, "Galerie vynikajících osobností Jindřicha Vaňka," *Historická fotografie* 4 (2004), no. 1, pp. 5–13.

22   See also Vít Vlnas, *Za zrcadlem: Čeští sochaři ve fotografiích a dokumentech*, Prague: National Gallery, 1993.

23   From Deml's letter, deposited in the Drtikol Papers, Museum of Decorative Arts, Prague.

24   Josef Kroutvor, "Fotograf se jménem antického boha," *Revolver Revue* (1993), no. 23, p. 147. Anton Josef Trčka, in Vienna, whom Kroutvor's article is mainly about, is a good example of one of the even younger photographers who in the 1920s still adhered to the view that was widespread before the First World War. For more on this, see Monika Faber, *Anton Josef Trčka 1893–1940*, Vienna: Christian Brandstätter, 1999.

25   Stein, "Jaroslav Rössler," p. 17.

26   Ibid.

27   From Rössler's letter to Kateřina Klaricová, 6 February 1987. In the private archives of Kateřina Klaricová.

28   Kroutvor, "Česká fotografická moderna," p. 69.

29   Kroutvor, *Česká fotografická moderna*.

30   František Drtikol, "Muž u fotografa," *Bulletin MG* (1992), no. 48, p. 96.

31   Quoted after Fárová, *Fotograf František Drtikol (tvorba z let 1903–35)*, p. 25.

32   Drtikol, "Muž u fotografa," pp. 95–96. See also Jeníček, "Na besedě u Františka Drtikola," p. 18.

33   Drtikol, "Muž u fotografa," pp. 95–96. See also Jiří David, *Skryté podoby*, Prague: Kant, 1995.

34   František Drtikol, *Oči široce otevřené*, Prague: Svět 2002, p. 67; in English, by the same publisher, as *Eyes Wide Open*.

35   An undated Czech draft of the correspondence is deposited in the Museum of Decorative Arts, Prague. The translation of another letter into English (also undated and in the Museum) reveals some prices: Drtikol was asking 60 crowns for a silver-bromide print and 260 crowns for a carbon print. His nudes were often made on 30 × 24 cm glass plates, and the prints are usually 1:1. Most of the commissioned portraits are contact prints on small-format silver-bromide paper, and mounted on card with the "Drtikol a spol." blindstamp.

36   Jeníček, "Na besedě u Františka Drtikola," no. 18.

37   Vladimír Birgus, *Fotograf František Drtikol*, Prague: Prostor, 1994, p. 34; Ibid, *František Drtikol*, Prague, Kant, 2000, p. 33. To get an idea of prices, for example, the "Bromograf" print *Salome* from the 1920s was sold at auction on 10 December 2004 for 35,200 Czech crowns (about US $1,574). See, "Antikvariát Dr. Prošek," *Art & Antiques* 4 (2005), January, p. 24.

38   Drtikol, "Muž u fotografa," p. 96.

39   A carbon copy of the German manuscript is deposited in the Museum of Decorative Arts, Prague.

40   Jeníček, "Na besedě u Františka Drtikola," p. 18.

41   Antonín Dufek, "Drtikolův neznámý text," *Bulletin MG* (1992), no. 48, p. 95.

42   Jana Šmejkalová, "Hamletovský odkaz Františka Drtikola," *Antique* 5 (1998), no. 5, p. 44.

43   Drtikol, *Duchovní cesta*, p. 289.

44   Quoted after the Czech drafts of Drtikol's inaccessible correspondence with the Royal Photographic Society, London. On the back of the third sheet of the typescript, which is deposited in

the Museum of Decorative Arts, Prague, is the title "O fotografii" (On Photography) written by
the artist in red pencil.

45 Jeníček, "Na besedě u Františka Drtikola," p. 18.

46 Drtikol, *Oči široce otevřené*, pp. 39, 19, 47, 61, 69.

47 See Karel Funk, *Mystik a učitel František Drtikol*, Prague: GEMMA89, 1993, p. 214.

48 Drtikol, "Muž u fotografa," p. 96. In the same article he differentiated between the art of the portrait
and "taking photographs in a mask": he accepted theatricality from actors made up for their
roles on stage, but otherwise he tried to capture the psychological traits of the sitter, which
meant getting under the masks that were being presented for admiration: "It is very difficult
to portray actors. I think it's hard for them not to perform. They have a thousand masks.
If they stand before the camera, it's as if they're already standing before an audience. They're
immediately playing the part of something or someone."

49 Wittlich, "Drtikolova mystika."

50 Otakar Hostinský, "Fotografie a malířství," *Pražská lidová revue* 1 (1905), no. 10, pp. 258–59.

51 Hana Volavková, "Moderní podobizna," *Eva* 8 (1935), no. 1, p. 14.

52 Ibid.

53 Drtikol, *Oči široce otevřené*, p. 16.

54 Anna Fárová, "František Drtikol: Magie imaginativního plození," *Výtvarné umění*, 1992, no. 2, p. 28.

55 Drtikol, *Duchovní cesta*, p. 201.

Portrétista František Drtikol

„Střed vesmíru je všude.“
František Drtikol[1]

Průčelí Drtikolova rodného domu na Václavském náměstí v starobylé stříbronosné Příbrami poutá pozornost pamětní deskou: *„V tomto domě měl v letech 1907–10 svůj první ateliér příbramský rodák František Drtikol (1883–1961), světoznámý fotograf a výtvarník.“*

František Drtikol je dnes stálicí globálního obchodu s uměním a sběratelskou tužbou kurátorů českých i zahraničních muzeí. Nebylo tomu tak vždy. Vývoj k dnešnímu stavu nasměroval sběratel Rudolf Skopec, když fotografa roku 1967 při veletrhu Interkamera připomněl výstavou v pražském paláci U Hybernů. Jím zorientovaná historička umění Anna Fárová vyzvedla Drtikolův odkaz z degradujícího uložení v hospodářské usedlosti v Uholičkách, kde se ocitl po vyřazení ze sbírky Uměleckoprůmyslového musea v Praze (1961). Toto absurdní zřeknutí se autorových darů, završených ve válečném ohrožení roku 1942, jde na vrub *„době, kdy Uměleckoprůmyslové museum jako součást Národní galerie nemělo dostatečně specifikovaný vlastní program“*.[2]

Anna Fárová převedla Drtikolovy fotografie z Národního technického muzea zpět do fondu Uměleckoprůmyslového musea v Praze (1970) a připravila zásadní monografickou výstavu. Přirozeně se k Drtikolovi nepřestala vracet. V polovině 80. let napsala jeho první velkou monografii a roku 1998 vybrala pro Galerii Rudolfinum autorovy metafyzické fotografie. Stanislav Doležal, iniciátor této výstavní akce, nabídl reprezentativní průřez Drtikolovou tvorbou malířskou. Zároveň vyšlo album *František Drtikol fotograf, malíř, mystik* rozšiřující obecně ceněné období prvních tří desetiletí Drtikolovy fotografické kreativity. Malby poprvé významněji rehabilitovala koncem 80. let historička umění Hana Rousová putovní výstavou *Linie / barva / tvar* a jejím katalogem.

Drtikolovské průřezy v anglickém i českém jazyce s obsáhlým propracováním životopisu v dobových souvislostech a s podrobným výčtem dostupných dat, jež vydal Vladimír Birgus, jsou všeobjímajícím zázemím specializovanějších drtikolovských studií a edic.

Kurátor fotografické sbírky Uměleckoprůmyslového musea v Praze Jan Mlčoch poznamenal v tiskovém komuniké *Fotografie z let 1901–1914 a album*

Z dvorů a dvorečků staré Prahy: „Umělecký odkaz českého fotografa Františka Drtikola, čítající několik tisíc prací, byl již mnohokrát výstavně připomenut. Hlavní zájem se vždy soustředil na období 20. let, kdy autor oslňoval publikum svými akty, komponovanými ve stylu art deco. [...] Co však dosud nebylo předmětem hlubšího zájmu, je období autorova mnichovského pobytu, prvního příbramského ateliéru a počátky pražské praxe, kdy vznikala jedinečná díla v duchu secesního piktorialismu, mající formu tzv. ‚obrazové fotografie‘.“ Tento výčet lze rozšířit i o nejširší pole Drtikolovy působnosti: portrétní tvorba se kupodivu dosud nestala námětem monografické publikace, byť ve většině alb došlo alespoň na její ukázky.

Perspektivu fotografické živnosti vytyčil Františku Drtikolovi otec. Mladík by byl volil studia malířství na akademii. K tomu však nenašel oporu. Vyrůstal jako třetí dítě v kupecké rodině, střádající na dvě věna.

Budoucí umělec strávil u příbramského fotografa Antonína Mattase tři nepříznivá učednická léta (1898–1901). V jeho ateliéru se inspiroval nanejvýš měsíčníkem *Das Atelier des Photographen*, zveřejňujícím práce portrétistů „*Nicoly Persheida* [sic], *M. R. Dührkoopa, Hugo Erfurtha, Erwina Rauppa, bratří Hofmeisterů, kteří všichni jsou rozhodnými zastánci názorů a myšlenek, formulovaných roku 1893 první mezinárodní fotografickou výstavou v Hamburku. Tehdy vilémovské Německo vidí,*“ píše Jiří Jeníček, „*jak se sloupy jeho zpátečnické, živnostenské i amatérské fotografie kácejí pod krumpáči nastupující, pokrokově orientované fotografické generace, jež hrdě prohlašuje: fotografie je umění!*“[3] Fotograf Rudolph Dührkoop nabádal kolegy, aby neuvažovali jen v šabloně osvětlení portrétů shora a zepředu, dané konstrukcí ateliérů. Ta přiváděla denní světlo do pracovní místnosti prosklenými partiemi stropu a jedné ze stěn. Dührkoop připomínal možnosti jiných směrů hlavního světla – horizontální, ale třeba i spodní. Cílem bylo obohacení starodávných schémat. V roce Drtikolova narození si Rudolph Dührkoop otevřel portrétní ateliér v Hamburku a svou praxí postupně dokazoval, že fotografie nemusí být ve svém výrazu odkázaná na ostatní výtvarné obory. Naopak, snažil se dosáhnout fotografičnosti podobizen a takzvané pravdy materiálu. Odtud vedla cesta k purismu a k ryzí fotogenii.

List *Das Atelier des Photographen* navedl Drtikola na dráhu inovací. Začala zahraničním studiem. V secesí pulzující bavorské metropoli Mnichově se školil na Učebním a výzkumném ústavu pro fotografii (1901–1903). Dosáhl na fotografa své doby špičkového vzdělání, neošizeného o průpravu v kreslení, v dějinách umění, ale také třeba v chemii a v účetnictví. V citovaném rozhovoru si Drtikol posteskl, že *„osvětlení hlavy, postavy a vůbec jakéhokoli předmětu se tehdy ještě dělalo po staru, podle Daguerrovy zásady: přední, horní světlo“*.[4] Sám se hned v Mnichově nerozpakoval úspěšně experimentovat s elektrickým světlem, i když musel používat malé stolní lampy. Ale zároveň neopomněl říci, že škola předváděla posluchačům – v důrazu na portrét – Rembrandta, Dürera, Lucase Cranacha staršího, Holbeina, van Dycka, Velázqueze. Pěstovala cit pro rozmanitost oválných tvarů tváře, rozdílnost pohledu týchž očí, různé polohy rukou či sklonů hlavy… Rozvoj uměleckého cítění mělo fotografům přinést pozorování rytin, kreseb a maleb v obrazárnách.

V Mnichově si fotograf přisvojil hledisko, že umění je v jádru jediné, byť podob má na tisíc: *„Ars una, species mille.“* Školu následovaly cesty za praxí do portrétních studií v německém Karlsruhe a švýcarském Churu, do turnovského ateliéru V. E. Grán a poté k pražské firmě Josefa Faixe. Z úsilí o mnichovský či pařížský pobyt sešlo. Vandrovní rok Drtikolovi ukázal, že by nemohl pracovat pro zaměstnavatele s menším rozhledem, než jakého sám nabyl. Cítil sebevědomí svrchovaného umělce: *„Ze školy jsem dostal místo v Karlsruhe,“* napíše po letech v autobiografii, dotažené do roku 1948: *„Tam jsem byl velice krátce, protože můj pan šéf, vzdor tomu, že byl dvorní fotograf, byl fotografický zaostalec.“*[5]

Vlastní kariéru zahájil František Drtikol po ukončení tříleté služby v rakousko-uherské armádě, když roku 1907 s otcovou pomocí otevřel portrétní studio v Příbrami. Bylo umístěno za domem, který Drtikolovi vlastnili od roku 1880. O případnou nerentabilitu ateliéru, tradovanou drtikolovskou literaturou, se ve frekventovaném poutním místě mohly přičinit umělcovy sklony k tvorbě aktů. Vždyť Drtikolovo studio převzal portrétista Václav Petřík (a ještě v roce 1948 tu provozoval živnost jeho syn Miroslav; za upozornění děkuji Haně Ročňákové, kurátorce Galerie Františka Drtikola v Příbrami).

Stálá expozice Drtikolových prací je umístěna v středověké rezidenci pražských arcibiskupů, vystavěné prvním z nich, důvěrným rádcem císaře Karla IV.: arcibiskup Arnošt z Pardubic od roku 1348 Příbram s okolím vlastnil a napomohl jí v konkurenci s českými kultovními okrsky tím, že svatohorské kapli věnoval sochu Bohorodičky. Podbrdským Athénám, jak se časem královskému hornímu městu a centru báňské vzdělanosti říkalo, dominuje Mariánský hrad. K němu za Drtikolova mládí stoupala po 365 schodech početná procesí. Z pouti se přirozeně vozívaly památky včetně upomínkových fotografií; ateliér ostatně vznikl přímo na úpatí posvátné akropole. Nechybělo mu horní denní světlo a vcházelo se do něj zahradou Drtikolova rodného domu s luxusní příslušností k Václavskému náměstí.

Na secesních pohlednicích se slavné kulturní ohnisko zdvihá z radioaktivního podloží průmyslového předměstí přes oblouk ocelového mostu nad železniční tratí a děkanský kostel k Svaté Hoře. Nad ní se klene duha: v pastelových pásmech pableskuje od růžového oparu do zlatava a škálou zelení k blankytu. Symbolika astrálních sfér, stvoření, Boží smlouvy s lidstvem a představy smíření u Posledního soudu… Drtikol měl v jinošství tato absolutní mementa denně na očích a fantazie jeho zralosti pak nepřestávala ohledávat prasíly Země i horizonty obratu *A Slovo se stalo tělem* (Jan 1.14).

Příbramské období neznamenalo podle Anny Fárové uměleckou stagnaci: „*Z těchto let se zachovaly až kaligraficky krásně psané výpisky z literatury – básně, próza a myšlenky filosofů. Výběr je inteligentní a svědčí o sečtělosti, rozhledu a literárním vkusu. Drtikol neztrácí čas. V těchto letech pracuje na sobě a vzniká řada fotografických obrazů z příbramských dolů (1908–09), které vydal u pražského Štence jako dopisnice začátkem svého definitivního nástupu do Prahy.*“[6] Spolu se záběry kladenské kamenouhelné těžby předá fotograf později negativy příbramských kovkopů České tiskové kanceláři. Původně je zpracoval tvárným olejotiskem. Nad malebností ale i tak převažovala informativní složka.[7]

O podobiznách z Příbrami se mnoho neví. V pražském Uměleckoprůmyslovém museu se „*zachovalo nemnoho dokladů. Jemná ženská krása byla zpodobňována v křehkém světelném oparu, jehož dekorativní účinek byl ještě podtržen citlivou prací s barevnými odstíny pozitivů.*“[8]

Fotografie představovala – hned s rozšířením daguerrotypie na přelomu 30. a 40. let 19. století – zvláštní případ roztržky mezi rukodělnými disciplínami řemesel či umění a průmyslovou výrobou. Mechanicky vznikající zboží se dlouho snažilo vyhovět zvykovým nárokům zdobnou úpravou, tedy alespoň navenek. Daguerrotypii přibližovaly malovaným miniaturám adjustace a případně i kolorování. V době Drtikolova nástupu ale médium fotografie postrádalo technologicky daný status jedinečnosti. Ten byl přiznáván výhradně dílům posvěceným dotykem z uměleckých pozic vedené ruky.

František Drtikol byl vyškolen v motivické i symbolické tradici klasicky orientovanými vyznavači umění. A dokázal ji umocňovat stylizací snímku včetně žádané zdobnosti vnější úpravy: „*Lepší a trvanlivější kopie, jako tisky pigmentové, platinové, oleje- i gumotisky adjustujeme pokud možno tak, aby činily dojem spíše práce grafické, nežli obyčejné fotografie. K tomu hodí se velmi dobře ruční papíry, japany atd.“*[9]

Secesní umělecká fotografie zůstávala závislá na rukodělných předobrazech, byť se lavinovitě šířilo laické fotografování, provozované coby povyražení. Roku 1888 byl zkonstruován jednoduše ovladatelný přístroj značky Kodak, nevyžadující stativ. V únoru 1900 se podařilo stlačit pořizovací náklady na jediný dolar a během roku prodat aparátů sto tisíc. František Drtikol si naproti tomu vždy zakládal na výtvarném talentu, jejž projevil hned ve školních škamnách. Anna Fárová upozornila na dětskou práci, *„kvalitní malý krajinný akvarel z roku 1893“*.[10] Piktoriální efekt tedy nebyl Drtikolovi pouhou povrchovou či dekorativní záležitostí, ale prorůstal od výchozí představy ke konečnému artefaktu.

Praha sice leží od Příbrami nedaleko, pulzuje však v docela jiném rytmu. To byl nejspíš rozhodující důvod, proč František Drtikol léta Páně 1911 přesídlil z rodného města do srdce Českého království.

Progresívní kruhy dodávaly kultuře 10. let v hlavním městě dynamiku. *„Ti, kteří se nechytí hlavního proudu a nezřeknou se včas literatury, jsou odsunuti stranou do vedlejších ramen. Není to ani jejich chyba, ani dílo neztrácí na vnitřní ceně, ale vývoj se zrychluje ve smyslu Rimbaudova požadavku absolutní modernosti.“*[11] K přehlídkám domácích skupin či volnějších sdružení byli zváni zahraniční hosté, rendez-vous mívala v Praze díla fauvistů, expresionistů, futuristů, kubistů… Nicméně v letech 1910–12 v ní působil i spolek druhé symbolistní generace *Sursum*, s jehož členy se Drtikol sblížil jednak zaměřením tvorby, jednak osobně: Josefa Váchala zvěčnil roku 1913, Jana Zrzavého 1919, Jana Konůpka 1928. Obecně platí, že symbolismus nevytvořil sloh. Leč v Čechách a na Moravě – oproti Paříži – obsahově poznamenal kdekoho včetně kubistů. *„Umění fotografie splynulo ve fotografické moderně s esoterickou vědou a tajemstvím světla jako prostředkem niterného sebevyjádření a zároveň zobrazením vnějšího světa.“*[12]

Jde o tvorbu zajímavou nejen historicky: vždyť Drtikolovy kreace se dočkaly revitalizace a dokázaly si podmanit nové diváky. *„Námětem je vlastně obsahová extenze, překročení hranic média, což také dnes představuje určitou výzvu vládnoucí umělecké mentalitě.“*[13]

Poměrně stabilně zařízený ateliér v pražské Vodičkově třídě – zcela opomíjející horní denní světlo – přinášel Drtikolovi zakázky, prestiž i prostor k volné umělecké práci. Ve stejné ulici ale sídlila vůbec největší konkurence, firma Jana Langhanse, jež si vysloužila přízvisko *„továrna na fotografie“*.[14]

František Drtikol lákal zákazníky slovy: „*Jasný paprsek světla řízený citem umělce věrně vytvoří v okamžiku jedinečnou upomínku Vám i Vašim milým pro památku navždy.*"[15] Zájemce vyvezla do čtvrtého podlaží Huliciova paláce zdviž. Z domovní chodby ho do předsíně bytového ateliéru uvedla sympatická asistentka. Svého času to byla fotografka Gertruda Fischerová, budoucí choť kolegy Jaroslava Rösslera. Byl-li někdo právě aranžován ve studiu zřízeném z dvou propojených pokojů, mohl příchozí listovat fotografickými a společenskými časopisy. Drtikol se pokoušel návštěvy vyhodnotit hned v efektně zařízené přijímací kanceláři, zdobené ukázkami jeho umění. Šlo mu o to, aby každého uviděl dříve, než se začal chovat strojeně: „*portretista se má v portretované osobě vyznat. Z tváře, pohybu očí má vyčíst psychickou tonalitu portretované osoby a vědět, koho má před sebou. Má dát přednost tomu, co je ve tváři podstatné, nepodstatné má považovat za rušivou složku a podle toho sklonit, naklonit hlavu, tělo a určit způsoby osvětlení.*"[16]

Z Jeníčkova vzpomínkového rozhovoru se dá vyčíst také Drtikolova optika: „*Měl jsem dva portrétní objektivy: jeden bez označení o f = 60 cm s takovou hloubkou ostrosti, že když jsem zaostřil na nos, byly ostré uši, oči, brada už ze vzdálenosti tří metrů. Druhý byl měkkýš, Darlote o f = 40 centimetrů. Pod tuhle ohniskovou vzdálenost jsem nikdy nešel, ať jsem pracoval na rozměrech 30 × 40 cm nebo na visitkový formát.*"[17]

Osobnosti nenechával Drtikol obsloužit nikým jiným. Tak je pamětnicky zaručeno autorství portrétů, které se dochovaly pouze v negativech postoupených České tiskové kanceláři.[18] Drtikol rád portrétoval při denním světle, proudícím arkýřem a okny nároží. Série třinácti záběrů herečky Anny Sedláčkové – v negativech z roku 1912 dnes deponovaných Národním archivem – uchovala intimitu prostředí, ba zabydlenost ateliéru. Jakožto výslovně umělecký přístup k žánru podobizny označil Drtikolovu konfesi již před první světovou válkou starosta Českého klubu fotografů amatérů Karel Anderle. V reportáži o fotografově novém pražském působišti převyprávěl autorův přístup k věci: „*Poukazuje k tomu, že v moderní portrétní fotografii uchýlili se umělci od dřívějších stereotypních ateliérů s vrchním světlem, že obrátili svou pozornost dík průmyslu optickému a strojovému na portrétování a reprodukování při osvětlení přirozeném, tak jak každý jednotlivec žije ve své domácnosti, bez jakýchkoli umělých nevkusných dekorací a pozadí. Ukázal nám prakticky na živém modelu veškerá možná osvětlení, bez jakýchkoli odstiňovačů, reflektorů a gardin, pouhým přemísťováním portrétované osoby v saloně.*"[19]

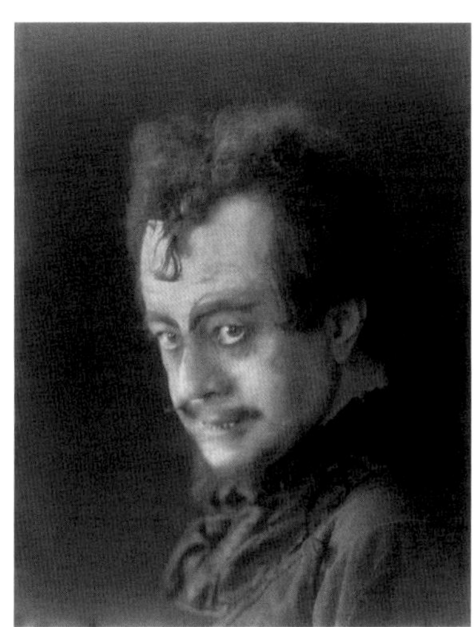

Václav Kliment, 1913 (NA 55672)

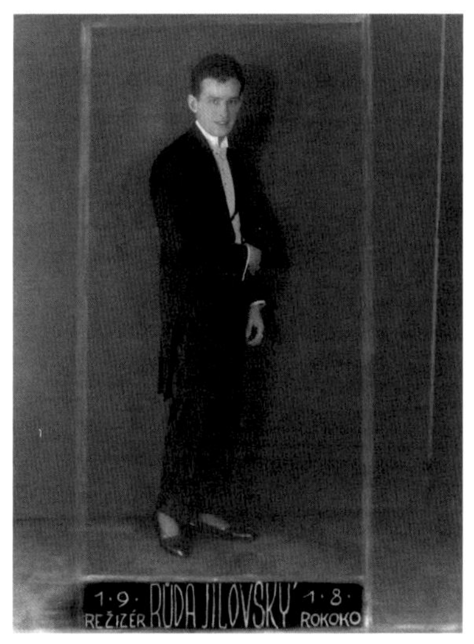

Rudolf Jílovský, 1918 (NA 56187)

Možnosti osvětlení Drtikol postupně rozvíjel a kompletní fázi popsal takto: „*Volil jsem osvětlení případ od případu. Nad hlavu portretované osoby jsem umístil žárovkovou lampu o 500 wattech, hned pod ni, za záda, rovněž 500wattovou žárovku, aby tělo, hlava byly v prostoru a nelepily se na pozadí, zleva zprava jsem měl dvě uhlíkové jupiterky o 2000 wattech, k tomu někdy třetí pro maximální jasy ve vlasech, a navíc ještě uhlíkovou lampu s kondensorem o 6000 wattech, kterou jsem postavil tam, kde jí bylo zapotřebí. Tou jsem vyrovnával, odstraňoval rušivé nepodstatnosti. Umělým i denním osvětlením jsem se snažil v tváři a v postavě vystihnout to, co do nich život vepsal.*"[20]

Je jasné, že Drtikolovi nešlo při rozšiřování světelného spektra výhradně o technické záležitosti. Zpřesňováním osvětlení měnil i určitost portrétů. Nad líbezně mlhavými nástiny raných obrazů s motivy tváře převládly individualizované podobizny nejen množstvím, nýbrž také významově.

Na způsob ambiciózních současníků i předchůdců přistoupil František Drtikol k založení kolekce podobizen významných představitelů kulturního a politického života.[21] Část souboru mínil jako *Český Parnas*. Většina série vznikala studiově, ale doplňoval ji i mimo ateliér. Třeba sochaře Stanislava Suchardu fotografoval roku 1913 u sebe i v pracovním prostředí. Zdánlivě bizarní podobenky s obnaženou hrudí vznikaly jako předlohy pro další výtvarnou práci. Například Eduarda Vojana (1913) a Marii Hübnerovou (1915) si objednal právě Sucharda, Růženu Kopeckou (1919) Jan Štursa.[22]

Neokázalému mobiliáři studia dominovala dvě pohodlná, avšak nefotogenická křesla neobyčejně dlouhé životnosti. Vzorem svých potahů ladila s kosočtverečným potiskem tapet. K základní výbavě patřil i černý paraván, usnadňující kreslení na negativní desky. Nikoli momentní, a proto někdy pohybově rozostřené, expozice byly v 10. letech bází, na níž Drtikol nejednou dál kreativně stavěl. Rozpon mezi původní autorskou interpretací negativů a strohými fakty, která dnes dokážeme v nejstarších skleněných matricích vidět, zůstává tím nepřekročitelnější, čím byly tvůrčí zásahy při převádění negativu v pozitiv větší. Zvláště výrazné je to u noblesního *Portrétu Anny Sedláčkové* (1913, negativ 1912) s domalbou pozadí na způsob předgiottovské krajiny. Rovněž meziválečným pracím dodával Drtikol ireálnou, technologií pigmentového přenosu zrcadlově obrácenou polohu. Dokonalou představu o různorodosti zpracování pozitivů poskytuje jedině sbírka Uměleckoprůmyslového musea v Praze. Nicméně reprodukování podobizen přímo z negativů je regulérní. Jednak k němu přistupoval sám Drtikol, když vydával bromografické rozmnoženiny pro sběratele; navíc předznamenal způsob vydání v knižnici FotoTorst tím, že portréty osobností vybral s ohledem na potenciál jejich budoucí publicity a po zrušení své živnosti je v negativech odevzdal České tiskové kanceláři.

Historizující nostalgie zůstávala v rozporu s předpoklady masovosti produkce fotografií jen do té doby, než se postupy spjaté s řemesly přežily a uvolnily pozice sériovým technologiím. Svár epoch vrcholil secesí a jejím překonáním. Maskování vlastností média fotografie se stalo zbytečným. Kněz a literát Jakub Deml 9. ledna 1916 z Jinošova u Brna požádal Drtikolovy spolupracovníky o nové vyhotovení pozitivu ze staršího negativu příznačnými slovy: *„Přál bych si však, abyste pozadí za tou hlavou změnili, resp. vynechali."*[23]

Josef Kroutvor obohatil charakteristiku Drtikolova vývoje o fázi fotografické moderny, jejíž znaky *„se objevují už před rokem 1910, pak následují nejplodnější léta přerušená válkou a dlouhé doznívání až do poloviny 20. let."*[24]

Činnost ateliéru Drtikol a spol. pokračovala i v mistrově nepřítomnosti během světového konfliktu. Drtikolův návrat do Prahy se udál po čtyřech letech, kdy kreslíval v duchu mytologizujícího umění. Protože hodlal dát finanční bilanci podniku do pořádku, hojně sahal ke starým negativům, jež znovu zpracovával. Pozitivy byl zvyklý označovat nikoli rokem expozice negativu, nýbrž letopočtem jejich finalizace, což je zásada trvající po celé jeho produktivní období. Přispěla k rozostření i bez toho volných přechodů mezi jednotlivými etapami volné tvorby a znejisťuje též dataci portrétů.

O setrvačnosti osvojených praktik, podporované provozními nároky, podal svědectví někdejší Drtikolův zaměstnanec Jaroslav Rössler. Svému prvnímu životopisci rozkryl Drtikolovy úpravy portrétu italského futuristy Marinettiho: Martin Stein napřed evokuje, jak Rössler Drtikola zaujal bromolejotiskovým *Imaginárním portrétem Ore Tarraco* (1922): *„několikrát se na něj přišel podívat. Nakonec prý prohlásil: ‚ale udělejte mi to na pigment‘, což není technicky možné. Jako by se chtěl ujistit o marnosti podobného úsilí.“*[25] Následujícího roku 1923 však Drtikol podobiznu *Filippo Tommaso Marinetti* ozvláštnil způsobem, který se dá rozmnožovat: *„Techniku použil stejnou jako dříve,“* píše Stein, *„když domalovával k aktům krajinné pozadí a pod. Na skleněnou desku negativu natřenou matným lakem nanášel štětcem barvu.“*[26] Podrobnosti uvedl Jaroslav Rössler v dopisu z 6. února 1987, adresovaném Kateřině Klaricové, která si vyžádala bližší osvětlení situace za příprav Drtikolovy monografie. Vyplývá odtud, že Drtikol byl *Imaginárním portrétem Ore Tarraco* přímo šokován a dodatečně se pokusil obdobný efekt vykouzlit zásahy *„na desce 18 × 24, polité mat. lakem, stěrkou a černou sypkou barvou. Nebylo možné tímto způsobem vyjádřit kubistické vzezření. Ty [tahy špachtlí] pak vyšly na pozitivu jako neostré šmouhy. Další dva členy M. doprovodu provedl také tímto způsobem. Nechápu, že tímto způsobem chtěl naznačit kubistický portrét.“*[27] Příklad dodatečně kubizovaného pozadí je spjat s podobiznou básnířky a operní pěvkyně Marie Calmy, vlastním jménem Marie Veselé (1922). Ale pomalu pětaosmdesátiletému Rösslerovi vadilo spíše to, co dokumentuje kubizace bezejmenného aktu, zachovaného sbírkou Uměleckoprůmyslového musea v Praze. Přestože Marinettiho portrét zůstává neznámý, Stein o něm nalezl zápis. Na kartotéčním lístku uvedeného muzea z roku 1942 jej objevil pod číslem 62 v *„Souboru 81 fotografických portrétů z atel. F. D. v Praze z let 1910–1930“*. Celkem jsou ve sbírce Uměleckoprůmyslového musea od Drtikola stovky podobizen všech jakostních vrstev – od umělecké tvorby k dětským podobenkám. Stein nakonec vysvětluje, že v meziválečných letech Drtikolem nejoblíbenější z ušlechtilých technik, pigment, je procesem, při němž autor nemůže – oproti bromoleji – tvarovat štětcem fantazijní podobu. Drtikol proto pigment považoval za ryzí fotografii.

I Jaroslav Rössler, který se v Drtikolově ateliéru vyučil (v letech 1917 až 1920), se zprvu musel vyrovnat s bromolejotisky, někdy s rozhodujícím podílem manuální práce. Proslavilo jej však průkopnictví abstrakce při avantgardním angažmá. Avantgarda programově zpřetrhala ikonografické vazby, jejichž kontinuita sahá k samým počátkům historie. Jakkoli se na ně zapomíná, právě revoluční záměry vymezily generaci, která nastupovala netoliko po Drtikolovi, nýbrž přímo proti němu. Jejím mluvčím byl Karel Teige. Věrozvěstové nových perspektiv se pokusili zbavit kulturního dědictví měšťanské společnosti a svými výstřelky odzvonit hranu oné jednotě umění o tisícovce drtikolovsky přijatelných podob. „*Generace moderny byla poslední generací, pro niž byly antické ideály ještě živým příkladem.*"[28] Je-li tedy někdy do jedné linie s obrazoborectvím avantgardy kladena evoluční kreativita Františka Drtikola, jedná se o naprosté neporozumění oběma svého času protikladným postojům.

Ač po první světové válce Drtikol upouštěl od potlačování fotografičnosti tvárnými procesy, přece zůstával pevně odhodlán vtisknout fotografovaným tvářím optiku své interpretace jejich niterného světa. To koresponduje s parametry fotografické moderny, definovanými Josefem Kroutvorem: „*Fotografická moderna myslí v básnických obrazech, což se nejsilněji projevuje v krajinách a symbolických scénách a nejméně u portrétů. Všichni fotografové moderny chtějí být v prvé řadě, a také jsou, básníky obrazu. Každý z nich má citlivou a jemnou duši básníka, kterou se snaží smířit s moderním světem a jeho technickou orientací. [...] Hermetici a vizionáři, první moderní fotografové, básníci a myslitelé, hledači moderní krásy, představují nejen originální umělce, ale také silné osobnosti. Jejich situace je zcela výjimečná: vidí už moderně, čistě fotograficky, ale myslí ještě starým způsobem. Nové poválečné generaci se nebudou zdát dostatečně moderní, avantgarda je vytlačí z hlavní scény. Fotografové moderny skončí jako samotáři, jejich dílo bude přehlíženo či zapomenuto a někteří se navrátí k malbě.*"[29]

Secesní předznamenání Drtikolova díla, jež ustupovalo s příchodem do Prahy moderně, se mělo v meziválečném čase rekvalifikovat v osobité pojetí slohu, kterému dnes říkáme art deco.

Roku 1918 navázal Drtikol na kompletování série tuzemských osobností. Po skončení světového konfliktu se s mnoha jinými umělci cítil povolán k vyjádření vztahu vůči české státnosti: „*takový ministr Beneš je zřejmě myšlenkami docela jinde, v Ženevě či v parlamentě, trochu nafukuje tvář, ovšem bezděčně; těká, spěchá. Tu je třeba říci náhle nějaké slovíčko, aby si povšiml skutečnosti a v téže chvíli exponovat.*"[30] O jakou dobu šlo, přiblíží heslo z průčelí jedné ostravské banky; pochází z roku 1923: „*Když vlast zlomila jařmo a zemí nesla se víra v silné příští, dům tento k podpoře práce v 5. roce nových dějin byl postaven.*"

Lidé s konkrétními rysy, které Drtikolův reflektor zbavuje přítmí raných šerosvitů a někdejších měkce idealizovaných pozadí, aby je modeloval v duchu nové doby, již nejsou poddanými Jeho c. k. Milosti, nýbrž občané republiky. A František Drtikol se stejně pozorně věnuje zahraničním návštěvám Československa. *„Nejvyššího oficiálního uznání se dostalo Drtikolovi zakázkou portrétu presidenta republiky Tomáše G. Masaryka,“* uvedla Anna Fárová následující citaci propagačního sloganu ze záložky v Emporiu vydané pětice snímků: *„F. Drtikol, z jehož fotografické dílny vyšly, jest z oněch málo průkopníků, kteří po řadu let snaží se vybavit portrétní fotografii z běžné šablony. V jeho dílech zjevny jsou oba znaky dobré fotografie: postižení charakteristiky osoby ve výrazu obličeje i postoji a solidní technická znalost bez hluché řemeslnické manýry. F. Drtikol vytvořil velkou řadu podobizen předních našich současníků z kruhů vědeckých, uměleckých a spisovatelských. Práce tyto mají cenu historickou, budou ale i svědky jeho uměleckého postřehu a zdatností.“*[31]

Portrétní fotografie z první republiky charakterizuje pokračující oprošťování. Důvěryhodně zní Drtikolovo opakované prohlášení, že retuše obrazu obličeje jsou zásadně nepatřičné a že se jich vlastně nikdy nedopouštěl.[32] Kolekce negativů v Národním archivu dokládá, že případné zásahy utvářely dekorativní nebo symbolické pozadí. Jestliže Drtikol vyřizoval již před první světovou válkou běžné zakázky přímočaře, ve 20. letech portrétoval v civilním prostoru i celebrity. Po roce 1922 odpadalo zdobné dokreslování snímků. Místo ornamentů i dodatečně geometrizovaného pozadí zaujal závěs s květovaným či abstraktním potiskem, popřípadě bez vzoru. Častěji býval přiznán prostý reál studia. Redukce iluzivního pozadí nešla do krajnosti, nicméně stylizace světlem modelovaného prostoru rozhodně nekonkurovala hře gest.

Ideálem byla vstřícně naladěná bytost v jednoduchých šatech: *„Poddá-li se pak do vůle fotografovy, je vyhráno. Neboť fotograf pak nejlépe vystihne, jak člověka portrétovati, zda z levé či pravé strany, s enfacu atd. Při té příležitosti podotýkám, že skoro každý člověk je s každé strany jiný. Existuje skutečně dvojí tvář člověka: obličej má dvě různé podoby, které profil odděluje, někdy je s jedné strany člověk hezký, ale není to typicky on. Anebo naopak.“*[33] František Drtikol rád uplatňoval důvtip, jímž zvyšoval renomé firmy. Invenčním pěstěním slohu art deco získal pověst vhodného reprezentanta etablovanosti československé republiky: v roce 1925 obdržel výzvu, aby zapůjčil fotografie na *Mezinárodní výstavu moderních dekorativních a průmyslových umění v Paříži.* Československý stát mu umožnil samostatné autorské vystoupení, jež bylo po zásluze oceněno porotou přehlídky v oboru fotografie a kinematografie.

Drtikol tou dobou užíval při fotografování geometrických dekorací, na míru vyráběných dílnami Národního divadla. Atraktivně je zúročil v aranžmá herečky Jarmily Horákové. Její portrét je ukázkou paralely volné a živnostenské tvorby. I abstrahující purismus konce 20. a první poloviny 30. let – etapa k fotografování vyřezávaných předloh – dostane protějšek v návrzích dekorativních svítidel.

Ušlechtilá náročnost zpracování negativu zůstávala Drtikolovi blízká rovněž ve fázi střídmé, leč o to nápaditější obraznosti druhé poloviny 20. let. *„Prostá, obyčejná lesklá fotografie je nejlepší prací,“* ujišťoval Drtikol začátkem 30. let posluchače svých kurzů.[34] Sám ale ctil vedle takto absolutizovaného bromostříbrného materiálu pozitivy provedené uhlotiskem. Dopisem Královské fotografické společnosti v Londýně doporučoval uhlotisk (neboli pigment) coby technologii vhodnou pro sběratelské účely: *„Zajisté by pak obrazy takové byly dobře zaplaceny, zvláště když by byl zhotoven od jednoho negativu jen určitý počet signovaných otisků, řekněme 10 a víc nic.“*[35]

O přitažlivosti věhlasné dílny Drtikol a spol. vypovídá množství dochovaných podobizen z 20. let: *„Však se u mne dveře netrhly,“* vzpomínal se zadostiučiněním fotograf.[36] Jenže nadcházel rok 1929 s krachem na newyorské burze. Zatímco v Paříži, tehdejší Mekce západního umění, nabízel nakladatel Antoine Calavas sběratelům první z nekončící série drtikolovských bibliofilií, podniku Drtikol a spol. klepal úpadek na dveře.

Pramenem zpráv o proměnách četnosti Drtikolových zakázek by jistě byly obchodní knihy. Jenže kde je jim konec?

Rámcově se ví, že finančním společníkem Drtikolovy živnosti byl po osm let (1913–21) stavební inženýr Augustin Škarda, amatérský fotograf i aktivista, povoláním úředník. *„V roce 1921 jsem se rozešel se svým společníkem, protože byly nějaké nejasnosti v hospodaření ateliéru za války a ty tři roky po ní,“* konstatuje Drtikol v již citovaném vlastním životopisu, archivovaném Uměleckoprůmyslovým museem v Praze. Nicméně ze slepotiskového razítka firmy přídomek „a spol.“ nezmizí, přestože finančního partnera Drtikol už nikdy nebude mít. Důkazem jsou spisy obchodních soudů uložené v pražském Státním oblastním archivu. Tak kupříkladu Krajský soud obchodní v Praze zaslal 11. května 1929 Magistrátu hlavního města Prahy dotaz stran ateliéru Drtikol a spol., přičemž vyplývá, že jediným majitelem zůstává František Drtikol: *„dle obchodního rejstříku nenastala od roku 1921 žádná změna při firmě.“*

Augustin Škarda odešel ze společného podniku koncem května vzpomínaného roku 1921 po trojici dramatických přelíčení, v nichž se neubránil Drtikolově žalobě. Pro pochopení sporu je důležitá následující pasáž Škardova podání Obchodnímu soudu v Praze z 13. prosince 1920: „*Navrhovatel totiž již dávno pracoval soustavně k tomu, aby se mne zbavil, jakmile seznal, že závod hlavně mým přičiněním se povznesl na umělecký podnik prvého řádu. Použil k tomu každého prostředku; k uskutečnění tohoto dávného plánu přispěla mu hlavně moje nervová choroba, která již před válkou následkem mé intensivní činnosti společenské vznikla a během mé vojenské povinnosti byla stupňována. Tato choroba ve spojení s notorickou nemožností opatřiti za války odbornou sílu ku vedení knih byla totiž jedinou příčinou, pro kterou obchodní knihy nebyly mnou vedeny způsobem dle čl. 28 obch. z.[ákonem] předepsaným, aniž by, jak zdůrazňuji, byla nějaká malversace zjištěna.*“

Drtikol reagoval 16. prosince 1920 doplněním svého podání z 29. listopadu téhož roku. Ve snaze ukončit společné vlastnictví podniku napsal Obchodnímu soudu v Praze: „*Bylo-li zjištěno všemi třemi instancemi ve sporu C III 69/20, že mne můj společník zkrátil o částku 13.696.53, jest úplně bezvýznamno, jestliže p. odpůrce tuto okolnost popírá. Co se pak týče částky 38.540 K, doznal p. odpůrce výslovně při stání dne 10/11. 1920 u tohoto soudu konaném, že po podání žaloby větší množství peněz v této přibližné výši si vybral a že je vrátiti nemíní. Ostatně nesporná částka 13.696 K 53 h, kterou bude nutno od p. Škardy sporem vymáhati, k odůvodnění kolise úplně postačí a není třeba touto druhou částkou, chce-li jí p. odpůrce popírati, nyní se zabývati.*“

Ze soudních spisů lze vyčíst, že během vleklé pře byla zaměstnankyní ateliéru Drtikol a spol. choť navrhovatele žaloby, paní Ervina Kupferová.

Drtikolovských nejasností zůstává ovšem celá řada. Vedle početnějšího zastoupení příbramské tvorby chybějí v Jeníčkově interview Drtikolem připomínaní první pražští zákazníci. Měli to být abiturienti, kteří si nechali zhotovit snímky pro šestnáct maturitních vývěsek.

Kolikrát asi musel Drtikol vyfotografovat podobenku (novo)manželů? Při válečné selekci negativů pro Českou tiskovou kancelář šly páry stranou. Z devětatřiceti dochovaných snímků Hany a Edvarda Benešových není ani jeden společný.

Negativy – zpravidla jednotlivých osobností – poznamenalo ledabylé zacházení ve 40. a 50. letech. Národní archiv je nyní opatruje ve vhodném teplotním režimu. Soubor neobsahuje volnou tvorbu, jež byla i v žánru portrétu relativně bohatá a zřetelně se liší od tvorby užité. Postrádat lze rovněž vlastní podobizny fotografa.

Nevíme, které osobnosti vydal Drtikol na pohlednicích a které v bromografických sériích. Kateřina Klaricová uvedla v umělcově monografii, že v polovině 20. let bromograficky publikoval 24 a začátkem 30. let na 120 aktů. Rozmnoženiny aktů značené na líci symbolem závodu Karla Podlipného Bromografia Lázně Poděbrady bývá ovšem na trhu vidět častěji než portréty i z toho důvodu, že jsou sběratelsky přitažlivější. Otázkou zůstává, jakého nákladu dosáhly. Pouze o pozdní svědectví Josefa Ehma se opírá údaj, že *„většinou šlo o individuálně zhotovované kopie v malých nákladech a nikoliv o průmyslově vyráběné bromografie"*.[37]

Namísto oficiózní vizáže vídeňského mocnáře fotografových začátků se na pořad dne dostaly zjevy němých biografů. Herečka Anny Ondráková si u Drtikola objednala portfolio široké výrazové škály – od sportovního převleku po glamour. Pózování u stolku s mísou umělého ovoce a s lyžemi před bílým závěsem však působilo anachronicky, byť šlo o stylizaci přiznanou. V epoše nástupu zvukového filmu a rázné vlády provozní funkce se v moderní Praze nedalo dost dobře lpět na starším pojetí aranžmá. I přesto, že třeba drážďanská etapa prominentního portrétisty Hugo Erfurtha (sahající až do roku 1934) se staromistrovstvím na poměrně čilé kulturní scéně menší zemské metropole úspěšně vystačila... Drtikolova živnost vyžadovala s 30. lety inovaci, pokud neměla opustit vrcholnou úroveň. Jenže Drtikolovi se nedařilo přehrávat do nových podmínek na způsob o čtyři roky staršího Američana Edwarda Steichena. Fotografická scéna měla napříště patřit funkcionalismu a momentce – protikladu ateliérového art deco. Rádoby divadelní estetika, imitovaná z technických důvodů ve snáze

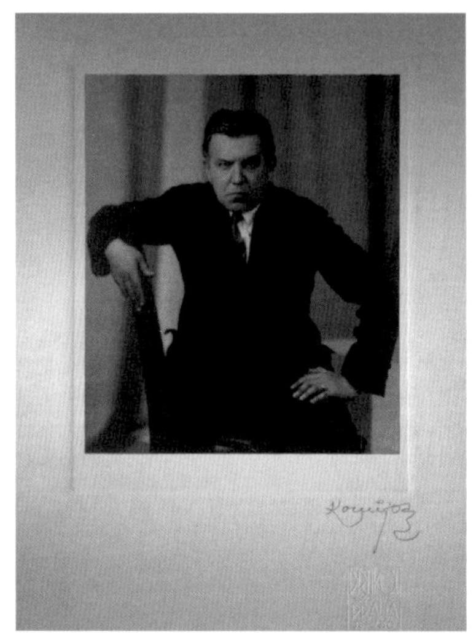

Jan Konůpek, 1928

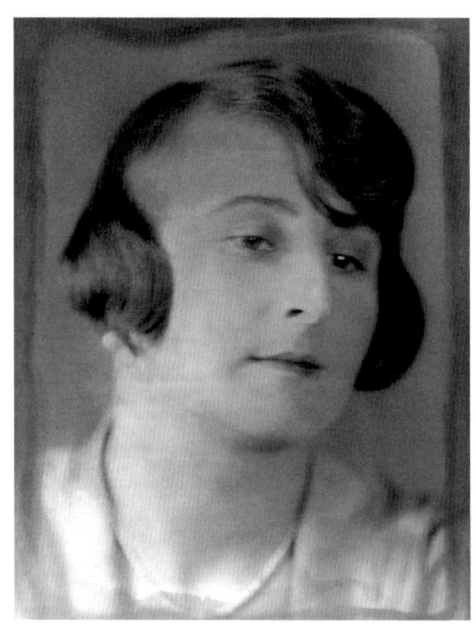

Libuše Freslová, 1922 (NA 55938)

42

zvladatelných světelných podmínkách ateliéru, brala za své. Jakmile se objevili mladí reportéři, kteří místo velkých skleněných desek pohotově exponovali v autentickém prostředí divadel reálné výstupy, odzvonilo teatrálním pózám. Tuto změnu nemohl Drtikol nevidět. Vždyť již roku 1924 do časopisu *Gentleman* napsal: „*Co se mne týče, portretoval bych člověka, kdyby to bylo možno, při jeho práci, ve chvíli, kdy vykonává své povolání. Tehdy má jeho tvář přirozený výraz, duše se vtěluje do charakteru hlavy. To jest, oč ve fotografii běží. Ale i když už tak portretovati nelze, řeknu, že by bylo dobře, kdyby muž přišel do atelieru jakoby mimochodem, náhodou, ve všedních šatech nebo těch, které nejraději nosí, nenaparáděn, nevyšvihnut, vždyť přece nechceme zvěčňovat jeho zevnějšek!*“[38]

Hodlal se však Drtikol s požadavky nové doby identifikovat? Dne 30. srpna 1930 přiložil k (vyžádané) zásilce fotografií do švýcarského časopisu *Camera* redaktorovi Adolfu Herzovi dopis, v němž stojí: „*Do současného směru nové věcnosti zabředla spousta fotografů, kteří teď nevědí, jak ven, protože jim nesvítí žádná nová hvězda.*“[39]

František Drtikol je z dnešního pohledu umělcem, ať už se vyjadřoval fotografií, kresbou anebo malbou. Pro jeho vrstevníky to stejně samozřejmé nebylo. Tvůrce svou zkušenost shrnul: „*Přicházely návštěvy z východu, západu, severu, jihu, ze zámoří, z celého světa. Zlaté, stříbrné i bronzové medaile, první i druhé ceny, diplomy, uznání, čestná členství – to vše je dnes v archivu Uměleckoprůmyslového musea v Praze, kam jsem odevzdal i negativy a obrazy. Bylo však i dost trpkostí. Už proto, že u nás byla a je fotografie považována za naturalistický obtisk skutečnosti. Co nespočetných hovorů jsem měl s našimi vůdčími uměleckými osobnostmi, leč kdekdo, až na výtvarného kritika J. R. Marka, se mne snažil přesvědčit, že fotografie je periferijní přívěsek kulturní lidské aktivnosti. Ať tak či onak, pro mne fotografie byla vždy uměním, nikdy dojnou krávou...*“[40]

Nevázanost volných Drtikolových portrétů cení historik umění Antonín Dufek: „*Možnost zdůraznit místo pravdy krásu či kouzlo osobnosti poskytuje větší prostor k manévrování, a proto formálně nejoriginálnější Drtikolovy portréty zobrazují ženy.*“ [41]

Rozumí se ovšem, že umělec neodkládal svůj mimořádný cit ani při hledání pravdy charakteru: „*Drtikolovo dílo ve skutečnosti tvoří jediný, nedělitelný celek, protože i fotografický portrét (manifestovaná viditelnost), kterému se Drtikol soustředěně věnoval, je výslednicí autorovy nezaměnitelné vnitřní zkušenosti.*“[42] Úsudek historičky umění Jany Šmejkalové podporuje nejedno Drtikolovo prohlášení.

„S jakou láskou a porozuměním je vytvořeno a kolik umělec do svého díla vložil své duše, sama sebe. – To rozhoduje, ne, jestli je to tak či onak vytvořeno, jestli je to tím nebo oním procesem zhotoveno. To je vedlejší.“[43]

„Proto také je tak skutečně málo pravých umělců, malířů, sochařů. Tvorba jejich je příliš rozumová – a ne citová. Zapomínají, že umění je věcí citu – a ne rozumu, a proto jestli tvořím obraz objektivem nebo štětcem, zůstává stejné. Hlavní věc je, když výsledek odpovídá tomu, co mi říká můj umělecký cit.“[44]

František Drtikol vztahoval své maximy také k portrétování: „Nikdy jsem člověka neofotografoval; snažil jsem se podat o něm zprávu výtvarně i psychologicky opravdovou.“[45] U podobizen, které vystavoval, naznačoval obecností názvů, že se mu jedná o volné umění: *Portrét* (1926), *Hlava* (1930), *Profil* (1930)... Jsou jeho rukou psány na ruby pozitivů, které věnoval Uměleckoprůmyslovému museu v Praze. Zakázková i volná tvorba se myšlenkově prolínaly, takže Drtikolovy sentence v mnohém platí pro obě části díla: „Fotografovat, to jest znovu a znovu se pokoušet z vnějších forem člověka podchytit to, co je náznakem, napověděním jeho duše, je mi chlebem samo o sobě, nejen prostředkem k jeho dosažení. [...] Pouhou formu se snažím zachytiti jen tehdy, když dělám fotografie modelů pro sochaře nebo malíře. Vložit do portrétu charakter – totiž jejich pochopení charakteru dotyčné osoby – je jejich věcí. Jinak se vždy namáhám zhmotnit to, co je v obličeji, v postavě nehmotného – charakter. [...] Zásadně: Co nejméně rekvisit, dekorací, pomůcek k vyvolání nálady. Předměty, jež mají tuto evokační sílu, protože se k nim připíná určitá představa, takové tradiční symboly svádí k banálním, zevšednělým komposicím. Sám jsem udělal smutné zkušenosti například s lebkou. [...] Dívám se třeba jen na kámen, na záhyb látky pod různým osvětlením: před mýma očima se ony věci pod jemnými prsty Světla mění, mění... [...] Dívat se je už samo o sobě uměním.“[46]

František Drtikol věřil, že každá bytost v sobě nese Božskou Jiskru,[47] a pokud to šlo, napomáhal její emanaci. Nicméně prakticky nemohl odmítat zakázky určené k povrchní reprezentaci v mezích panujícího vkusu: „Ale má-li portret býti vskutku tím, čím se člověk pouze zdá, pak pochopíte, jak těžkou práci má fotograf, aby udělal věc, která se líbí nejen vám, ale i mně.“[48]

U podobizen nepřekvapí, že výrazně převažuje vertikální orientace záběru. Kompozice se opíraly o střídání polopostav a celých figur, případně o charakteristiky typů atributy, jakými jsou nástroje u hudebníků, knihy u lidí pera anebo náznaky divadelních stylizací u hereček či baletek... Je dobře známé, čím Drtikol evokoval dojem pohybu statických postav v žánru aktu: dynamiky docíloval uvolněnou režií póz modelek a komponováním po diagonálách.

Z tanečních sérií je cítit puls spolupráce fotografa a baletek i vzájemnou důvěru v zhodnocení vlastních vkladů. Proměny opakovaných portrétních aranžmá zase prozrazují hledání nejvýstižnějšího niterného výrazu nasvícením rysů i psychologizující spoluprací se subjekty sezení: *„vznikla pozoruhodná série portrétů tváří známých i neznámých, zachycujících vždy s velkou citlivostí duševní potenciál 10. a 20. let“.*[49]

Někteří zákazníci se časem vraceli a lze tudíž sledovat nevyzpytatelné efekty stárnutí. Příkladně u historika umění V. V. Štecha, který je pověstný tím, že s fotografií zacházel jako s dokumentací a umělecké možnosti jí upíral. S jeho stanoviskem – ale ani s výlučně estetickými hledisky – nad odkazem Františka Drtikola nevystačíme. Názor profesora estetiky na Karlově univerzitě Otakara Hostinského na fotografickou podobenku stojí za připomenutí i proto, že se utvářel v čase zdobné secese, leč v progresivním duchu: *„fotografie se svým mechanismem opticko-chemickým neuprosně zaznamenává a neodčinitelně ustaluje všechno, cokoliv se v době exposice děje [...] jsou-li pak chvíle, v nichž jeví se povaha člověka v jeho tváři cele a plně, jako v zrcadle, vůbec vzácné, tím vzácněji dostavují se v ateliéru fotografově, a přece jenom když takový vzácný šťastný okamžik nastane, možno nadíti se opravdu zdařilé fotografické podobizny.“*[50]

O tři dekády později konstatuje historička umění Hana Volavková, že výtvarní umělci nechali žánr portrétu zplanět: *„Úsilí o nový styl vyčerpávalo tvůrčí duchy našeho století, že přenechali podobiznářství, kde hraje tak důležitou roli přímý styk s objednavatelem, umělcům, kteří se pramálo starali o dnešek a jeho duchovou náplň. Většina portrétů, které nacházíme dnes v rodinách, můžeme bez jakýchkoli skrupulí zařaditi do kategorie umění konvenčního.“*[51] Článek Hany Volavkové se o fotografování nezmiňuje, nicméně právě médium fotografie skýtalo východisko z probíraného dilematu: *„Jak je možno, aby člověk moderní se nechal portretovat formou tak včerejší a tak neaktuální, jak je možno nechat se na dlouhý čas zaklíti do obrazu nebo sochy, která už dnes působí bizarně svou neupřímností a strojeností.“*[52]

Z Drtikolových textů, psaných během fotografické praxe, připomeňme zakázkovou činnost relativizující zmínku: *„Není možno vyhnouti se tomu, aby ze sta portrétovaných lidí několik jich fotografu nezůstalo lhostejných.“*[53] Přestože dochované kolekce podobizen obsahují rovněž popisné snímky, Drtikolovo úsilí vyhnout se šablonám neinspirovaných konvencí bylo často úspěšné. Po desítky let ale zůstávalo skryto a nedoceněno, jakkoli známe mnohé tváře české prvorepublikové elity výhradně z anonymních reprodukcí Drtikolových snímků.

Soubor podobizen od Františka Drtikola byl zanedbáván neprávem. Už proto, že v Drtikolově fotografování akty nepřevládaly. Ale i proto, že tu jde o svéráz projevu mezinárodně význačného autora, jenž stál u zrodu české umělecké praxe v oboru fotografie. Anna Fárová k tomu poznamenala: *„Vztahy malířského pojetí a fotografické specifiky spolu se zvláštními obsahy, se zdůrazněním vztahu Erose a Thanata, spolu s mýtem ženy, byly něčím neopakovatelným a otevírajícím nové cesty tomuto novému médiu u nás a jak vidíme dnes, i ve světě."*[54]

Nejhledanějšími díly Františka Drtikola samosebou zůstávají fotografické akty. Jedná se zejména o pigmenty z posledních dvou třetin 20. let. Umělcova výtvarná práce ovšem pokračovala ještě dlouho poté, co se ztratil veřejnosti z dohledu. Adorace uměleckého potenciálu média však nejednou opomíjejí, že to bylo jeho služebné nasazení, jež přivedlo fotografy během 19. a 20. století k převzetí společenské iniciativy v soutěži s výtvarníky. Nakonec i negativy drtikolovských portrétů přežily díky své informativní složce – a nikoli kvůli jejich dlouho zapomenutému tvůrci.

Samo Drtikolovo dílo je založeno harmonicky. Vyjadřuje sounáležitost mentality s tělesností a překlenuje tím propast mezi idealismem a materialismem.

Obrazovou část portrétní monografie Františka Drtikola by mohlo otevírat motto: Každý z otištěných obrazů propojuje vysokou kulturu formy s plným výrazem Ducha. Anebo jinak, Drtikolovými slovy řečeno: *„Uznávám-li, že Bůh je všudypřítomný, pak je mi nejblíže v mém nitru, ve mně samotném."*[55]

Poznámky

1   František Drtikol: *Duchovní cesta*, Praha, Svět 2004, s. 36.

2   Anna Fárová: *Fotograf František Drtikol (tvorba z let 1903–35)*, Praha, Uměleckoprůmyslové museum 1972, s. 10. Blíže: Josef Moucha: Dvě otázky pro Annu Fárovou, *Ateliér* 10, 1997, č. 24, s. 3.

3   Jiří Jeníček: Na besedě u Františka Drtikola, *Československá fotografie* 6, 1955, č. 2, s. 16–17.

4   Tamtéž, s. 17. Srov.: „*jelikož bez světla rozptýleného nelze si správně osvětlený portrét vůbec ani mysliti, tu musíme v takovém případu, když střecha atelieru jest příliš krátká, sáhnouti ku prostředkům umělým, abychom světla rozptýleného dosíci mohli.*" Bohumil Markl: Praktické upotřebení světla a stínu v atelieru, *Fotografický obzor* 8, 1900, č. 10, s. 152.

5   Šéfem se rozumí Theodor Schuhmann. Dosavadní drtikolovská literatura v jeho jméně chybovala. Opis nedatovaných vzpomínek archivuje Uměleckoprůmyslové museum v Praze.

6   Anna Fárová: *Fotograf František Drtikol (tvorba z let 1903–35)*, Praha, Uměleckoprůmyslové museum 1972, s. 19.

7   Drtikol vyjadřuje vkus *belle époque* nedatovaným pojednáním o gumotisku, jehož korektury deponované Uměleckoprůmyslovým museem v Praze čítají 67 stran, ale postrádají titul: „*Retuše, hlavně co se portretu týče, užijeme co možná nejméně a vždy uvažujeme napřed, chceme-li nějaký tah vinout anebo úplně vyretušovat, zda nezmění se celý charakteristikon té či oné osoby. Ovšem objektiv vidí příliš mnoho jednotlivostí, vrásek, skvrnek, které nemají žádného vlivu na podobu, mohou se vyretušovat.*" Dle formátu stránek by se mohlo jednat o sešit velké řady knižnice *Nauk o fotografii*, o jejímž nerealizovaném edičním plánu se Drtikolova heslovitá biografie v přítomném svazku FotoTorstu zmiňuje k roku 1918.

8   Jan Mlčoch: *Fotografie z let 1901–1914 a album Z dvorů a dvorečků staré Prahy*, Praha, Uměleckoprůmyslové museum v Praze & Kant 1999, s. 17–18.

9   Vladimír Jindřich Bufka: *Katechismus fotografie. Úvod do fotografie pro fotografy amateury*, Praha, Hejda & Tuček 1913, s. 165.

10   Anna Fárová: *Fotograf František Drtikol (tvorba z let 1903–35)*, Praha, Uměleckoprůmyslové museum 1972, s. 34. Reprodukci viz: Jan Mlčoch: *František Drtikol. Fotografie z let 1901–1914 a album Z dvorů a dvorečků staré Prahy*, Praha, Uměleckoprůmyslové museum v Praze & Kant 1999, s. 11.

11   Josef Kroutvor: *Česká fotografická moderna*, Praha, Uměleckoprůmyslové museum v Praze 1989, nestránkováno.

12   Josef Kroutvor: Česká fotografická moderna, *Revue Fotografie* 34, 1990, č. 3, s. 70.

13   Petr Wittlich: Drtikolova mystika, *Ateliér* 11, 1998, č. 9, s. 16.

14   Pavel Scheufler: *Stará Praha Jana Langhanse*, Praha, Baset 2000, s. 19.

15   František Drtikol: *Moderní umělecká fotografie*, Praha, reklamní leták firmy Drtikol a spol., nevročeno.

16   Jiří Jeníček: Na besedě u Františka Drtikola, *Československá fotografie* 6, 1955, č. 2, s. 18.

17   Tamtéž.

18   Srov. Martin Stein: *Jaroslav Rössler*, Praha, Závěrečná teoretická práce na katedře fotografie FAMU, 1984, s. 10, 12.

19   K. A. [Karel Anderle]: Klub návštěvou v atelieru Drtikolově, *Fotografický obzor* 20, 1912, č. 3, s. 71–72.

20   Jiří Jeníček: Na besedě u Františka Drtikola, *Československá fotografie* 6, 1955, č. 2, s. 18.

21   Srov. Pavel Scheufler: *Jindřich Eckert*, Praha, Odeon 1985. Pavel Scheufler: *Jan Langhans*, Praha, Torst 2005. Libor Jůn: Galerie vynikajících osobností Jindřicha Vaňka, *Historická fotografie* 4, 2004, č. 1, s. 5–13.

22 Srov. Vít Vlnas: *Za zrcadlem. Čeští sochaři ve fotografiích a dokumentech*, Praha, Národní galerie 1993.

23 Z Demlova dopisu archivovaného Uměleckoprůmyslovým museem v Praze.

24 Josef Kroutvor: Fotograf se jménem antického boha, *Revolver Revue*, 1993, č. 23, s. 147. Vídeňský Anton Josef Trčka, k němuž především se Kroutvorův článek vztahuje, budiž příkladem, že se i mladší fotografové ve 20. letech drželi nazírání, rozšířeného před první světovou válkou. Srov. Monika Faber: *Anton Josef Trčka 1893–1940*, Wien, Verlag Christian Brandstätter 1999.

25 Martin Stein, *Jaroslav Rössler*, Praha, Závěr. teoretická práce na katedře fotografie FAMU, 1984, s. 17.

26 Tamtéž.

27 Z Rösslerova dopisu Kateřině Klaricové, datovaného 6. 2. 1987.

28 Josef Kroutvor: Česká fotografická moderna, *Revue Fotografie* 34, 1990, č. 3, s. 69.

29 Josef Kroutvor: *Česká fotografická moderna*, Praha, Uměleckoprůmyslové museum v Praze 1989, nestránkováno.

30 František Drtikol: Muž u fotografa, *Bulletin MG*, 1992, č. 48, s. 96.

31 Cit. dle Anna Fárová: *Fotograf František Drtikol (tvorba z let 1903–35)*, Praha, Uměleckoprůmyslové museum 1972, s. 25.

32 František Drtikol: Muž u fotografa, *Bulletin MG*, 1992, č. 48, s. 95–96. Srov. Jiří Jeníček: Na besedě u Františka Drtikola, *Československá fotografie* 6, 1955, č. 2, s. 18.

33 František Drtikol: Muž u fotografa, *Bulletin MG*, 1992, č. 48, s. 95–96. Srov. Jiří David: *Skryté podoby*, Praha, Kant 1995.

34 František Drtikol: *Oči široce otevřené*, Praha, Svět 2002, s. 67.

35 Nedatovaný český koncept korespondence archivuje Uměleckoprůmyslové museum v Praze. Z překladu jiného (tamtéž uloženého a opět nedatovaného) dopisu do angličtiny vyčteme ceny: za bromostříbrný pozitiv žádal Drtikol 60, za pigment 260 korun. Drtikolova díla v žánru aktu často pocházejí ze skleněných desek 30 × 24 centimetrů a bývají to průměty ve velikosti 1 : 1. U zakázkových portrétů převažují kontakty na bromostříbrné papíry menších formátů, adjustované na kartonu a opatřené slepotiskovým razítkem Drtikol a spol.

36 Jiří Jeníček: Na besedě u Františka Drtikola, *Československá fotografie* 6, 1955, č. 2, s. 18.

37 Vladimír Birgus: *Fotograf František Drtikol*, Praha, Prostor 1994, s. 34. Týž: *František Drtikol*, Praha, Kant 2000, s. 33. Pro cenovou představu: dne 10. prosince 2004 byla vydražena bromografie Salome z 20. let za 35 200 Kč. Srov. Anonym: Antikvariát Dr. Prošek, *Art & Antiques* 4, 2005, leden, s. 24.

38 František Drtikol: Muž u fotografa, *Bulletin MG*, 1992, č. 48, s. 96.

39 Průklep strojopisu v němčině archivuje Uměleckoprůmyslové museum v Praze.

40 Jiří Jeníček: Na besedě u Františka Drtikola, *Československá fotografie* 6, 1955, č. 2, s. 18.

41 Antonín Dufek: Drtikolův neznámý text, *Bulletin MG*, 1992, č. 48, s. 95.

42 Jana Šmejkalová: Hamletovský odkaz Františka Drtikola, *Antique* 5, 1998, č. 5, s. 44.

43 František Drtikol: *Duchovní cesta*, Praha, Svět 2004, s. 289.

44 Citováno z české předlohy Drtikolovy nedostupné korespondence Královské fotografické společnosti v Londýně. Na rubu 3. listu strojopisu, archivovaného Uměleckoprůmyslovým museem v Praze, je rukou umělce poznamenán červenou pastelkou titul *O fotografii*.

45 Jiří Jeníček: Na besedě u Františka Drtikola, *Československá fotografie* 6, 1955, č. 2, s. 18.

46 František Drtikol, *Oči široce otevřené*, Praha, Svět 2002, s. 39, 19, 47, 61, 69.

47 Srov. Karel Funk: *Mystik a učitel František Drtikol*, Praha, GEMMA 89, 1993, s. 214.

48 František Drtikol: Muž u fotografa, *Bulletin MG*, 1992, č. 48, s. 96. Stejným článkem odlišil umění portrétu od „*fotografování v masce*": u herců nalíčených pro divadelní roli teatrálnost akceptoval, jinak se však pokoušel o vystižení psychických rysů portrétované osoby, což znamenalo pronikat pod ony škrabošky stavěné na odiv: „*Velmi nesnadno je portretovati herce. Myslím, že je jim zatěžko vůbec nehráti. Mají tisíc masek na obličeji. Stojí-li před aparátem, je jim stejně, jako by již stáli před obecenstvem. Hned něco neb někoho představují.*"

49 Petr Wittlich: Drtikolova mystika, *Ateliér 11*, 1998, č. 9, s. 16.

50 Otakar Hostinský: Fotografie a malířství, *Pražská lidová revue 1*, 1905, č. 10, s. 258–259.

51 Hana Volavková: Moderní podobizna, *Eva 8*, č. 1, 1935, s. 14.

52 Tamtéž.

53 František Drtikol: *Oči široce otevřené*, Praha, Svět 2002, s. 16.

54 Anna Fárová: František Drtikol. Magie imaginativního plození, *Výtvarné umění*, 1992, č. 2, s. 28.

55 František Drtikol: *Duchovní cesta*, Praha, Svět 2004, s. 201.

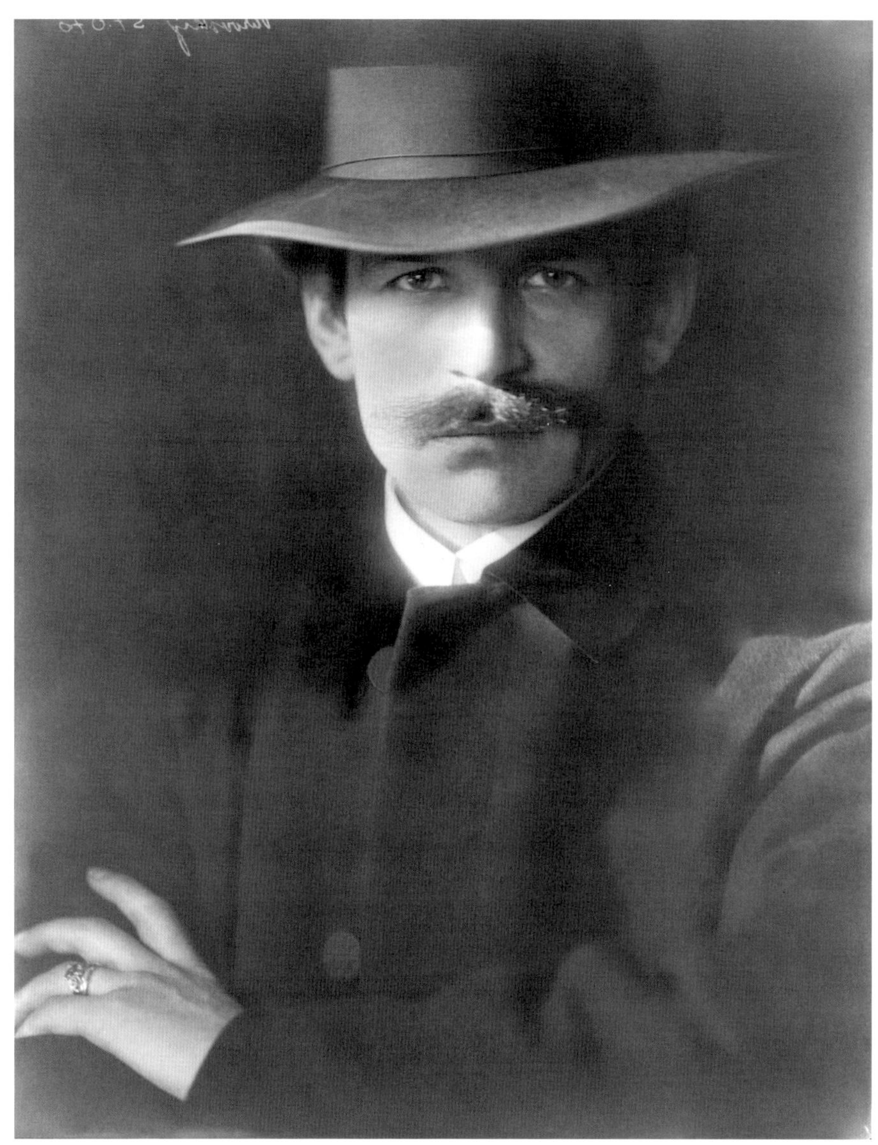

1 **Jakub Obrovský** 1913

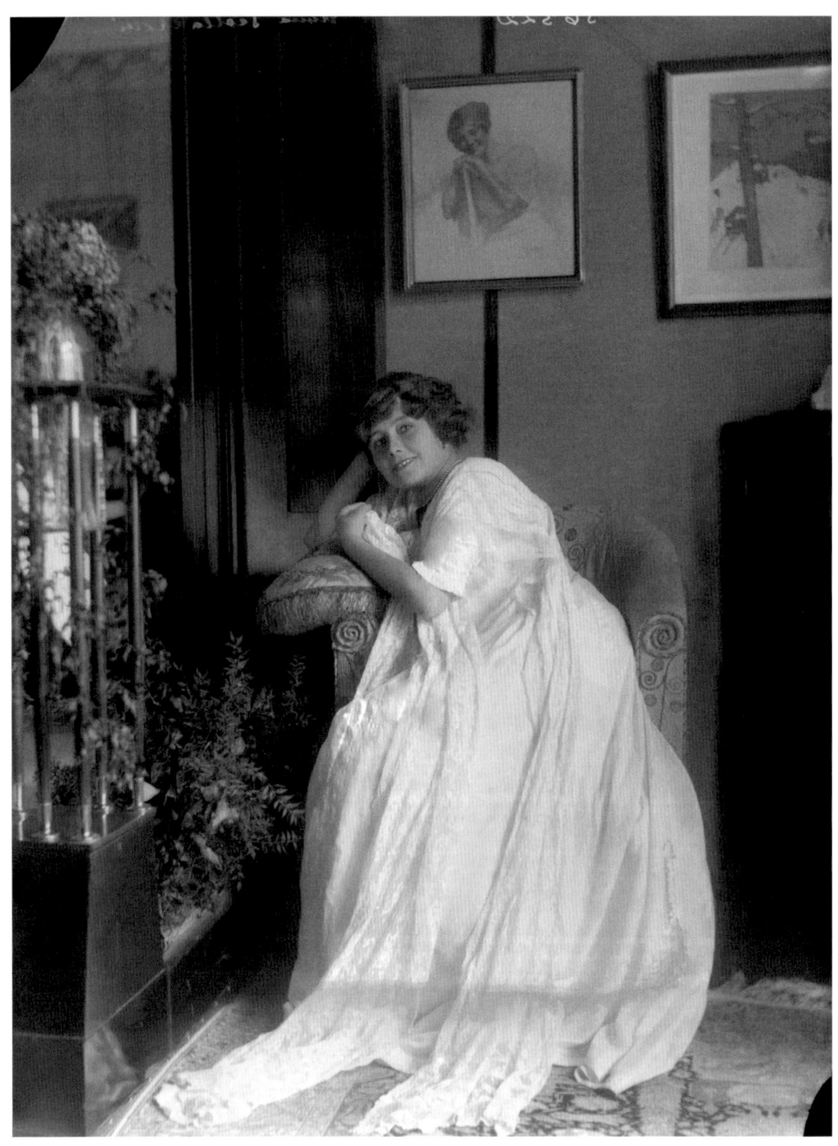

2 **Anna Sedláčková** 1912

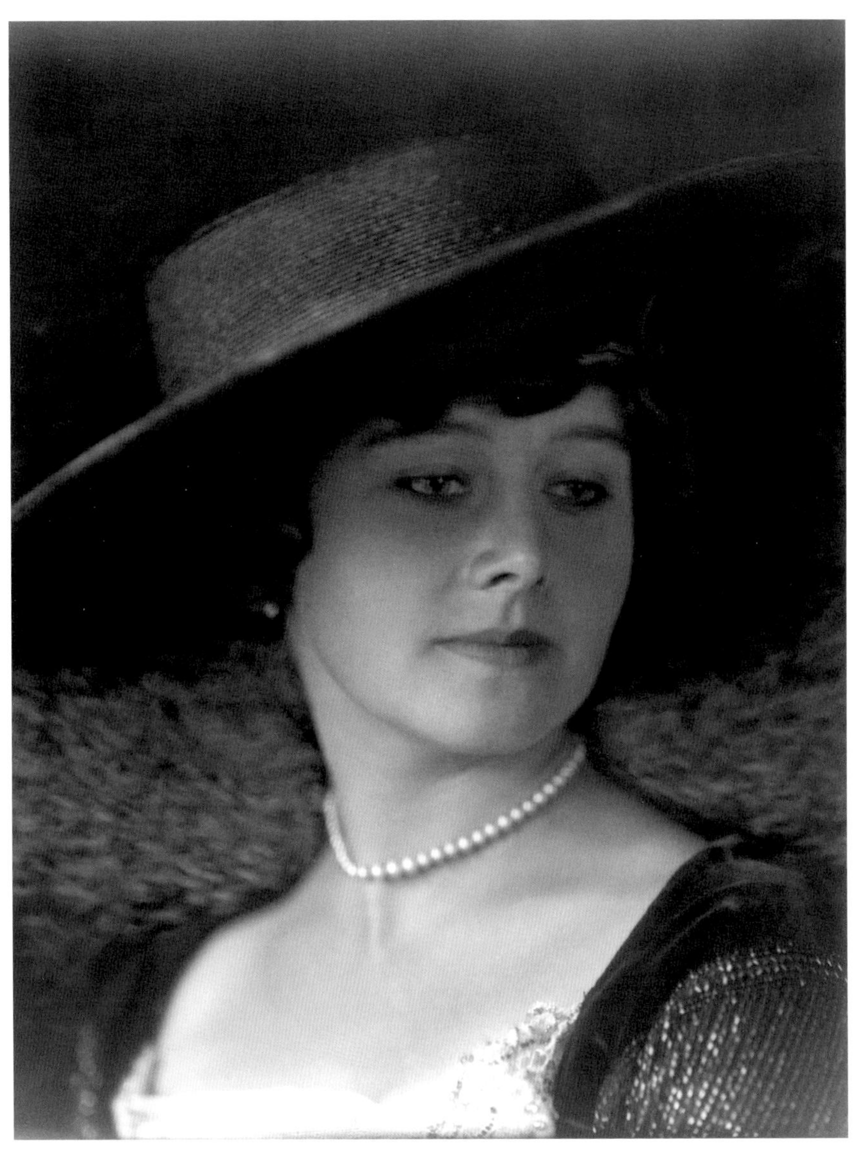

3 **Anna Sedláčková** 1912

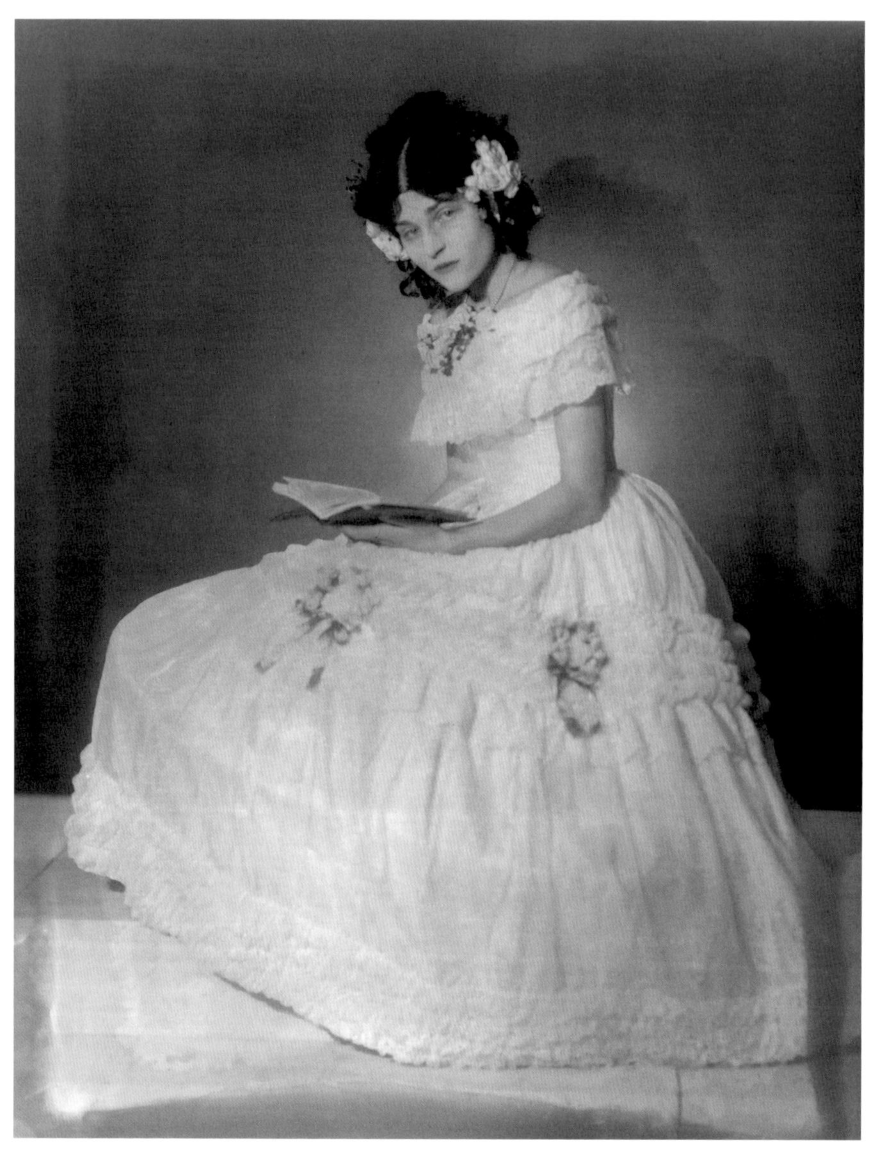

4 **Jarmila Bechyňová** c. 1925

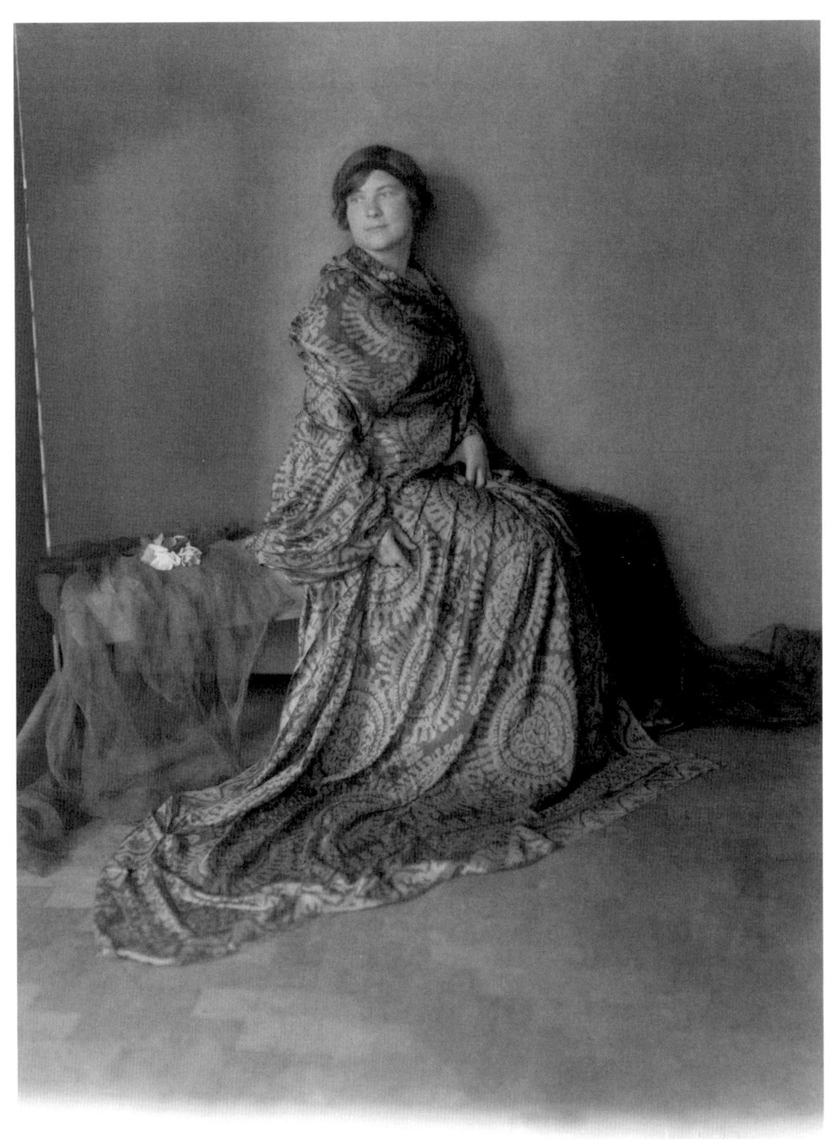

5 **Marie Majerová** c. 1913

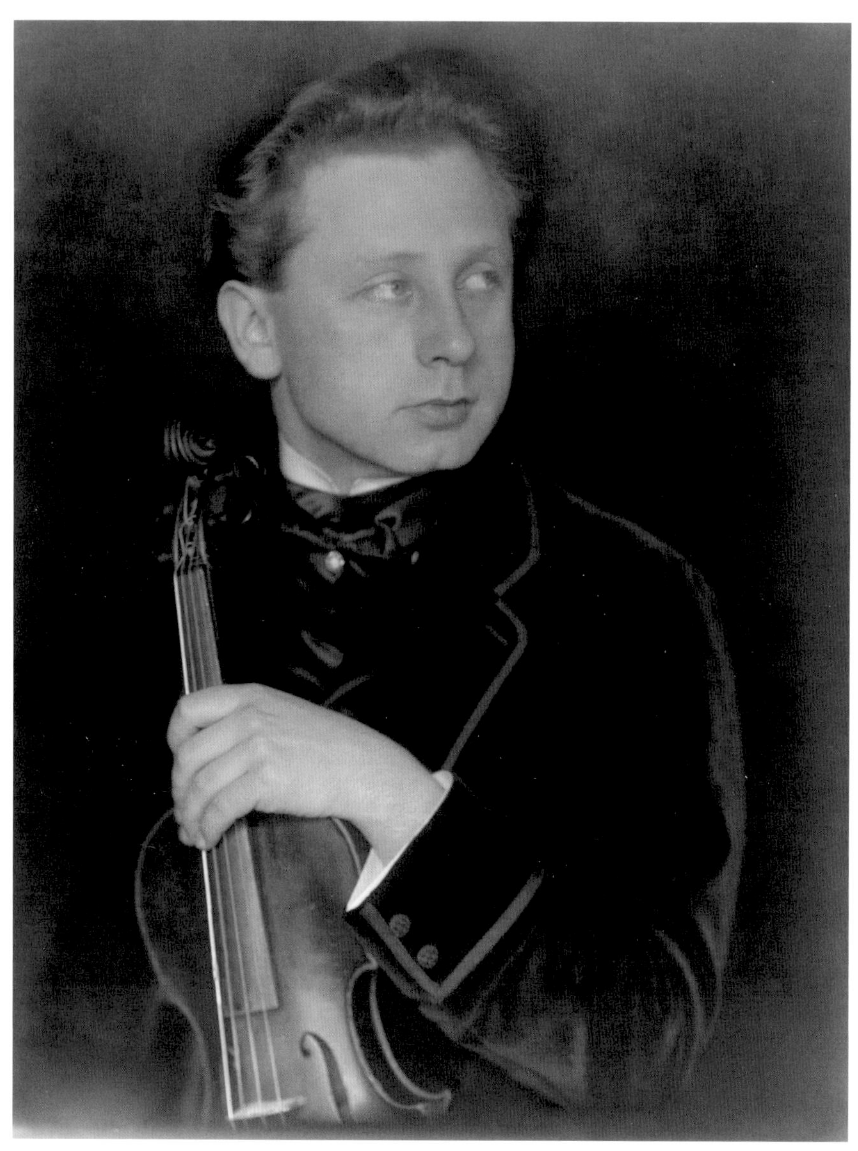

6 **Jaroslav Kocian** 1913

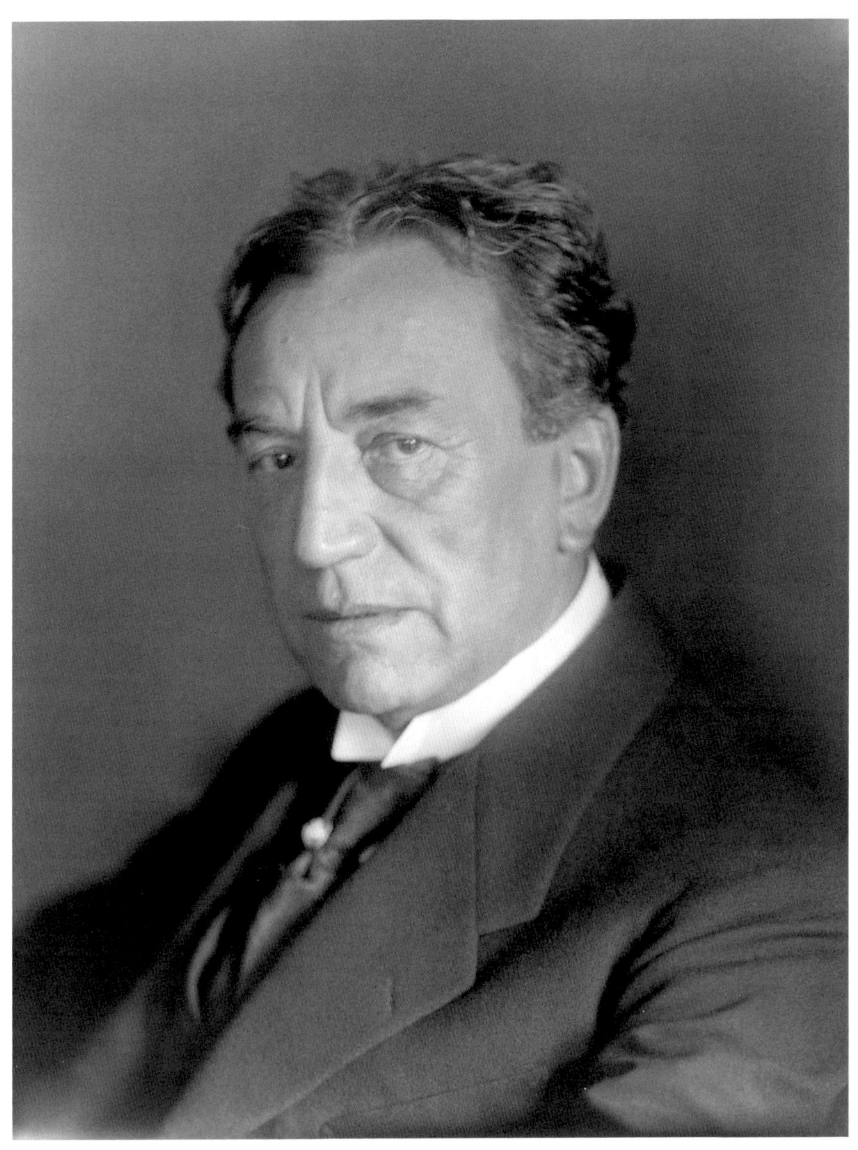

7 **Eduard Vojan** 1913

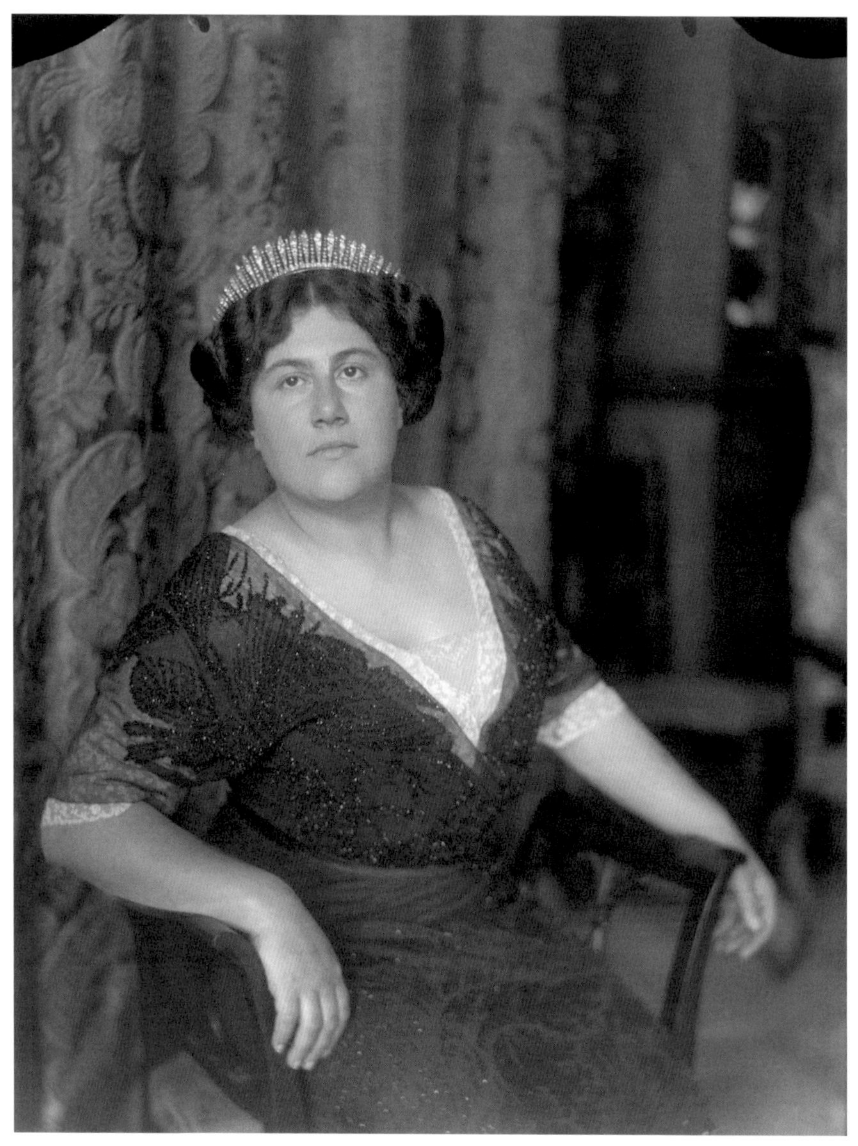

8 **Ema Destinnová** 1914

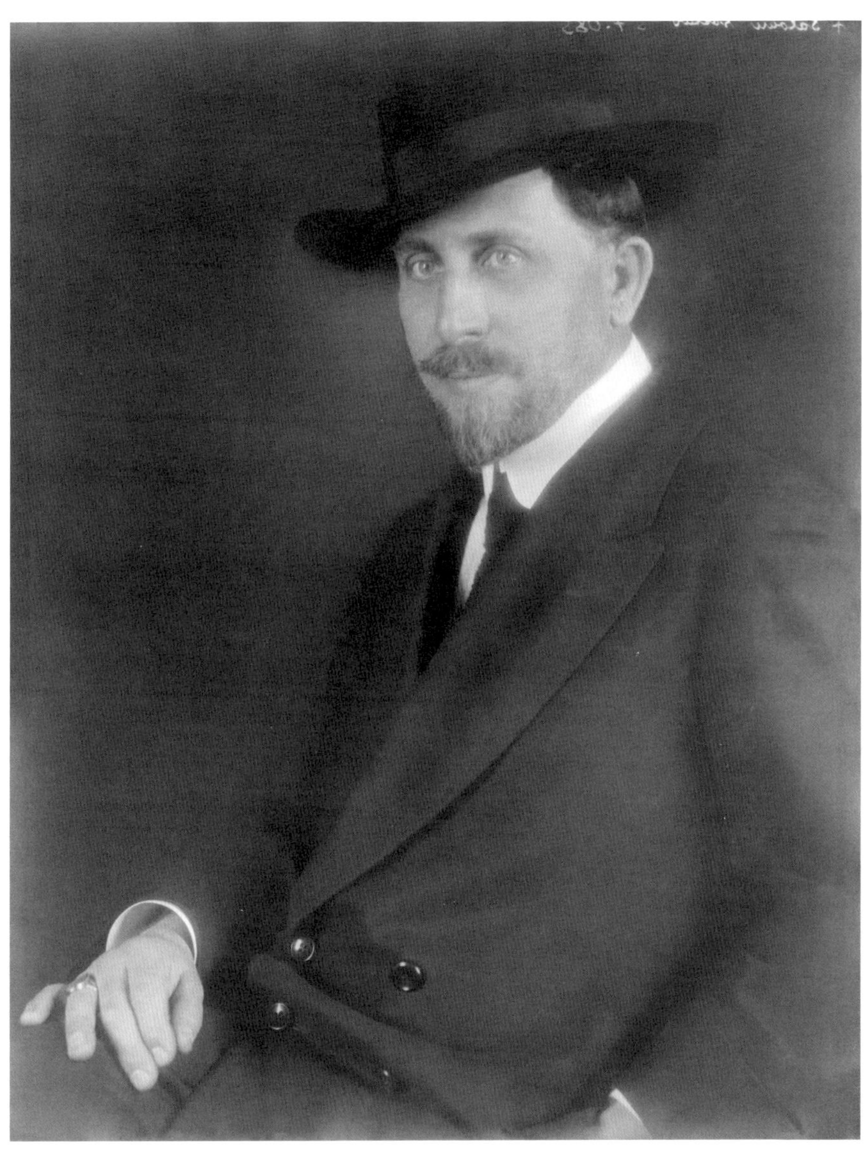

9 **Ladislav Šaloun** c. 1914

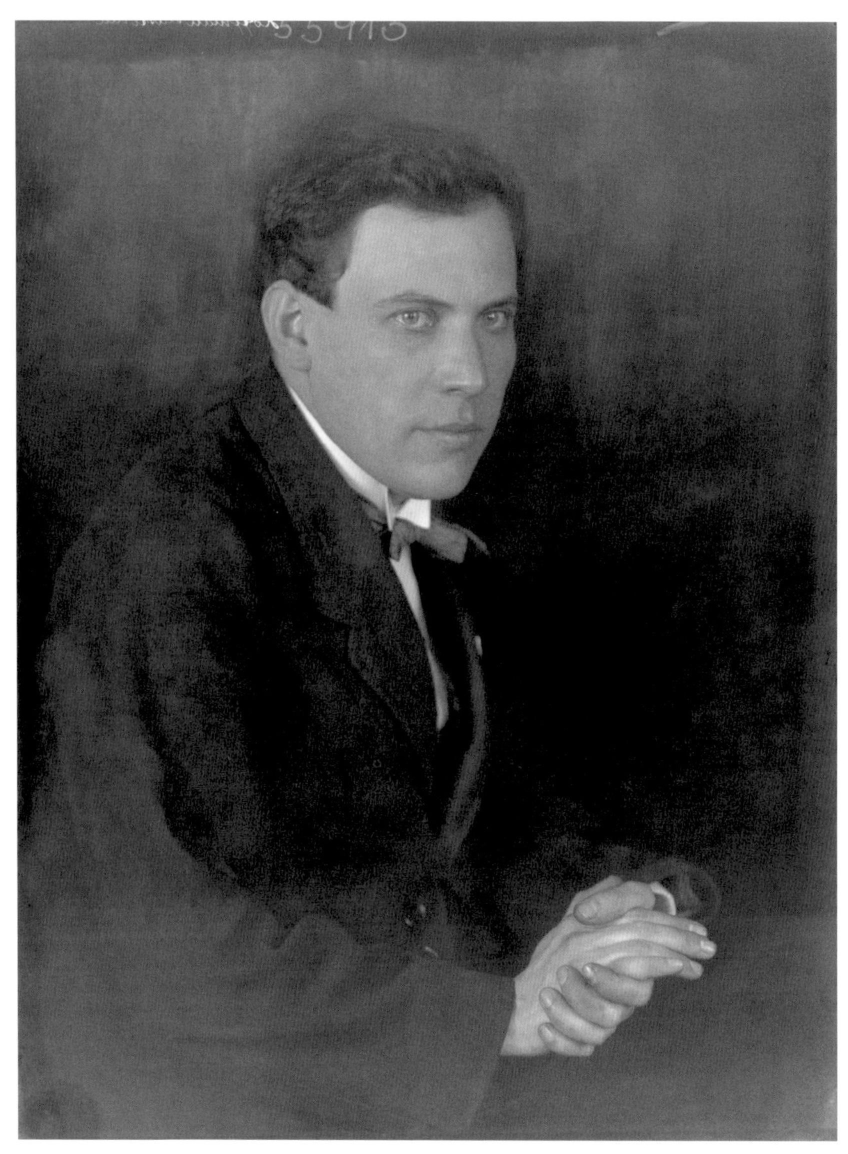

10 **Vlastislav Hofman** c. 1919

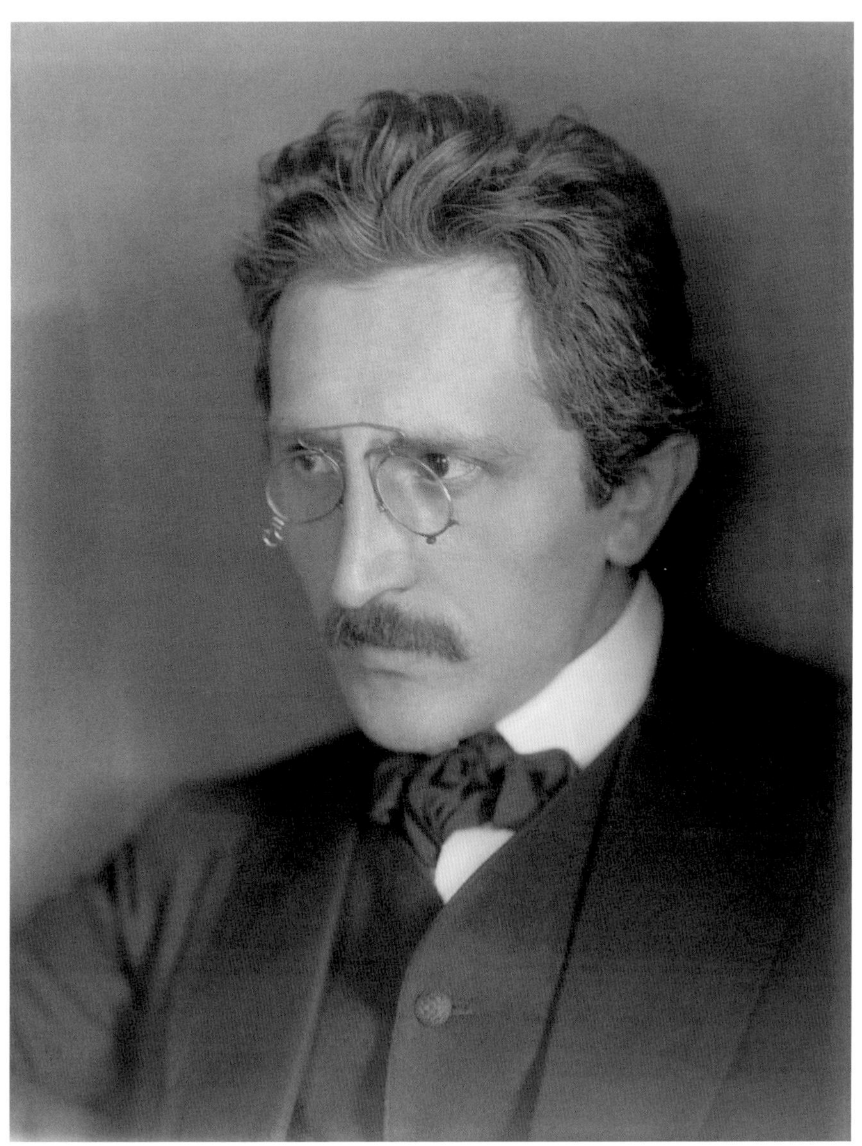

11 **Josef Váchal** 1913

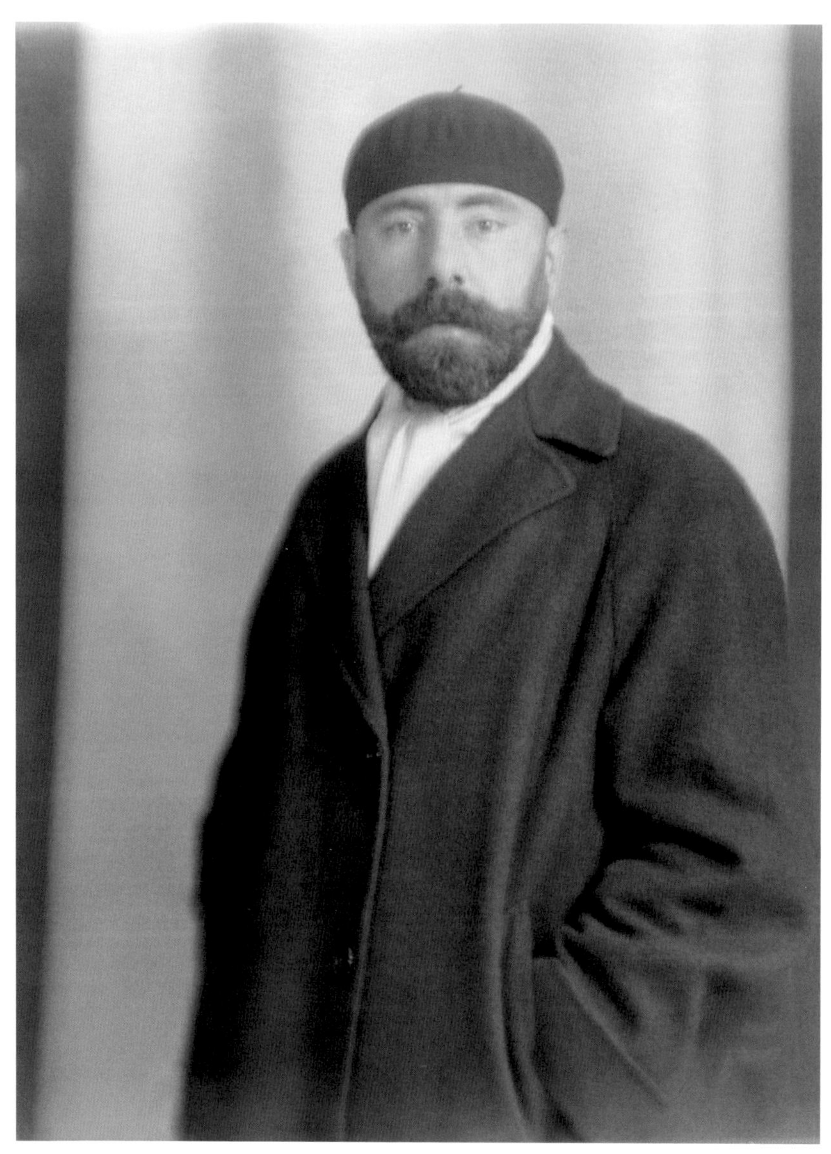

12 **Jan Zrzavý** 1919

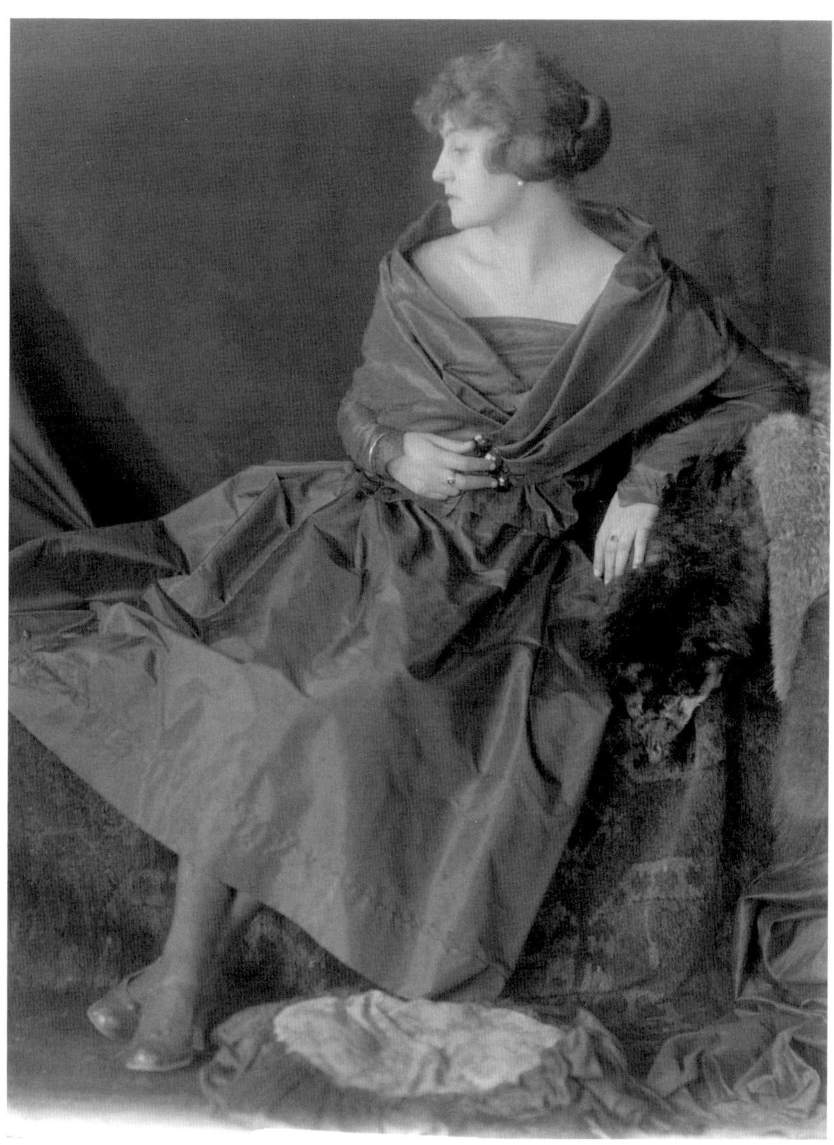

13 **Lydie Kamenská** 1919

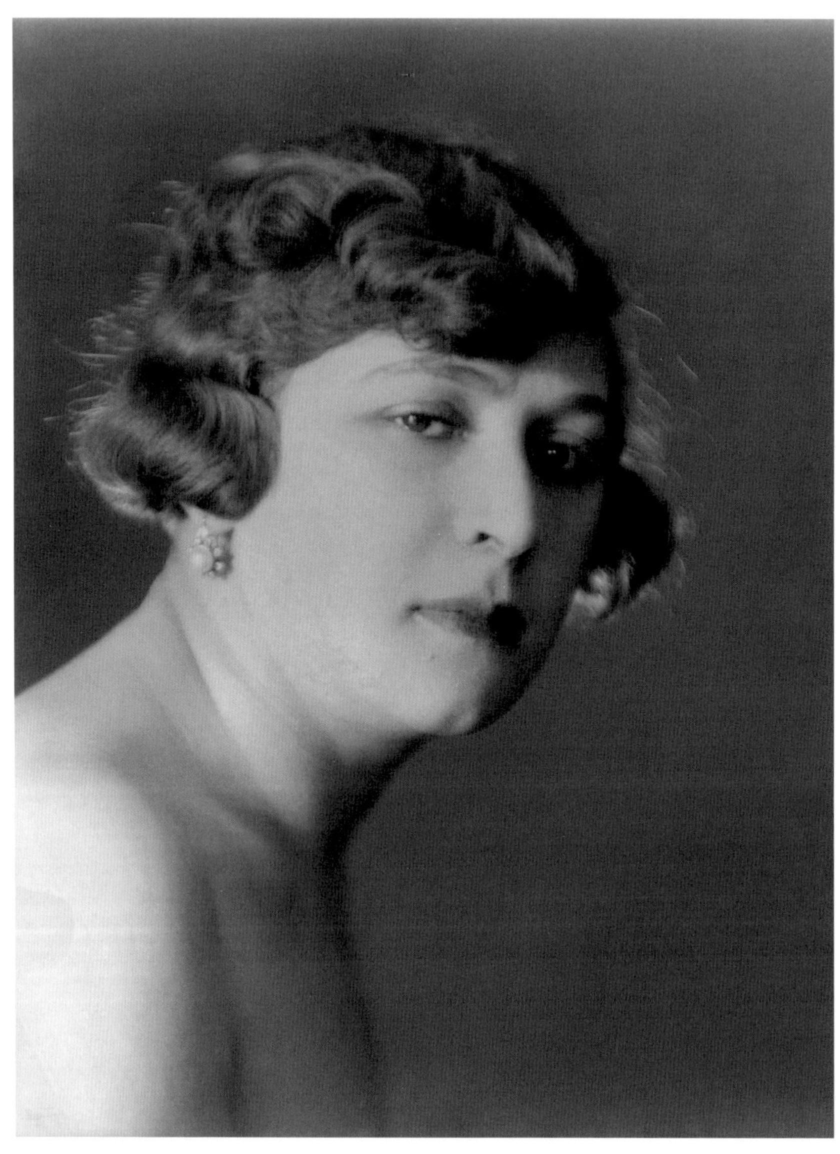

14 **Duška Vronská** c. 1925

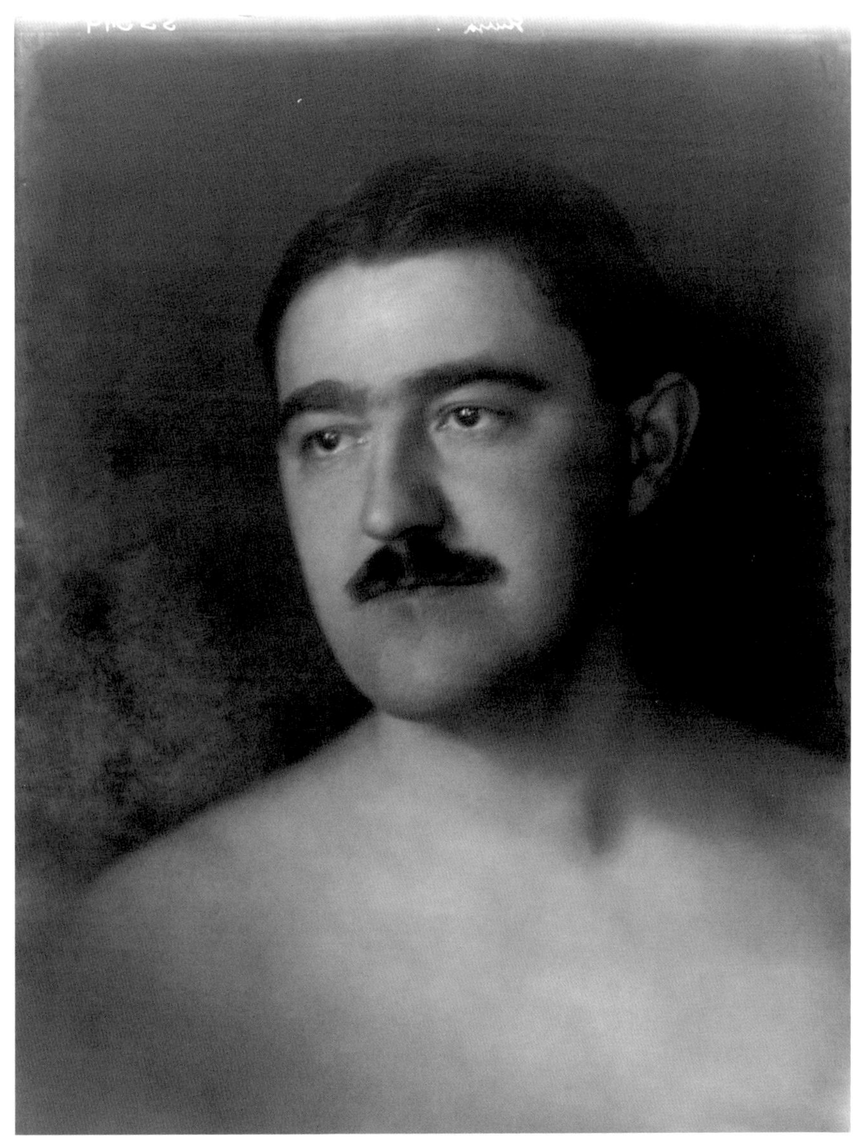

15 **Jan Štursa** c. 1912

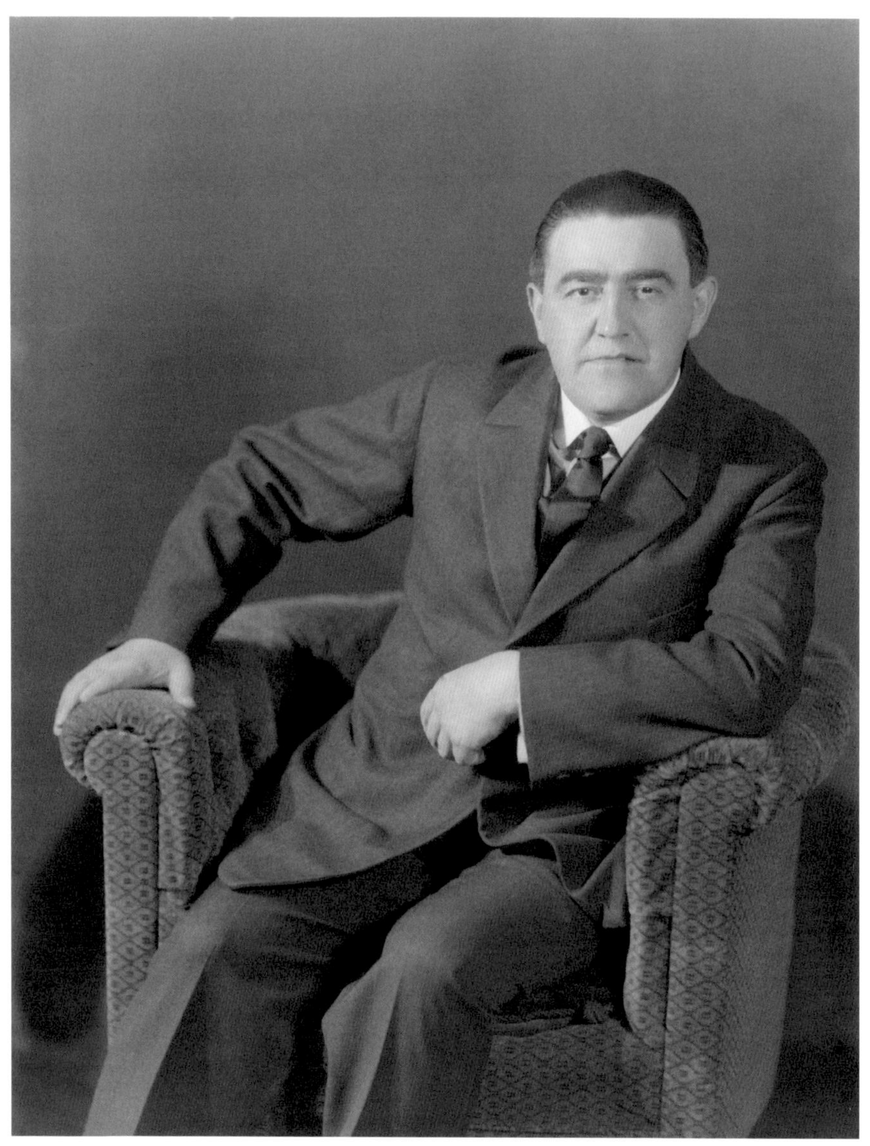

16 **Jan Štursa** 1924

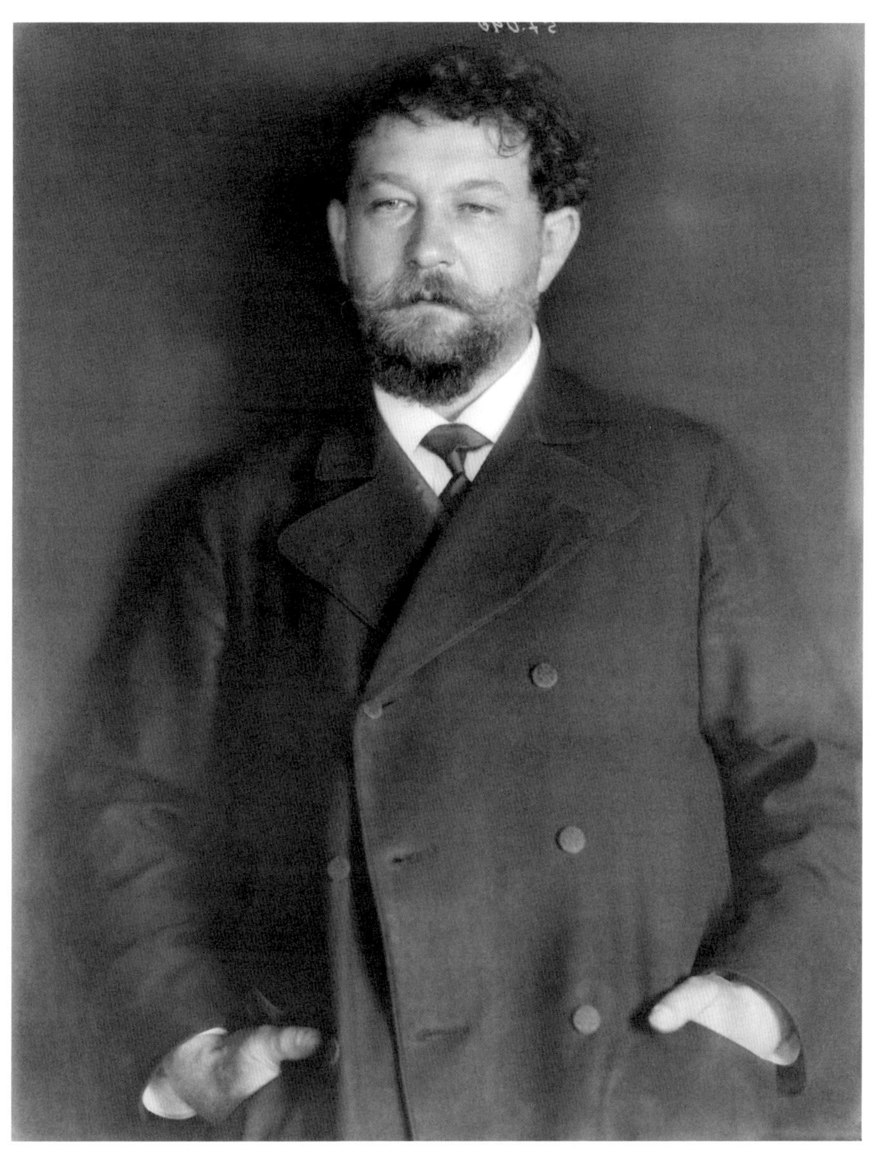

17 **Josef Mařatka**   c. 1912

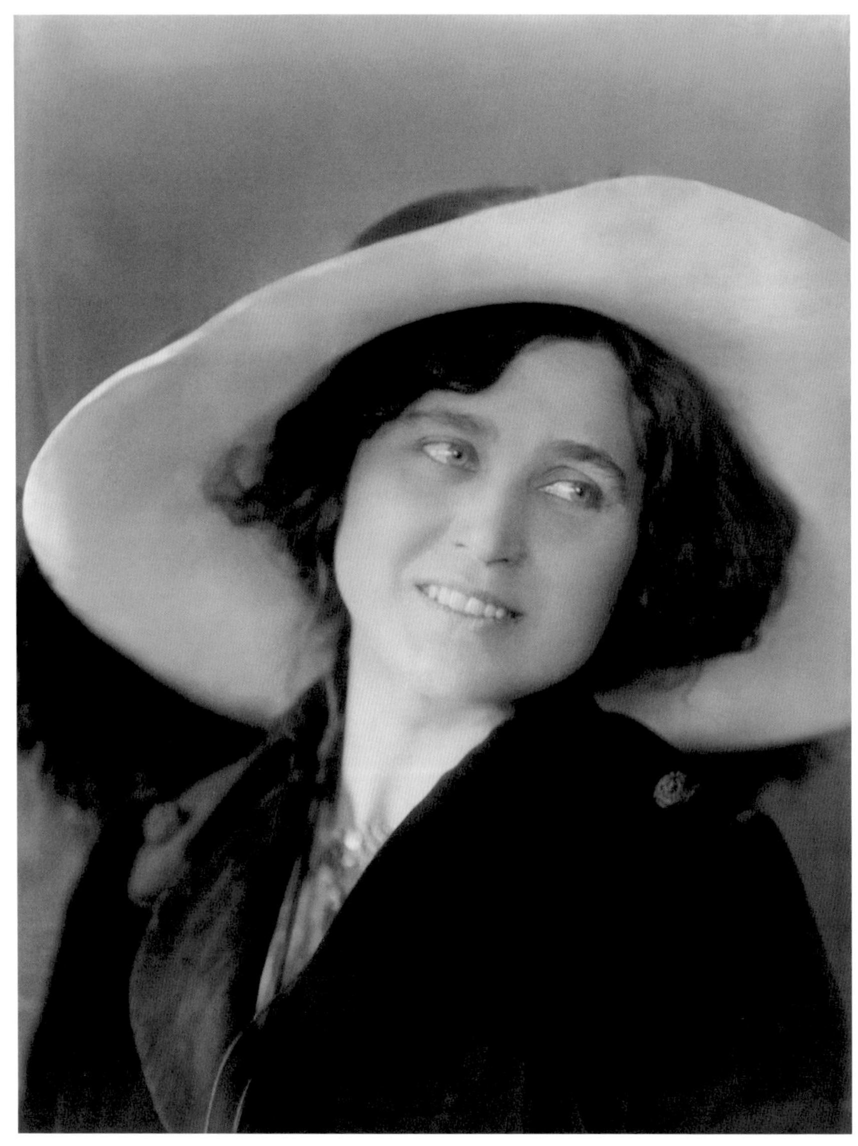

18 **Leopolda Dostalová** c. 1914

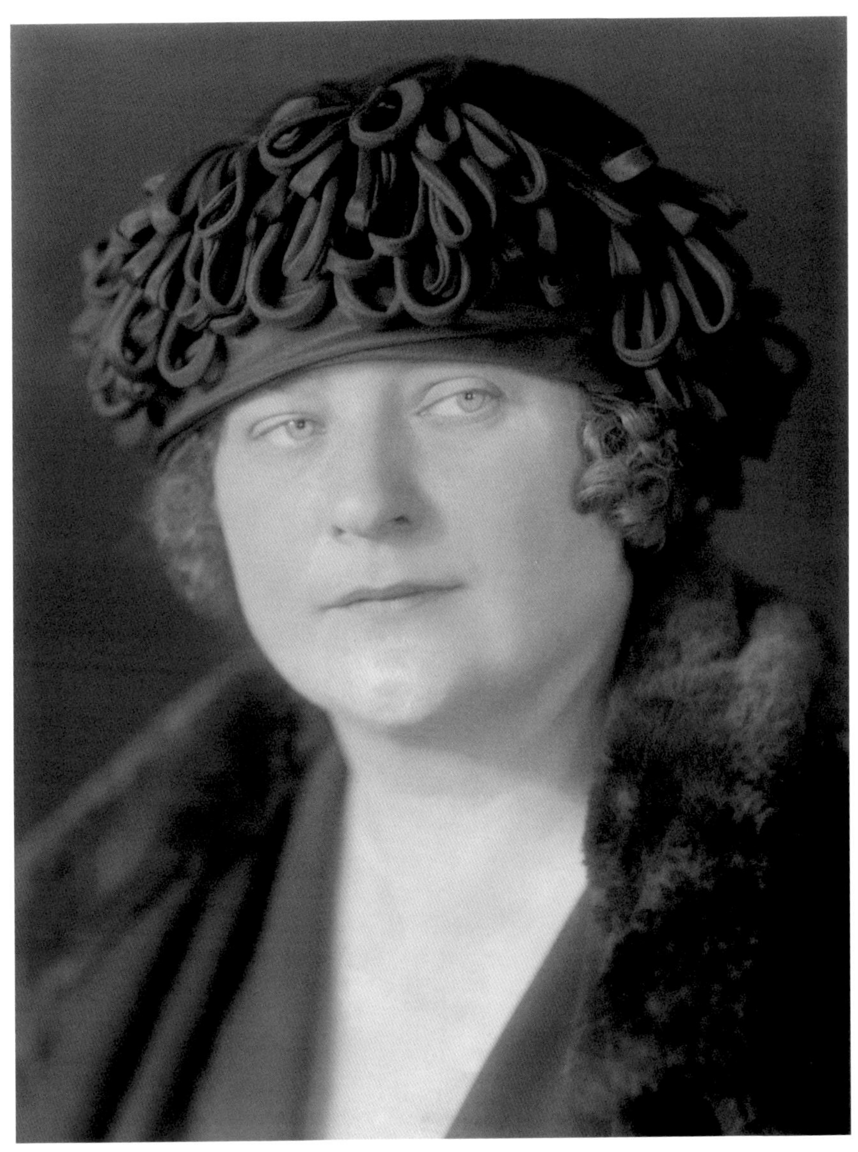

19 **Růžena Nasková** c. 1920

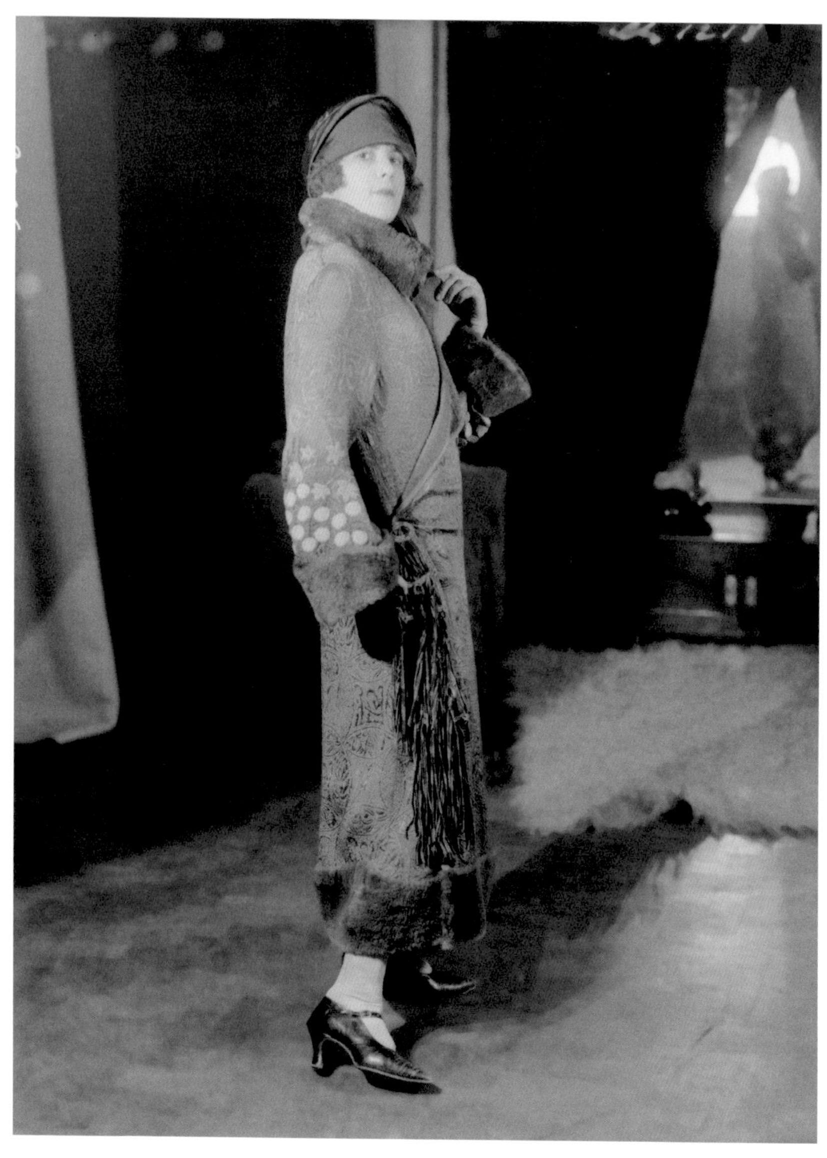

20 **Jarmila Novotná** 1928

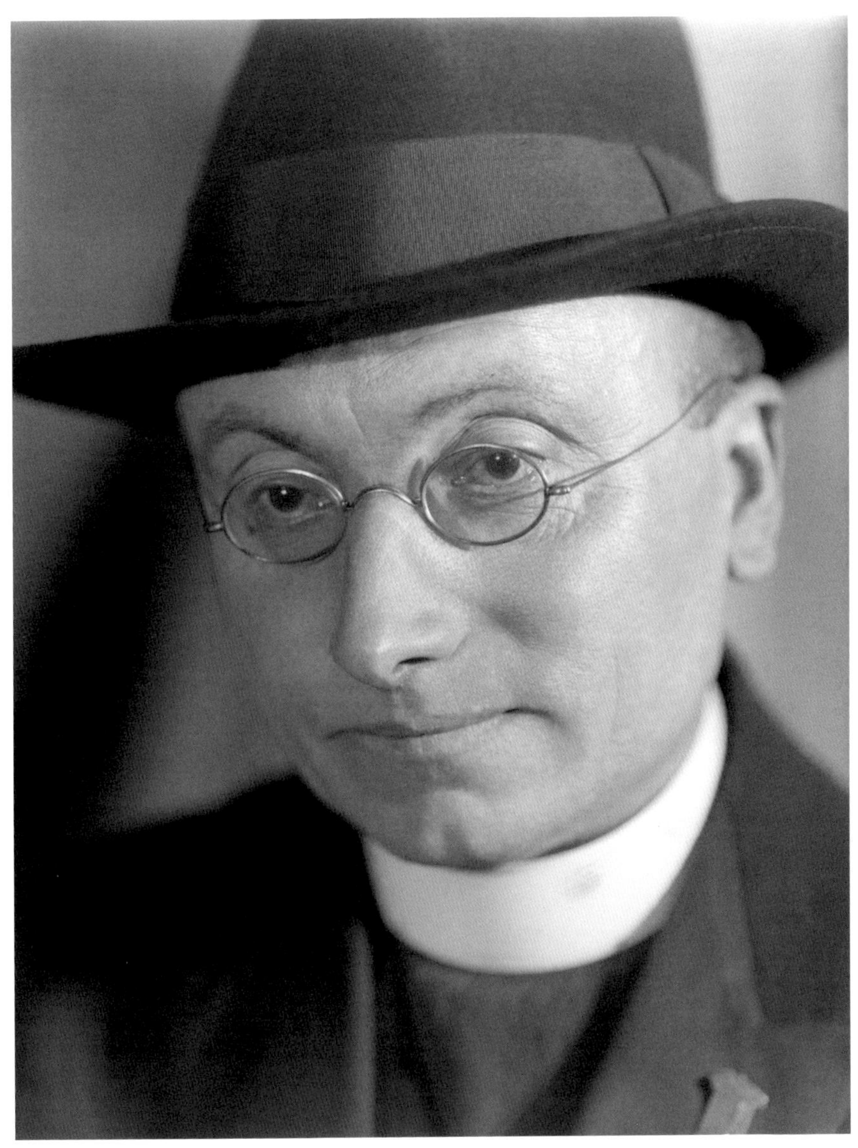

21 **Jakub Deml** c. 1914

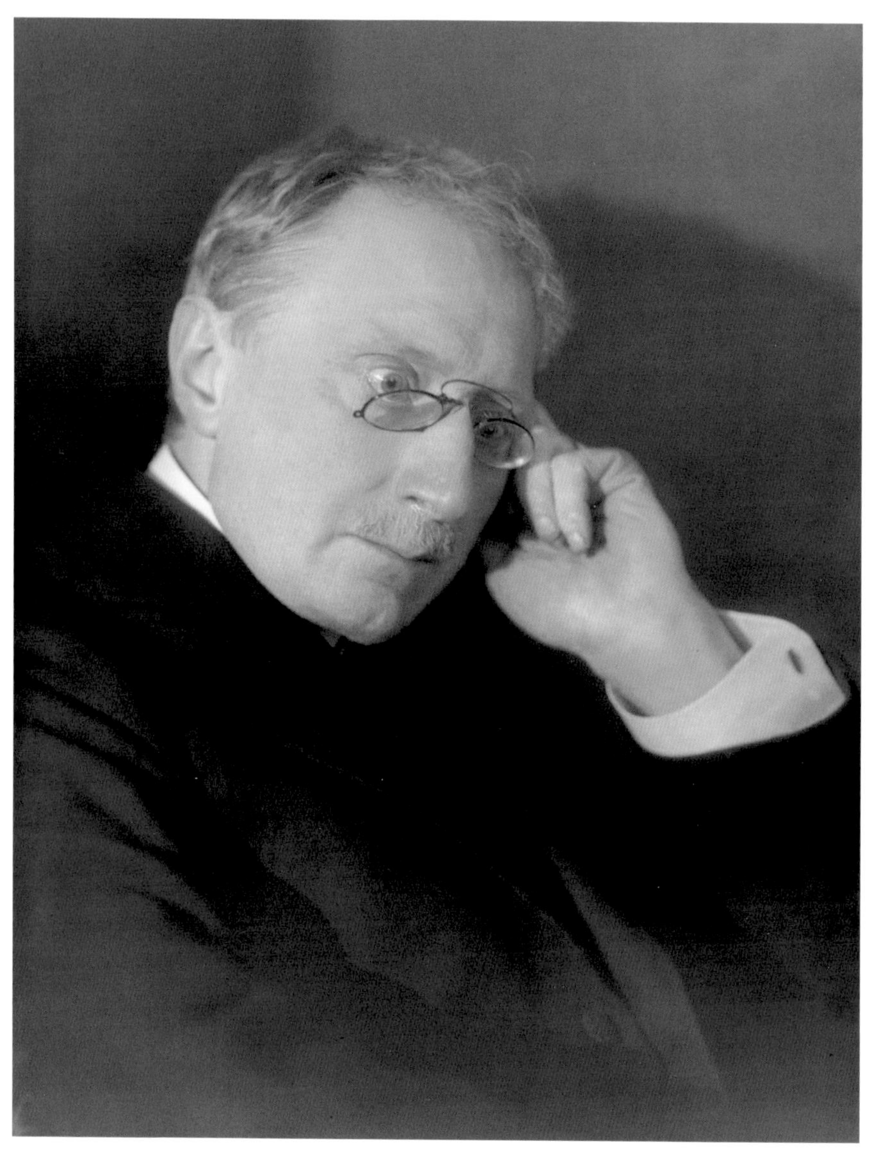

22 **Antonín Sova**   c. 1920

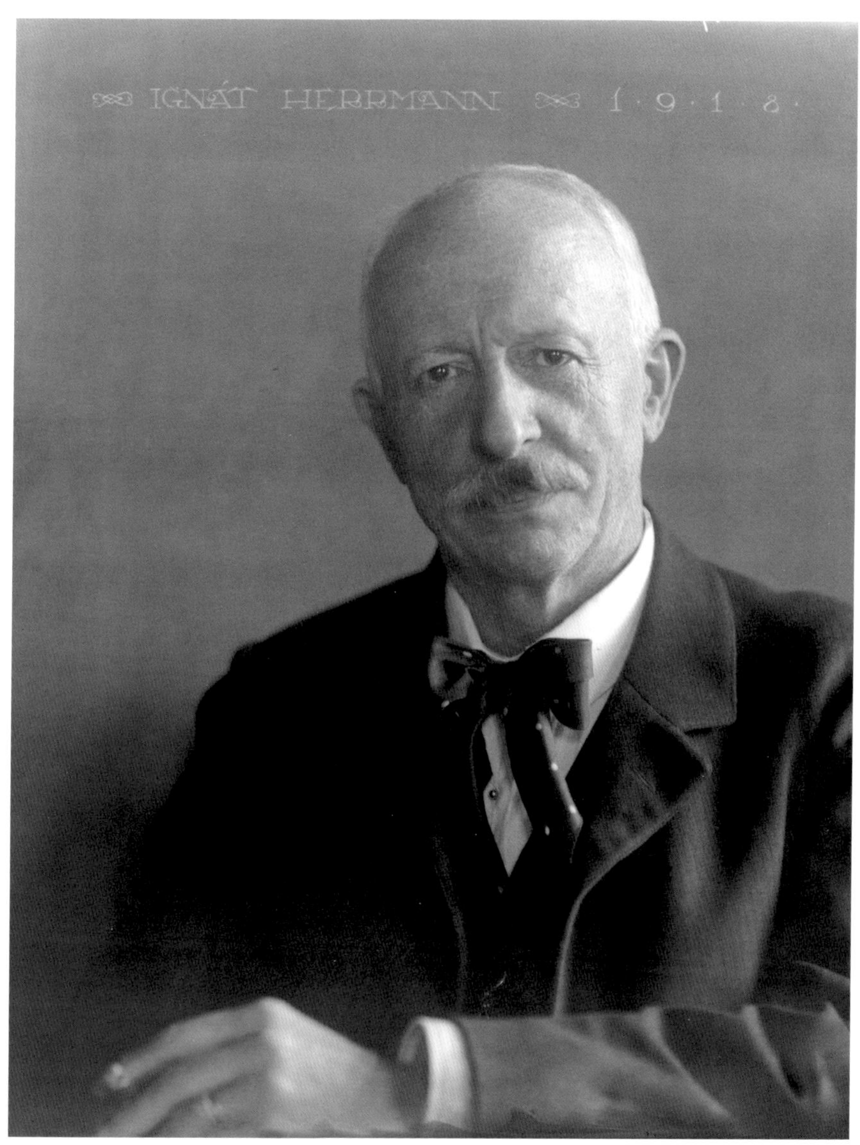

23 **Ignát Herrmann** 1918

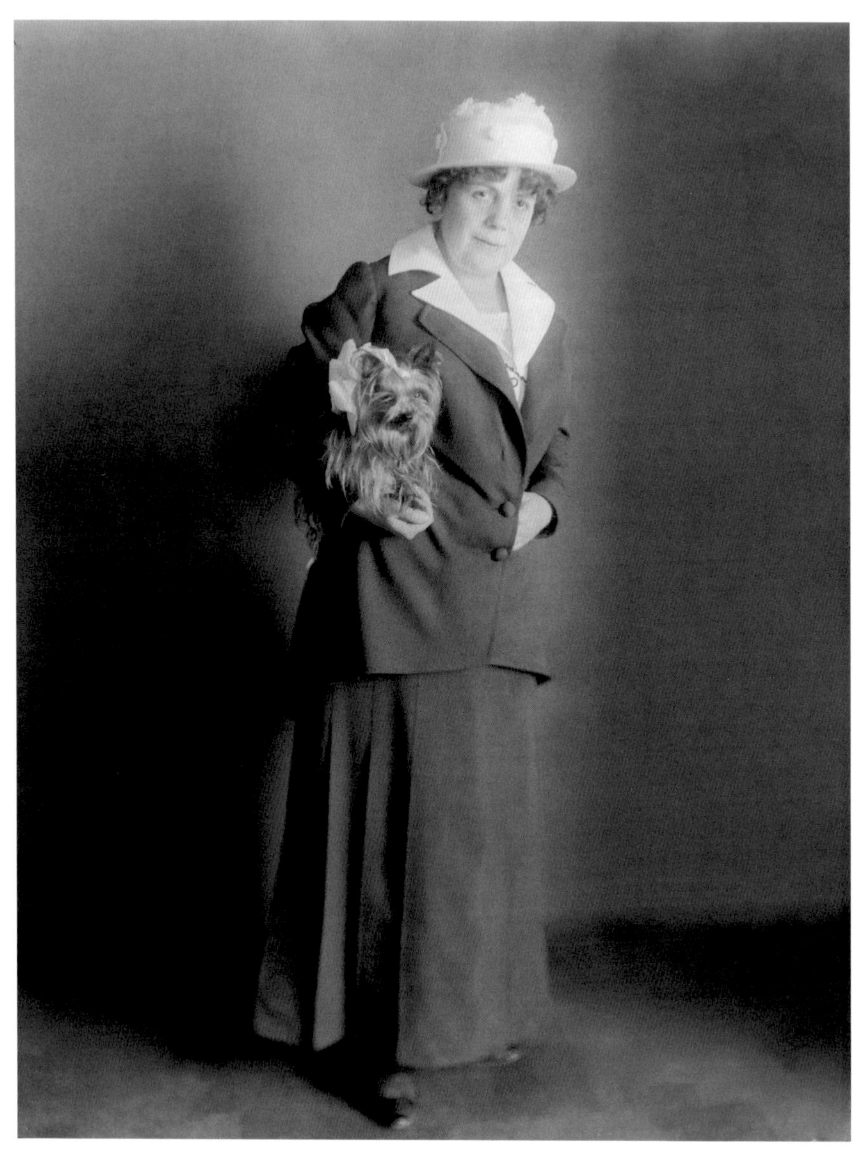

24 **Marie Hübnerová** c. 1925

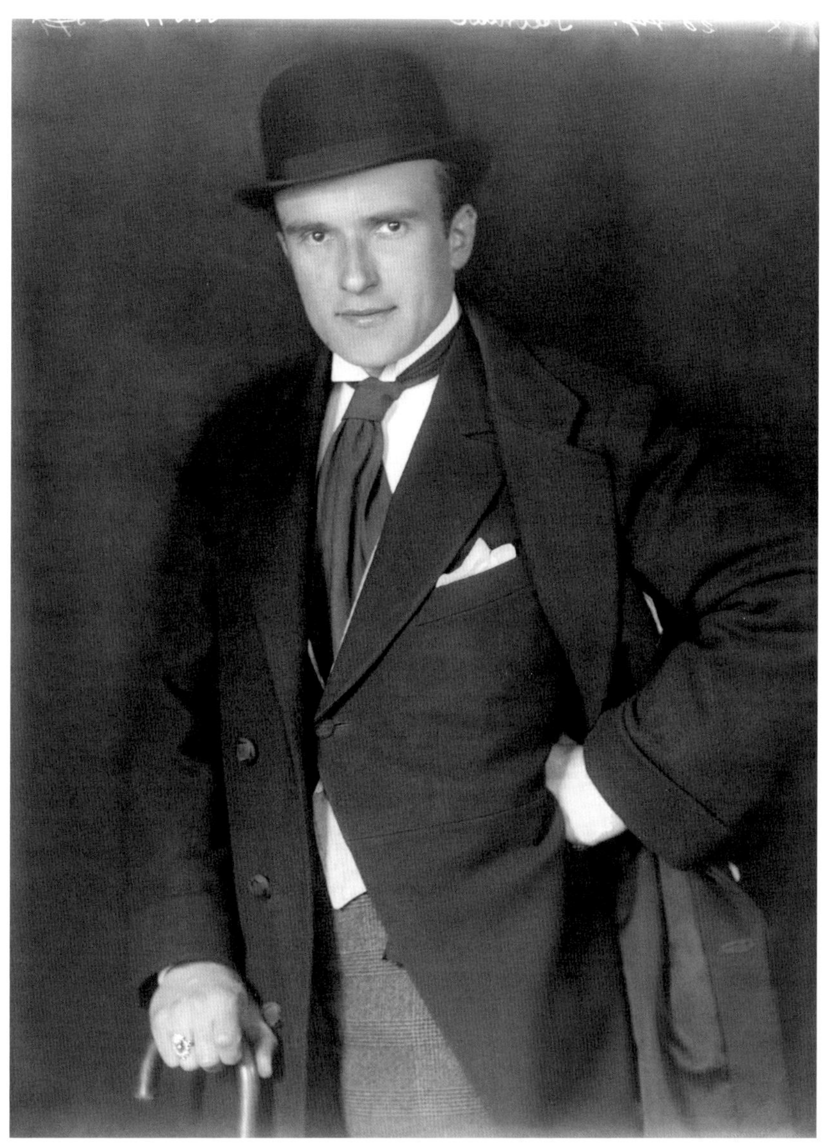

25 **Jiří Steimar** c. 1922

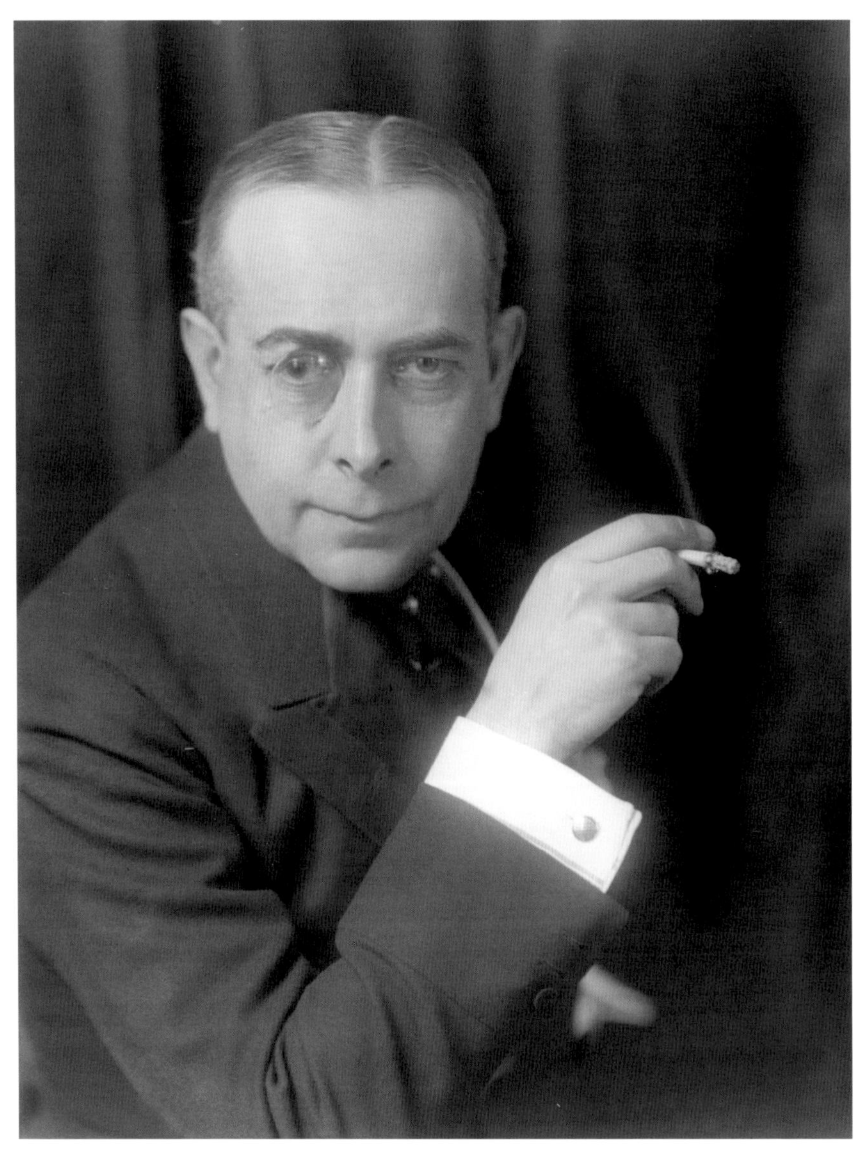

26 **Vojtěch Mastný** 1921

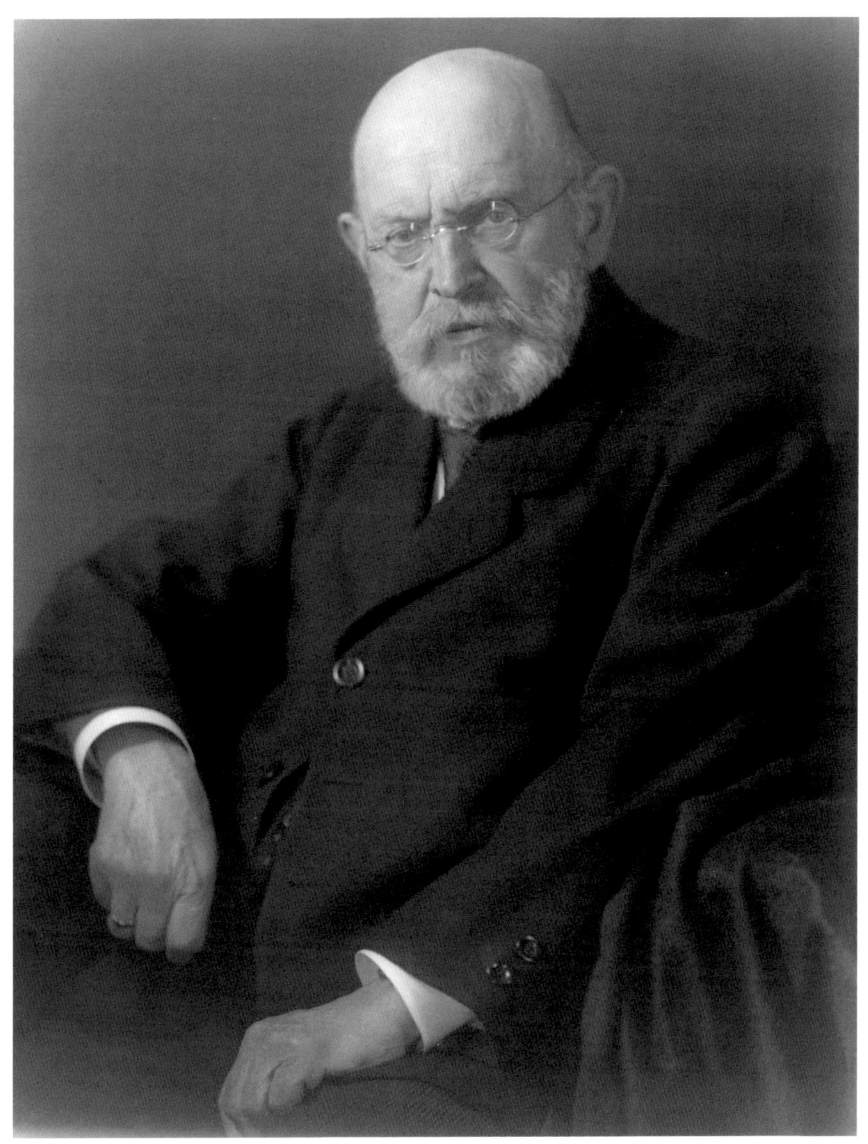

27 **Alois Jirásek** 1919

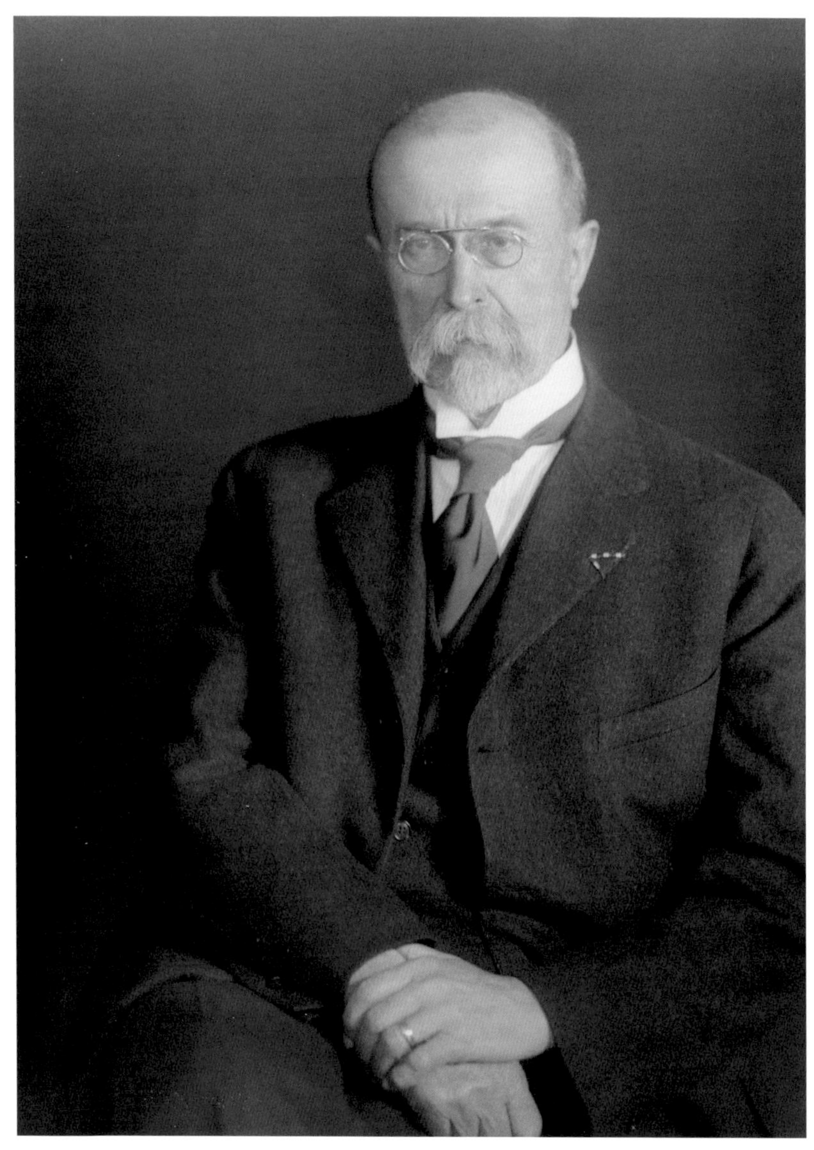

28 **Tomáš Garrigue Masaryk** 1919

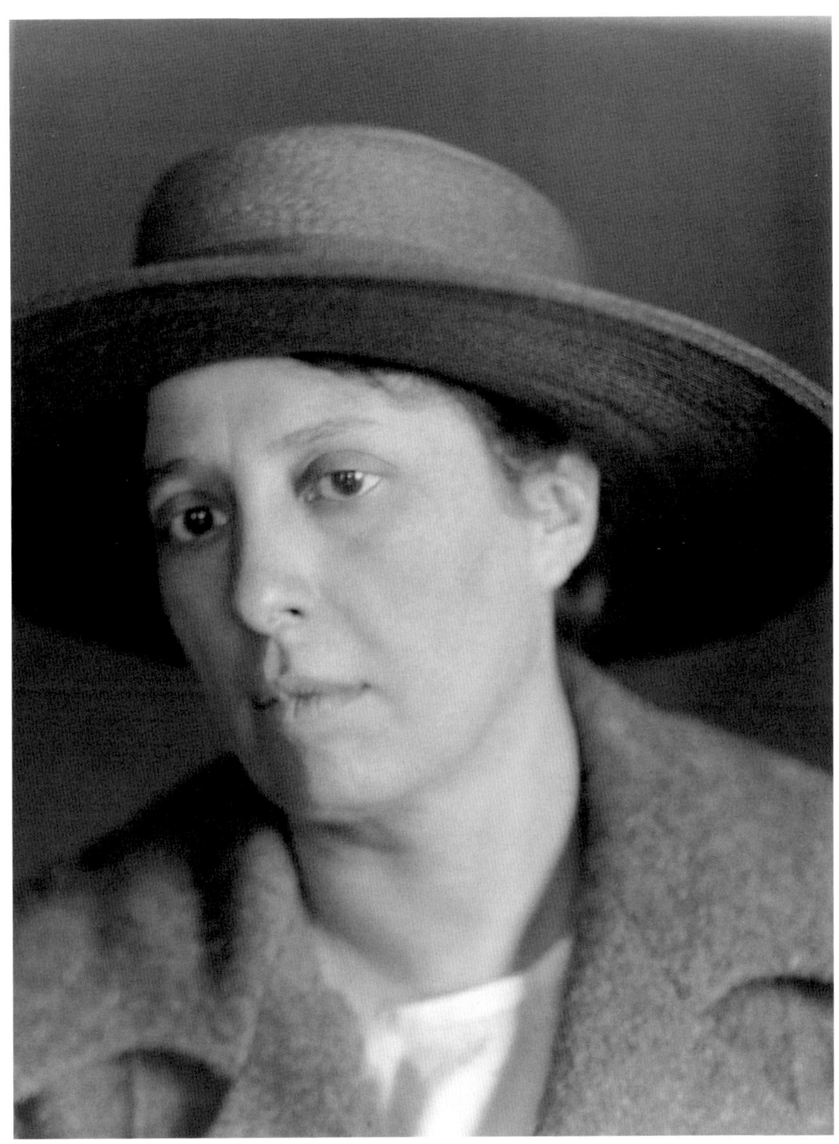

29 **Alice Masaryková** 1919

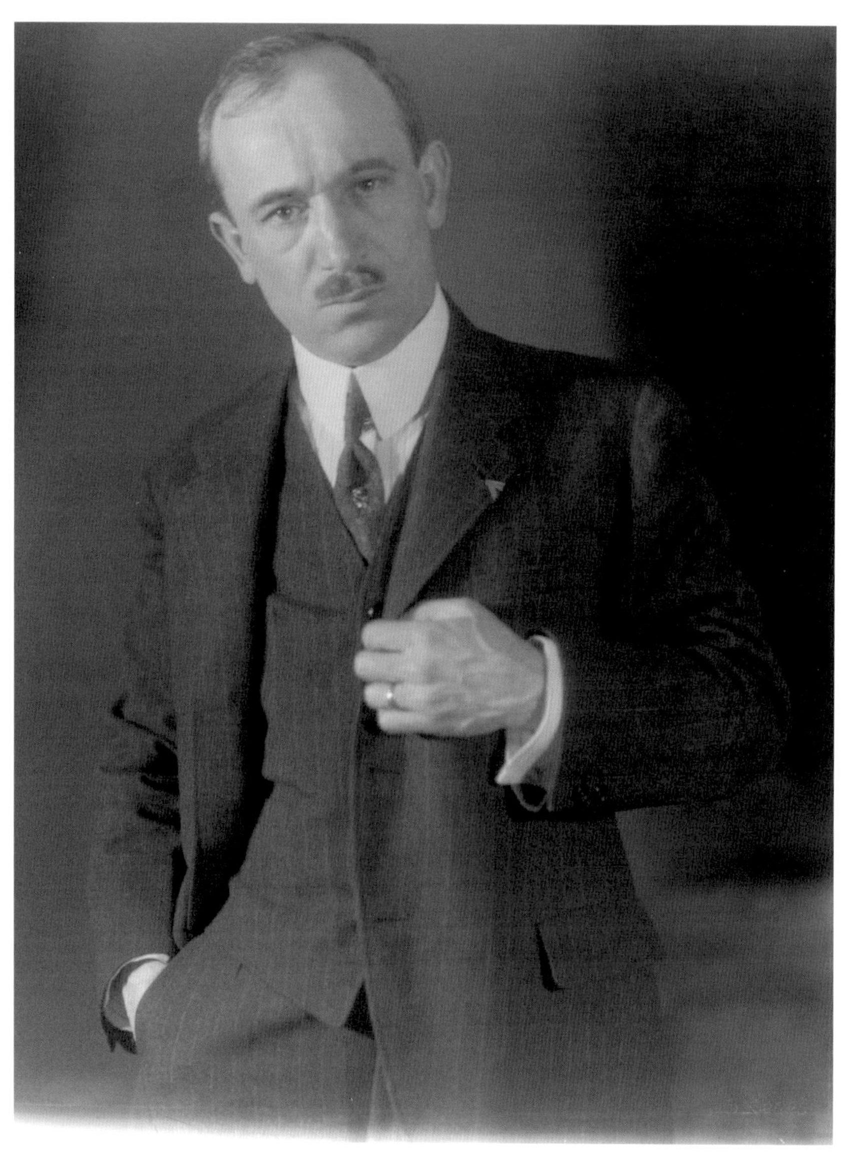

30 **Edvard Beneš** 1921

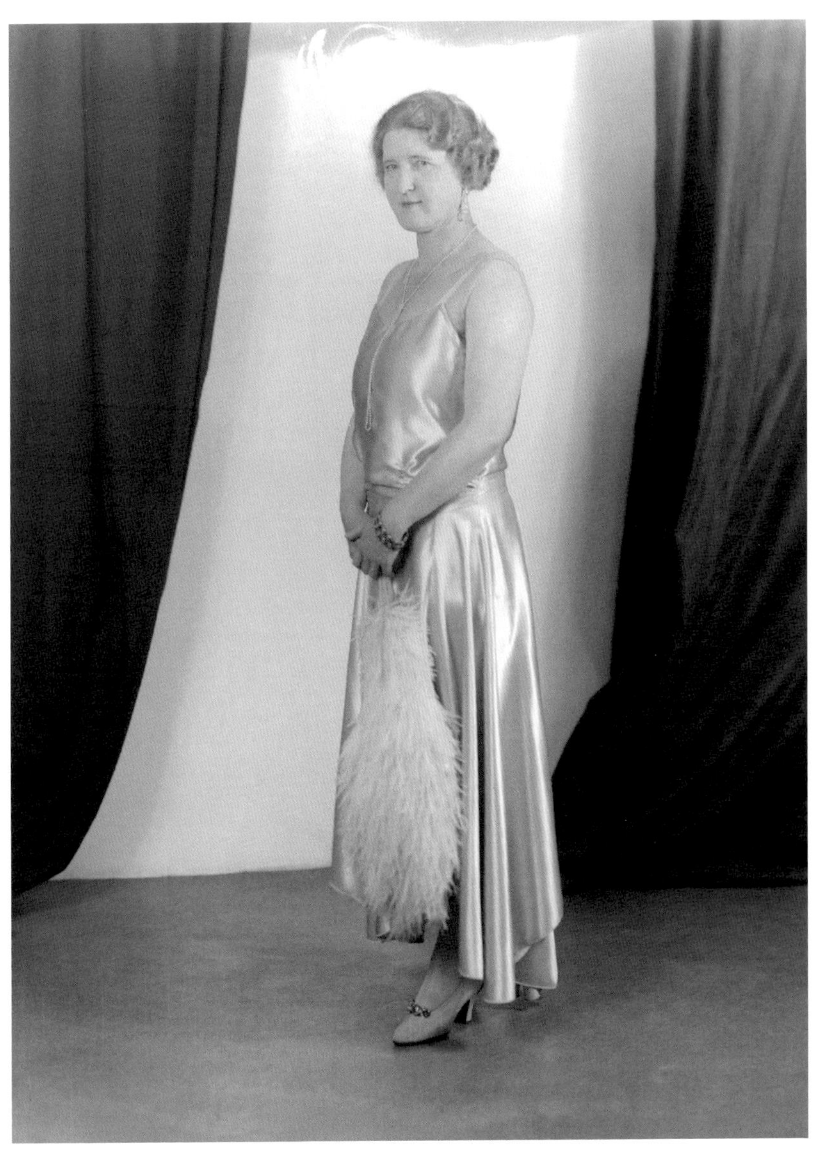

31 **Hana Benešová** 1929

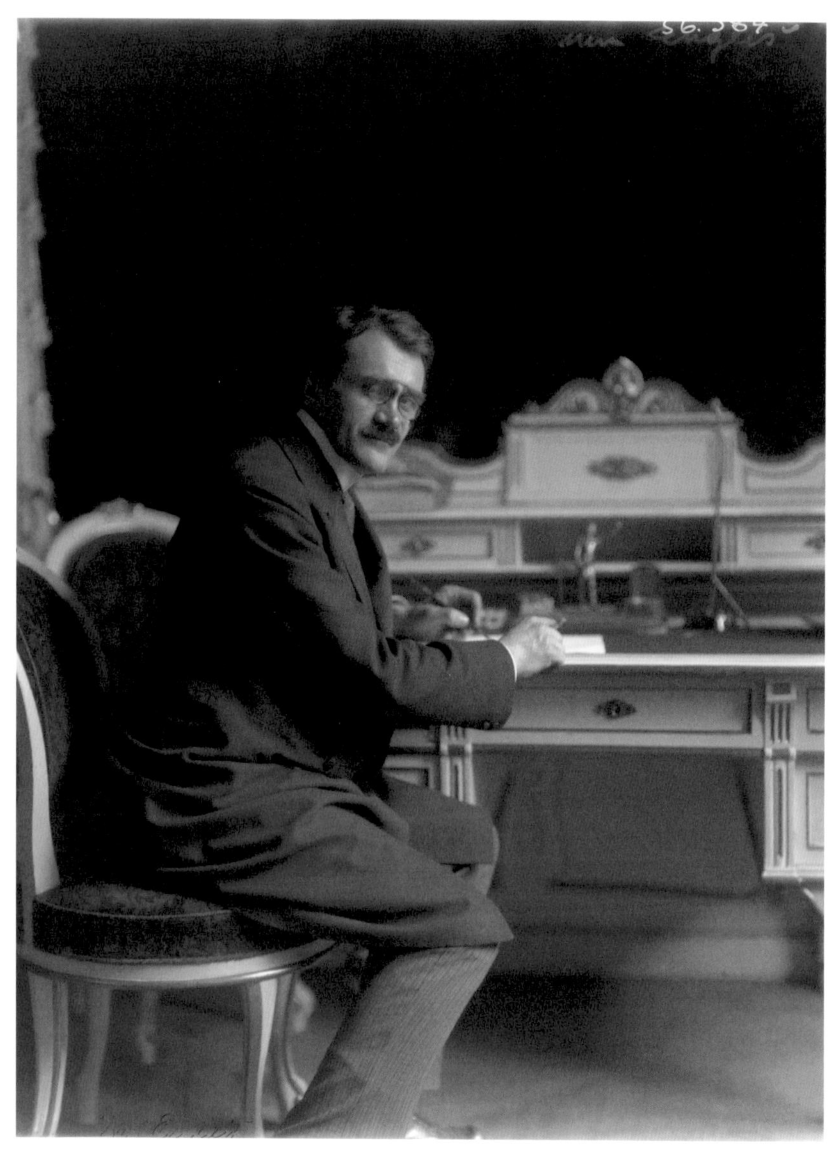

32 **Karel Engliš** c. 1920

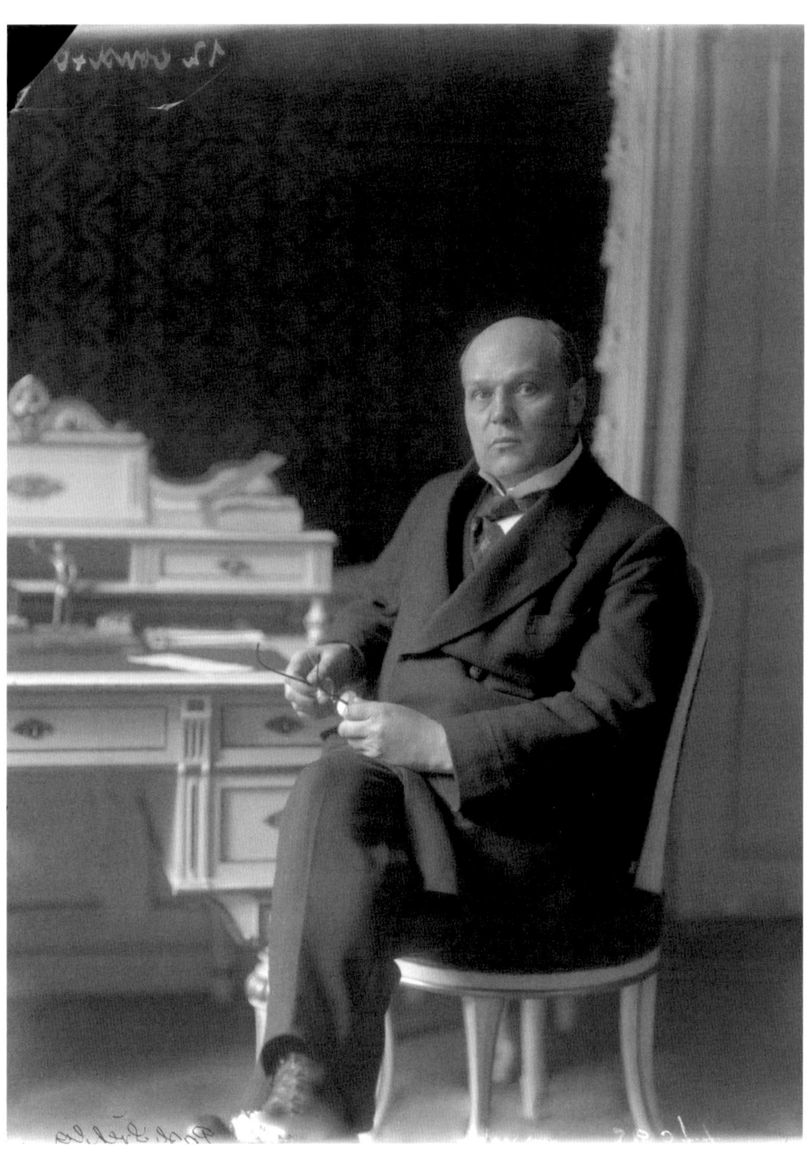

33 **Antonín Švehla** c. 1920

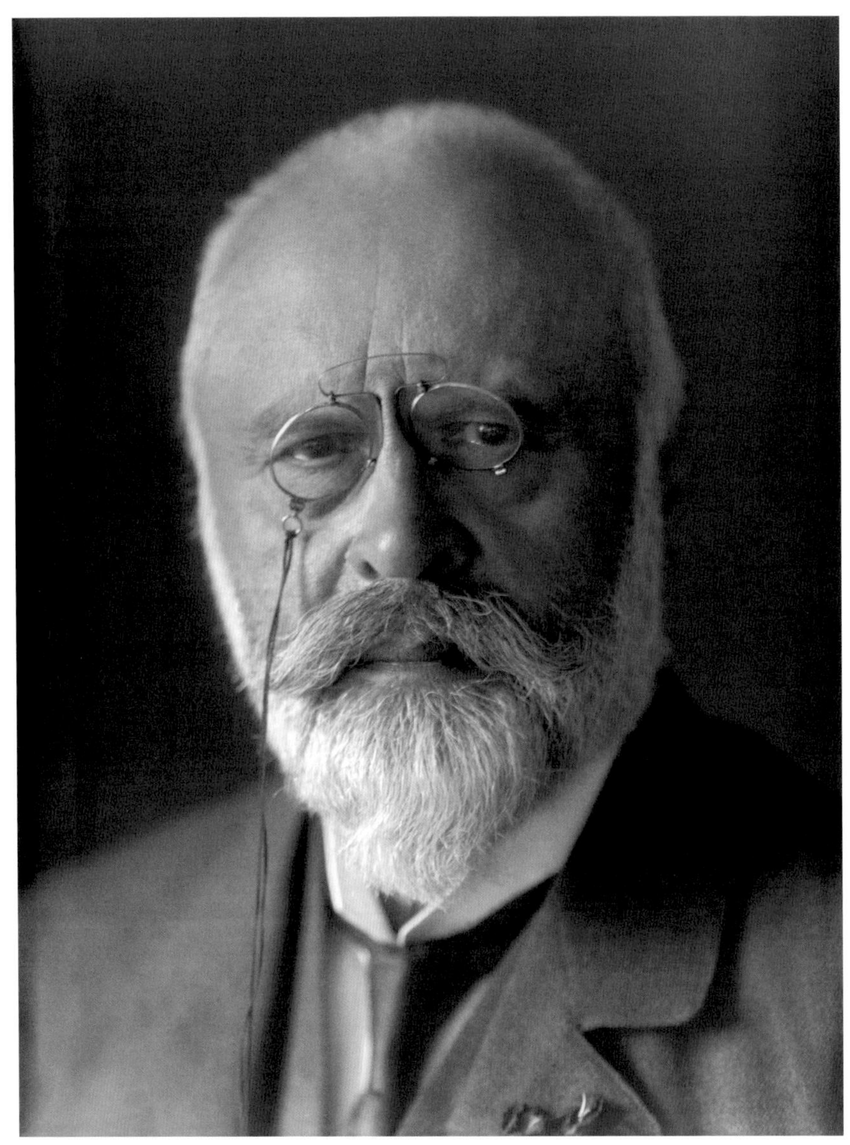

34 **František Topič** c. 1930

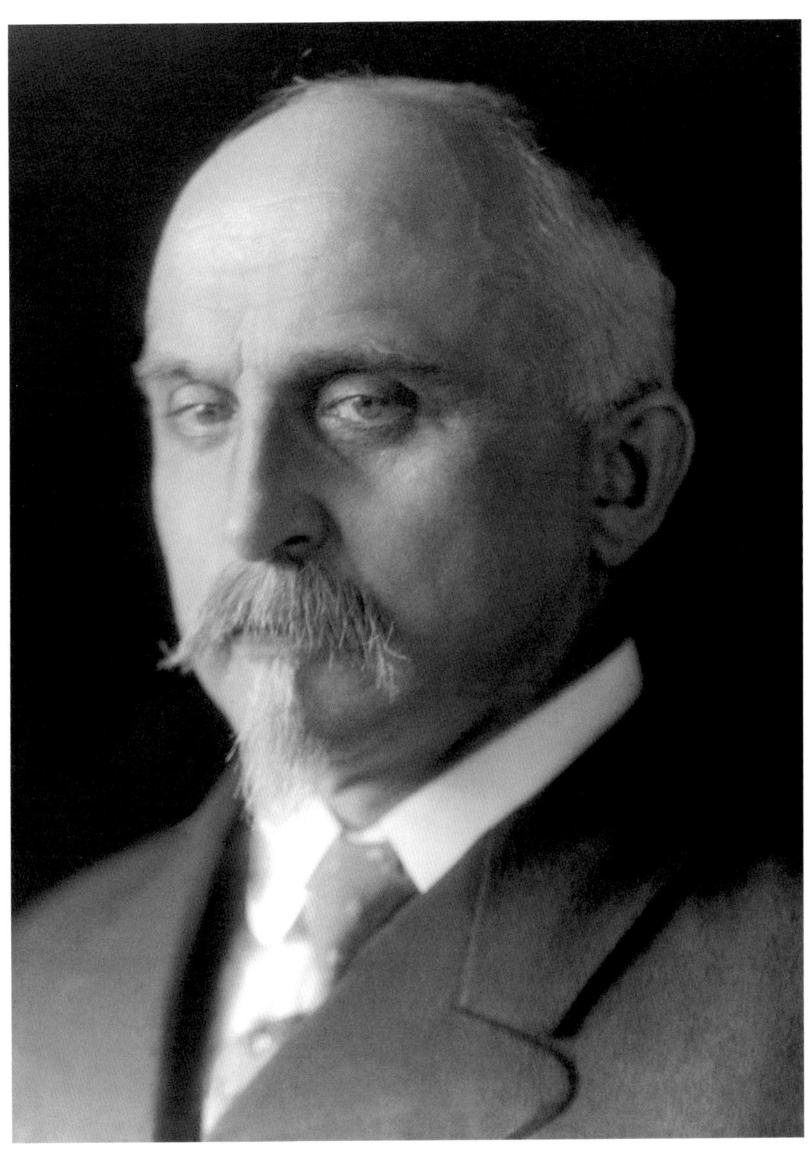

35 **Alois Rašín** c. 1921

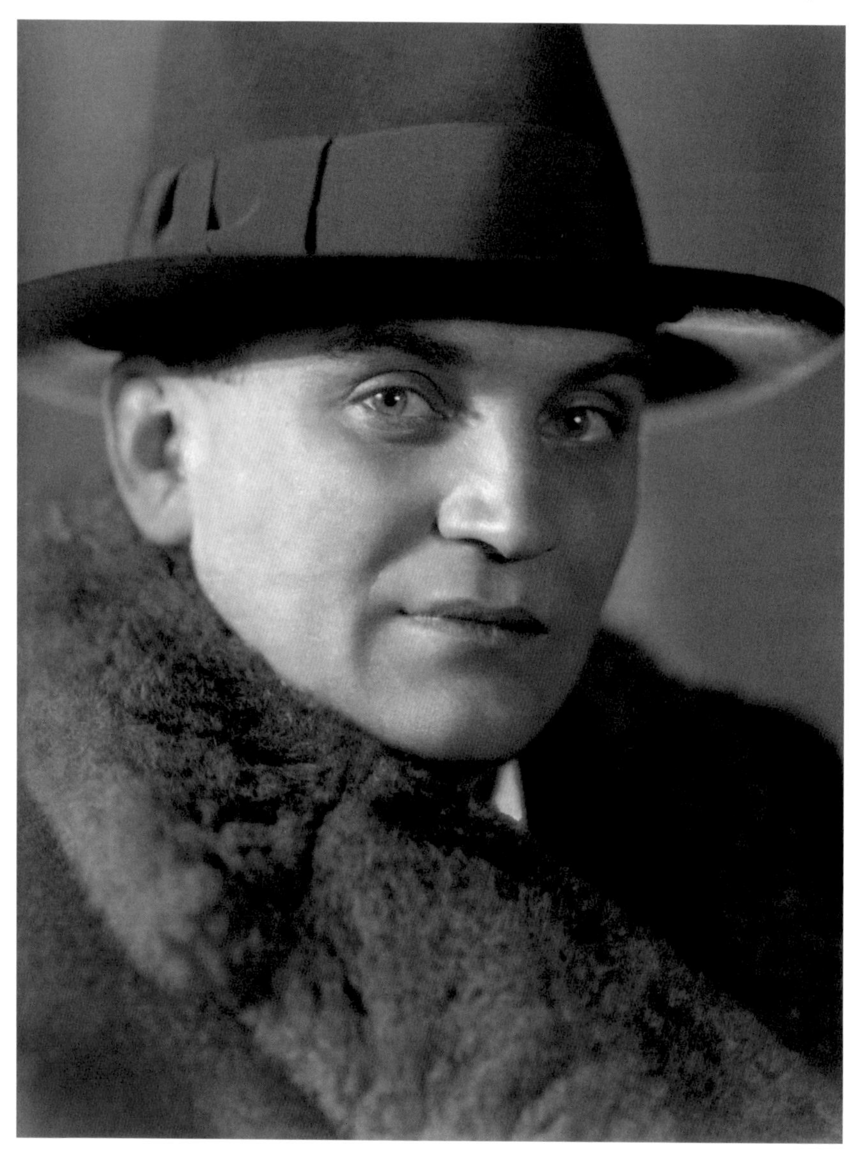

36 **Jiří Kroha** c. 1925

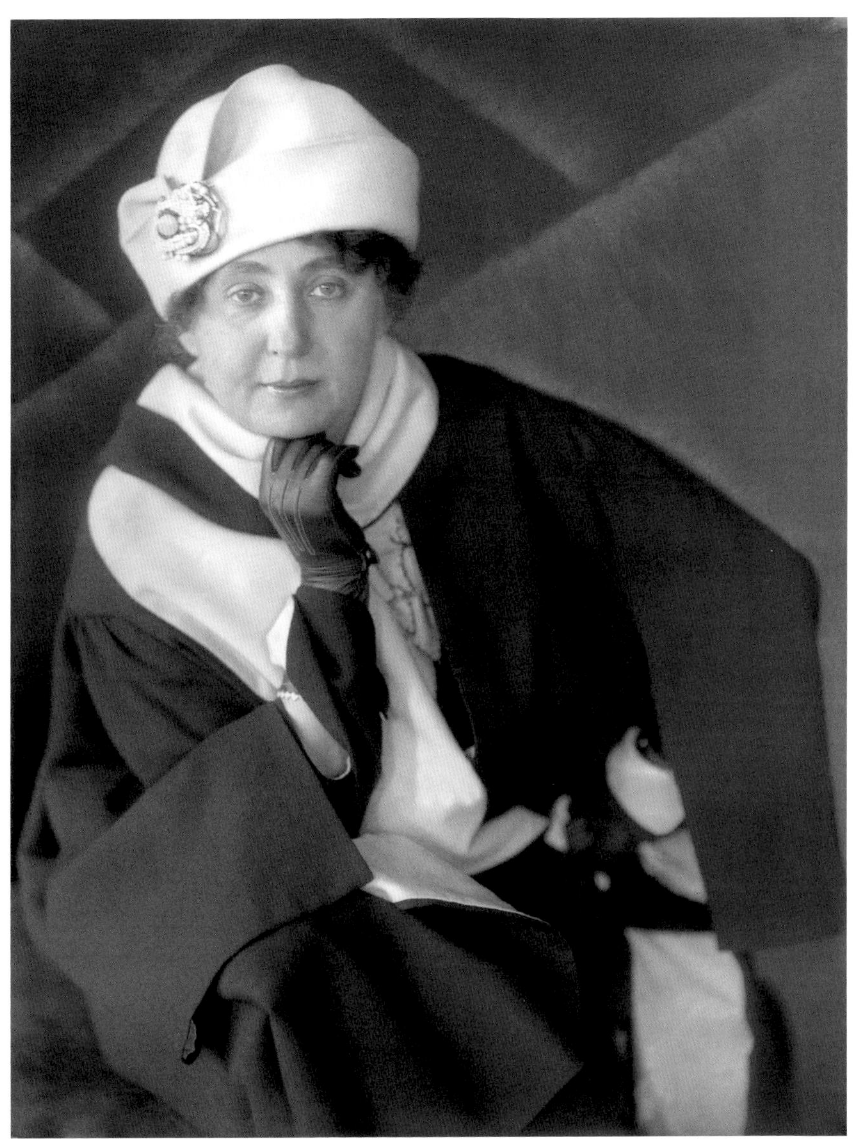

37 **Marie Calma** 1922

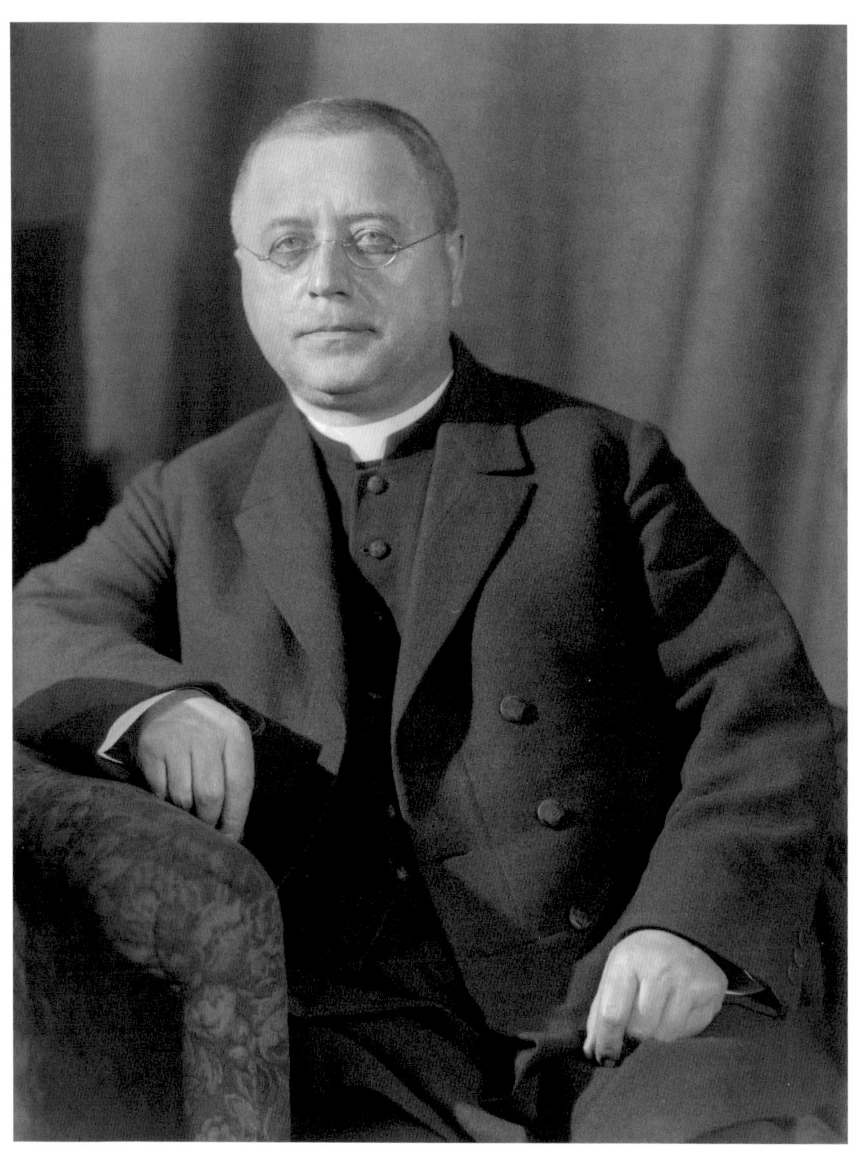

38 **Jan Šrámek** c. 1925

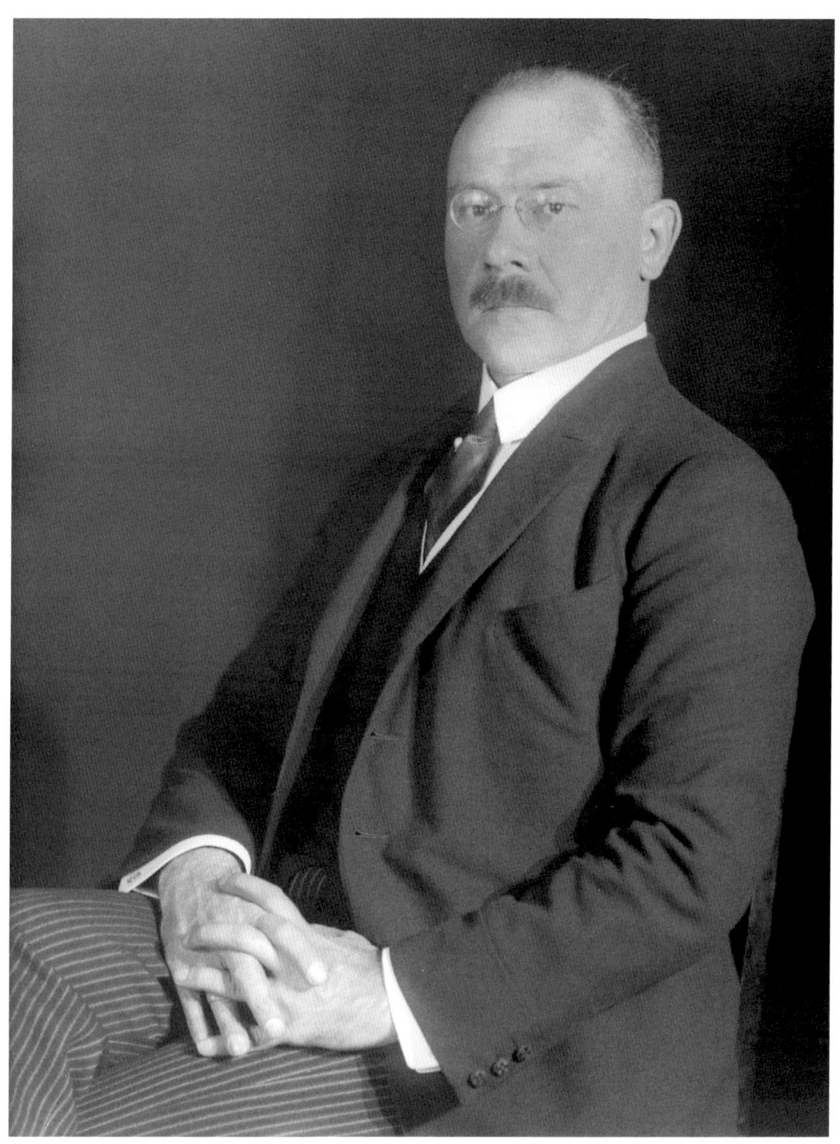

39 **Milan Hodža** c. 1928

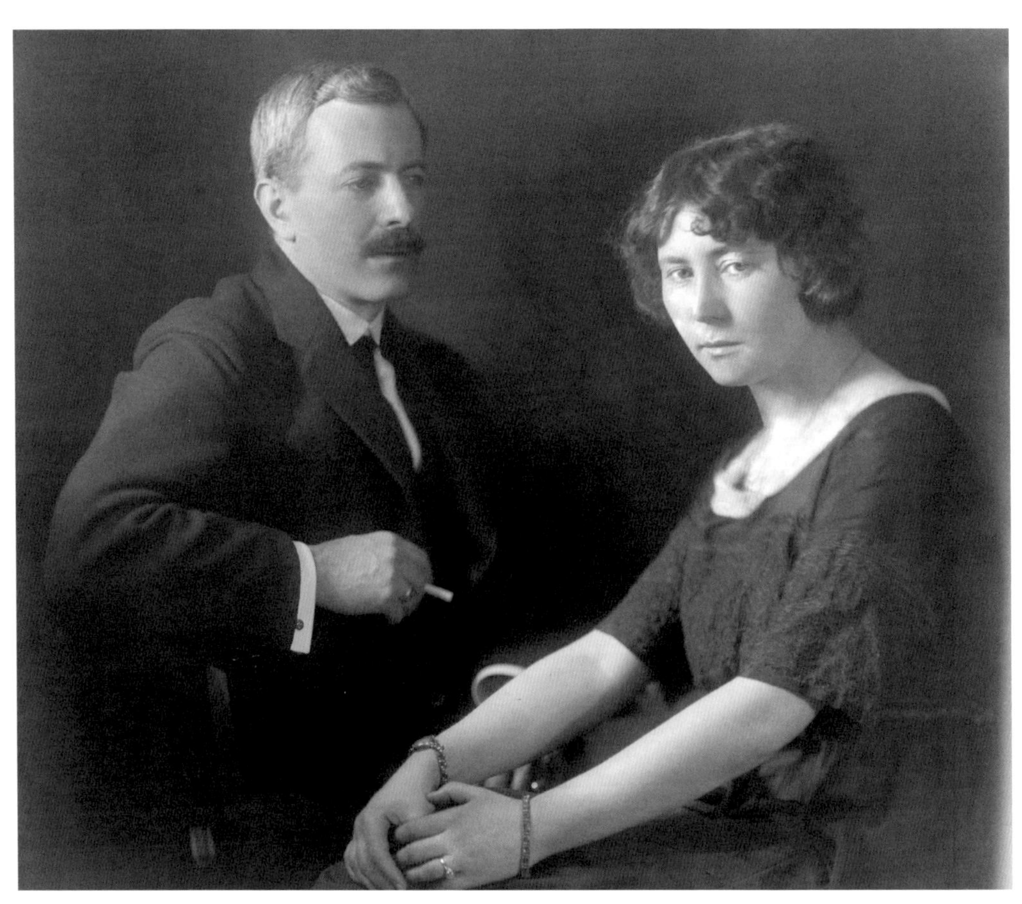

40 **Ferdinand Josef Lobkowicz, Klotylda Leopoldina Volková** c. 1921

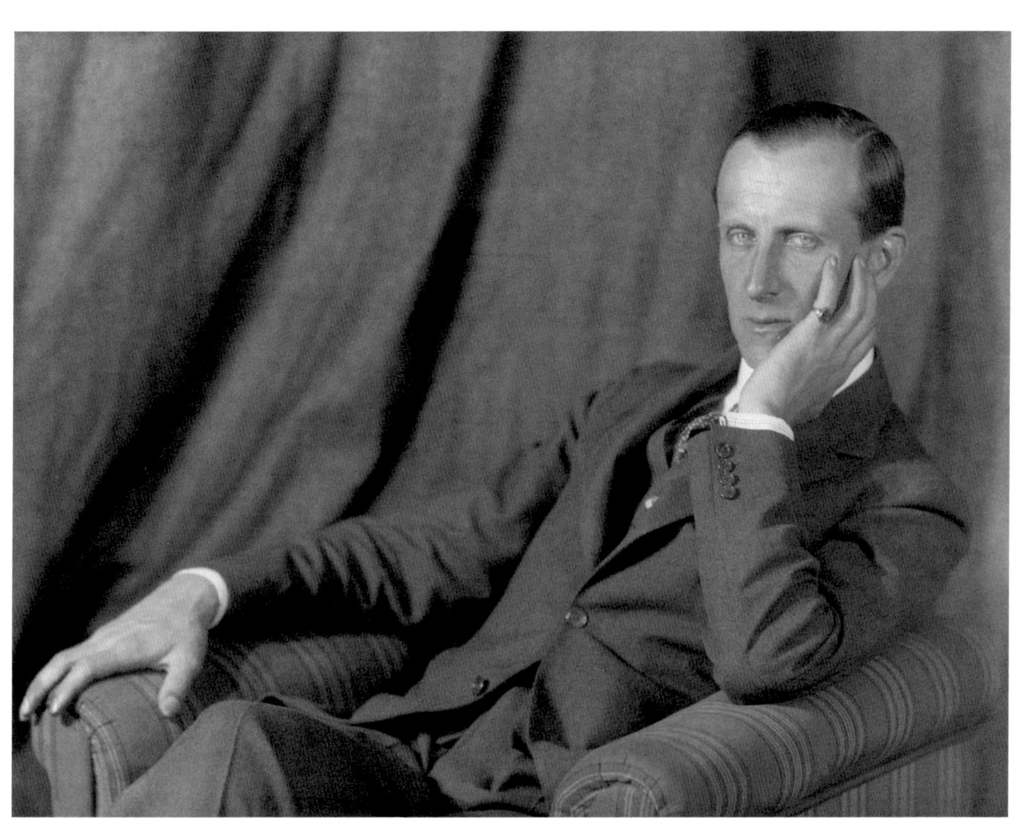

41 **Maxmilián Lobkowicz** 1925

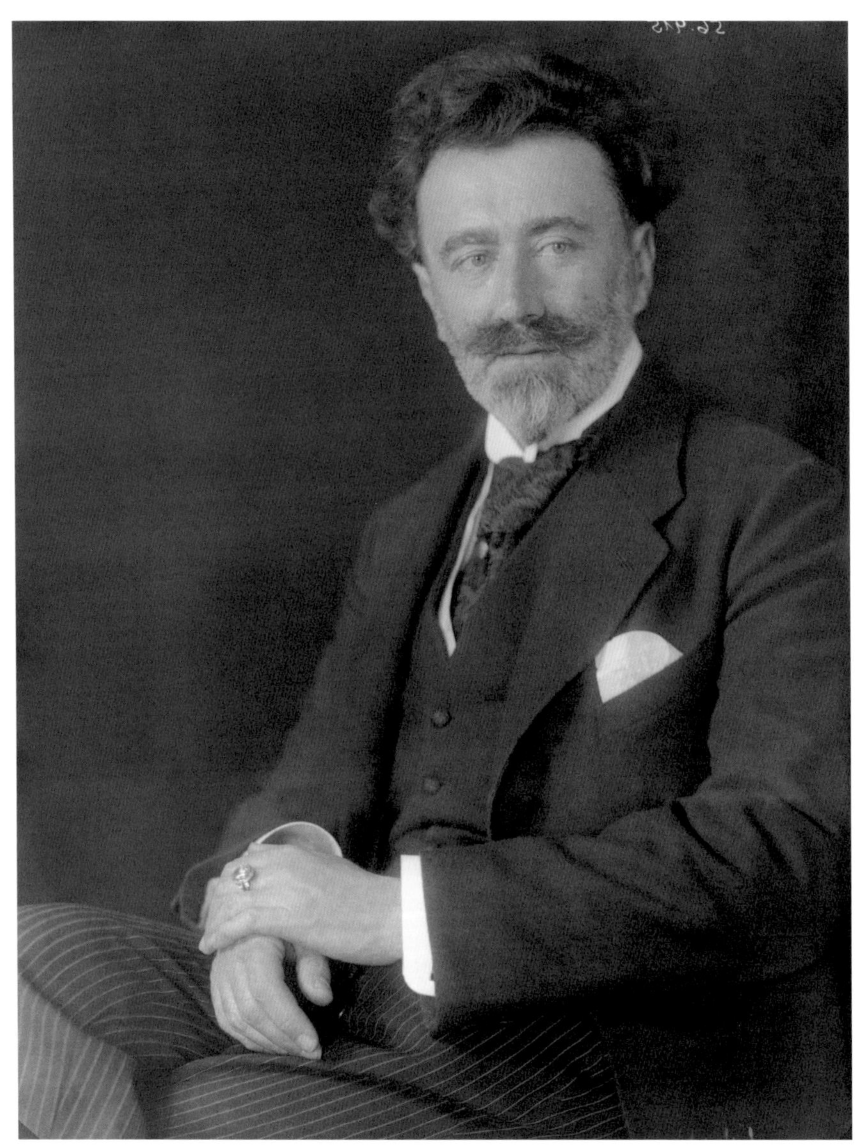

42 **Max Švabinský** 1922

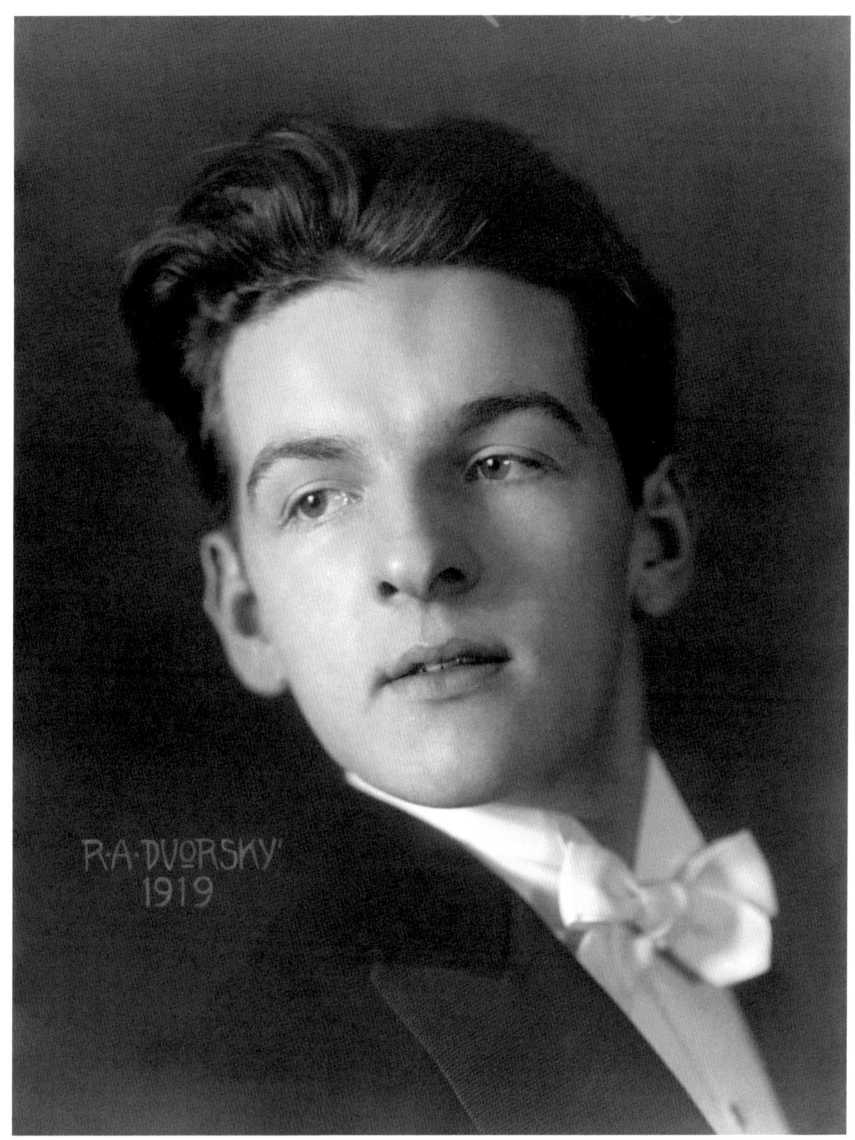

43 **Rudolf A. Dvorský** 1919

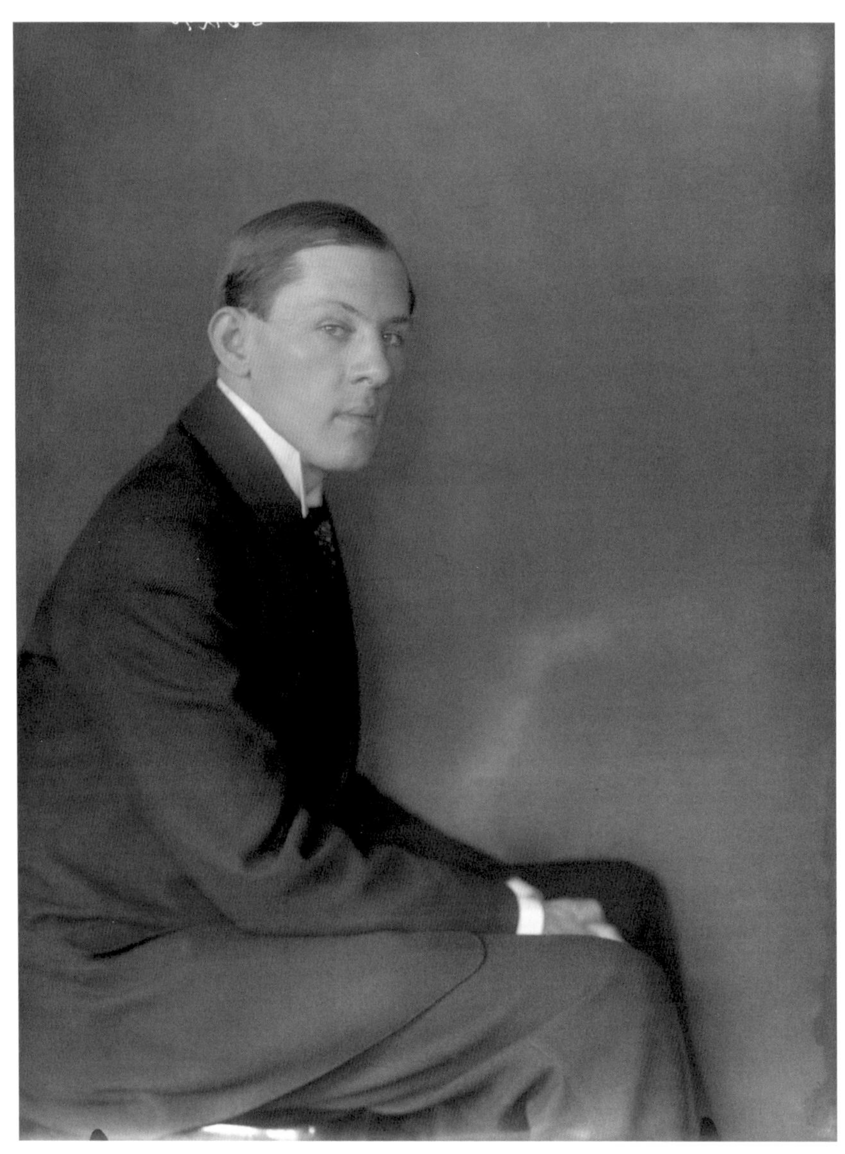

44 **Václav Vilém Štech** c. 1914

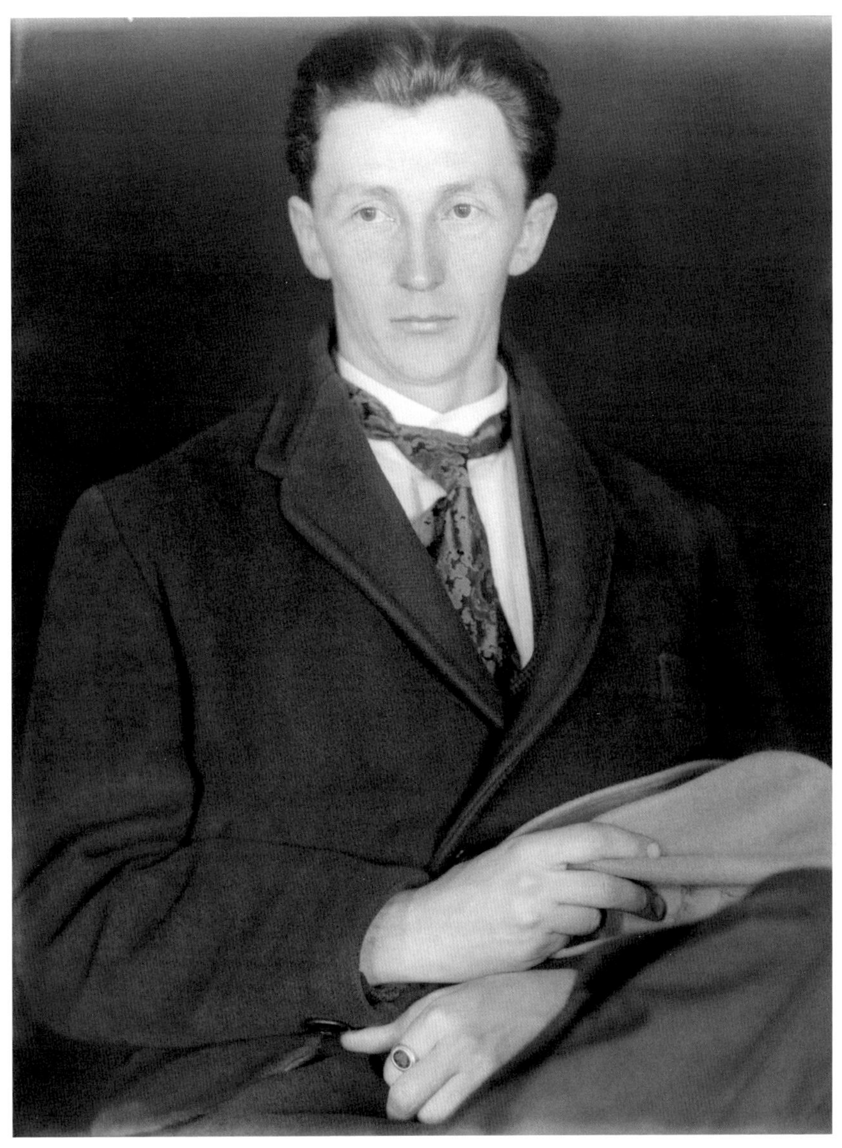

45 **Jaroslav Horejc** c. 1918

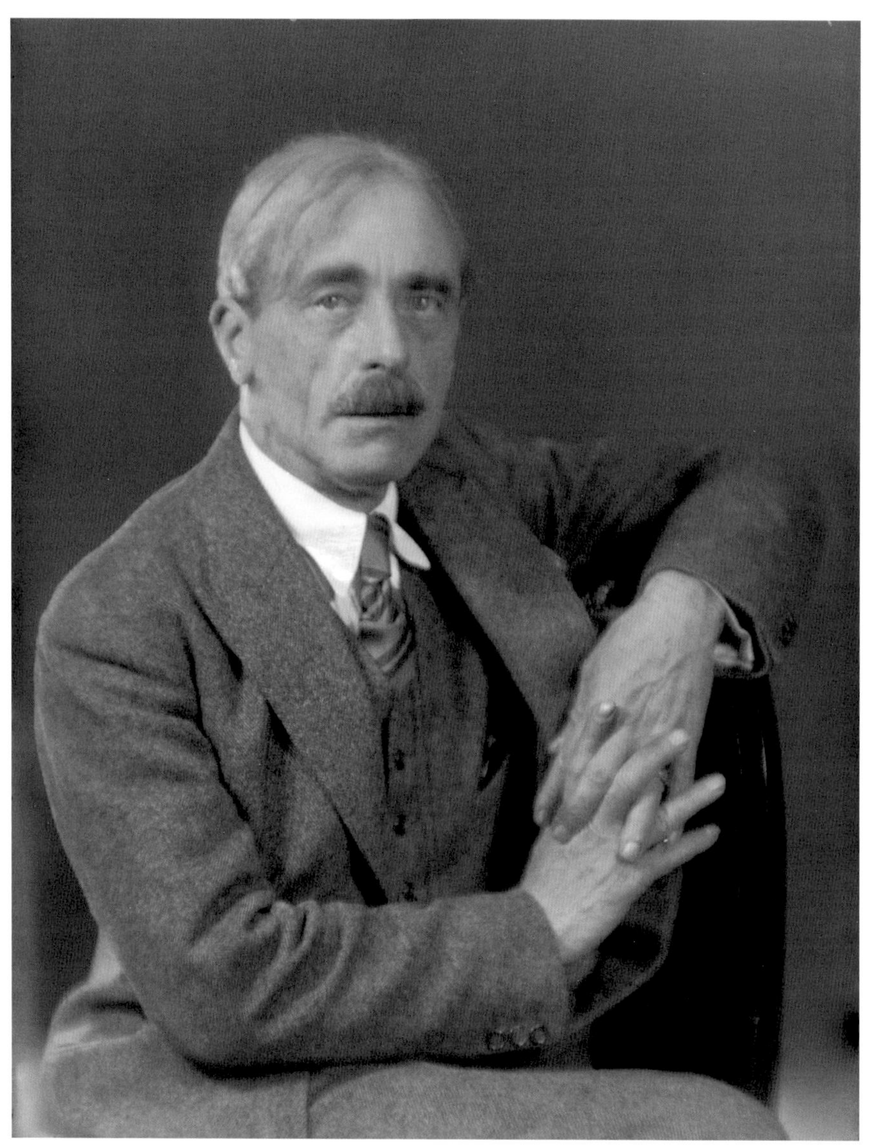

46 **Paul Valéry** c. 1920

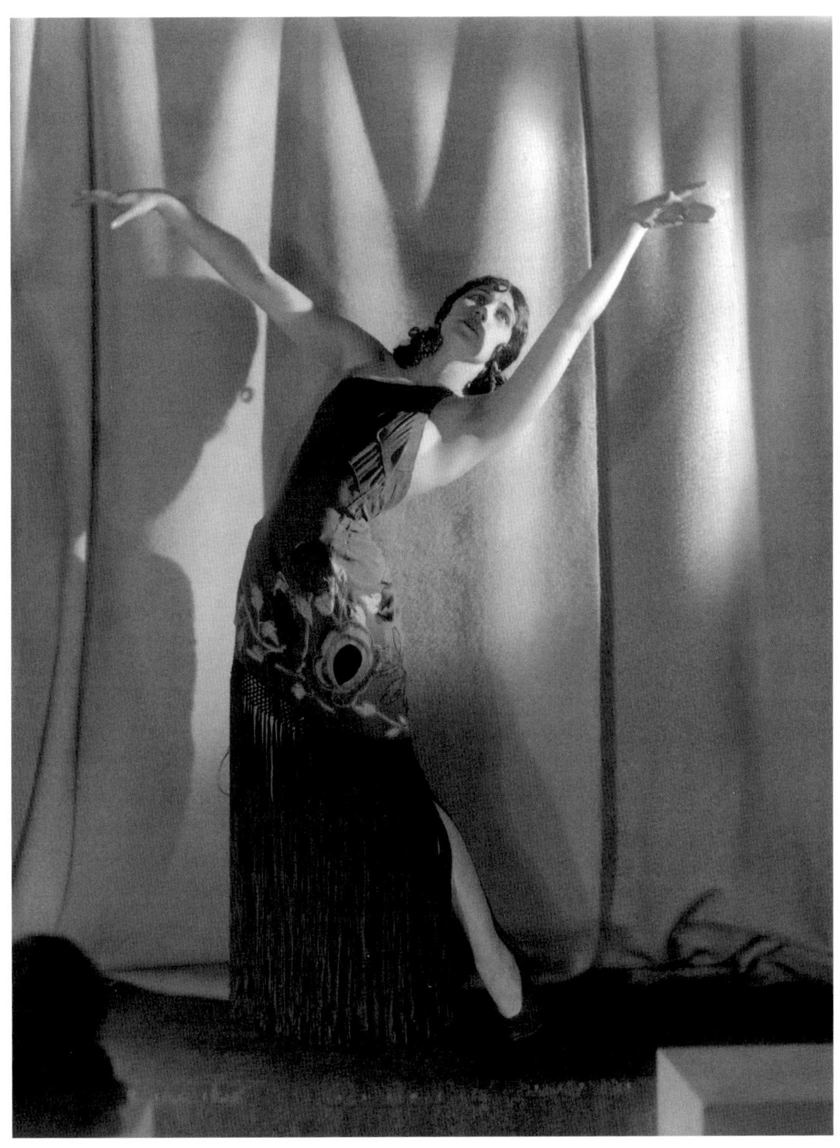

47 **Jelizaveta Nikolská** c. 1924

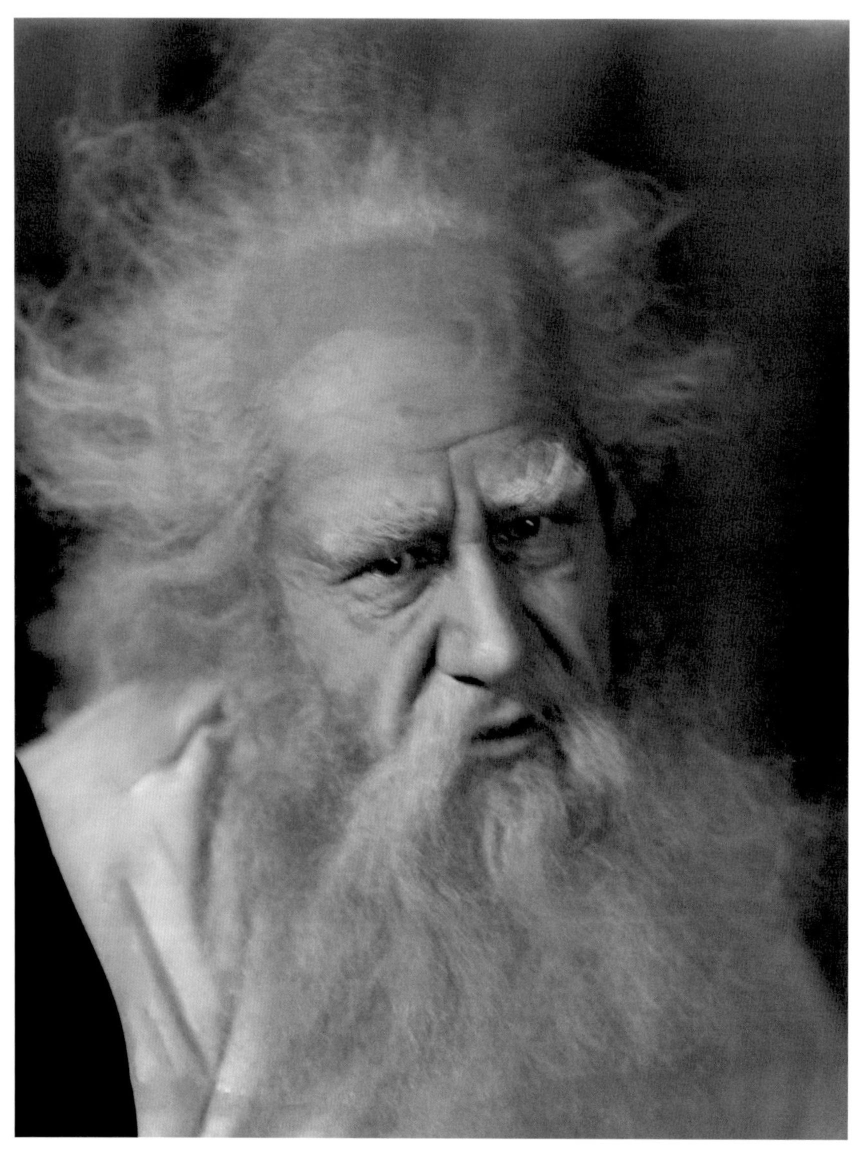

48 **Jan Vávra** c. 1919

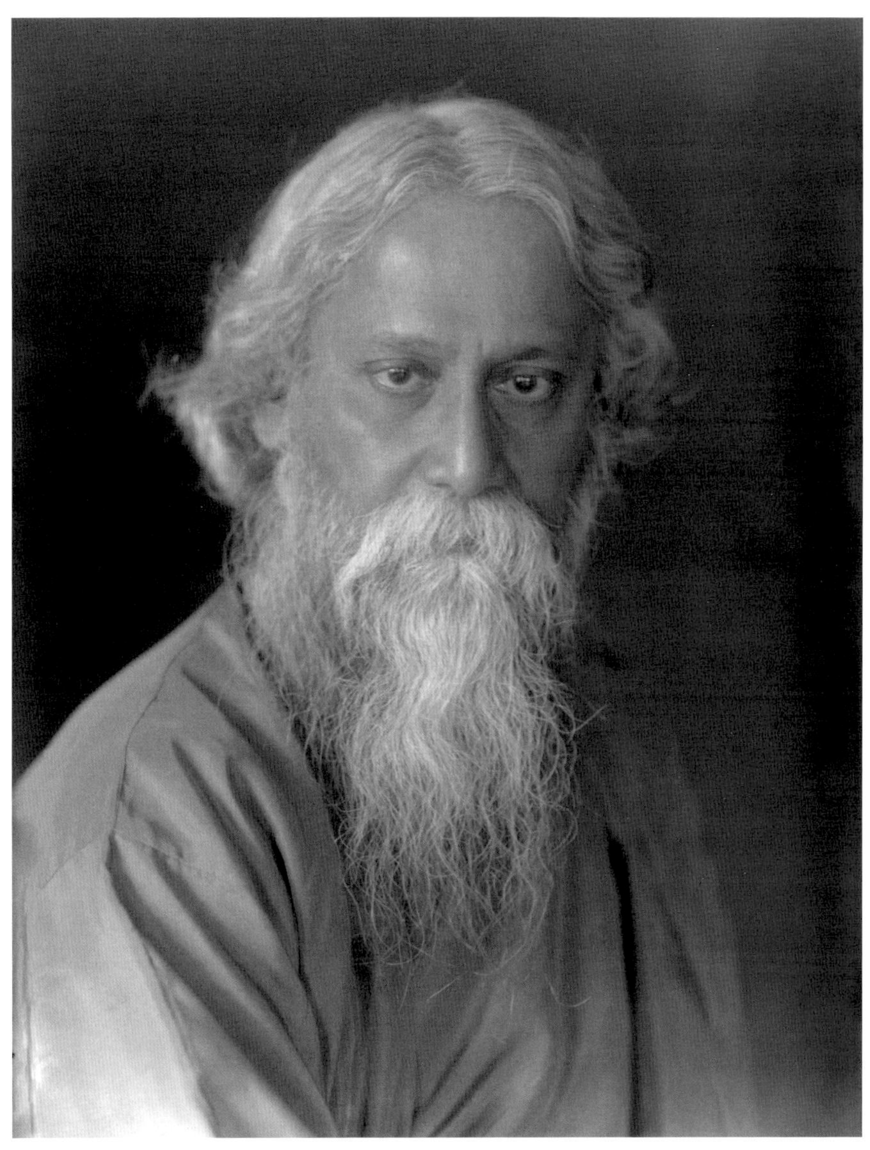

49 **Rabindranath Tagore / Rabíndranáth Thákur** 1921

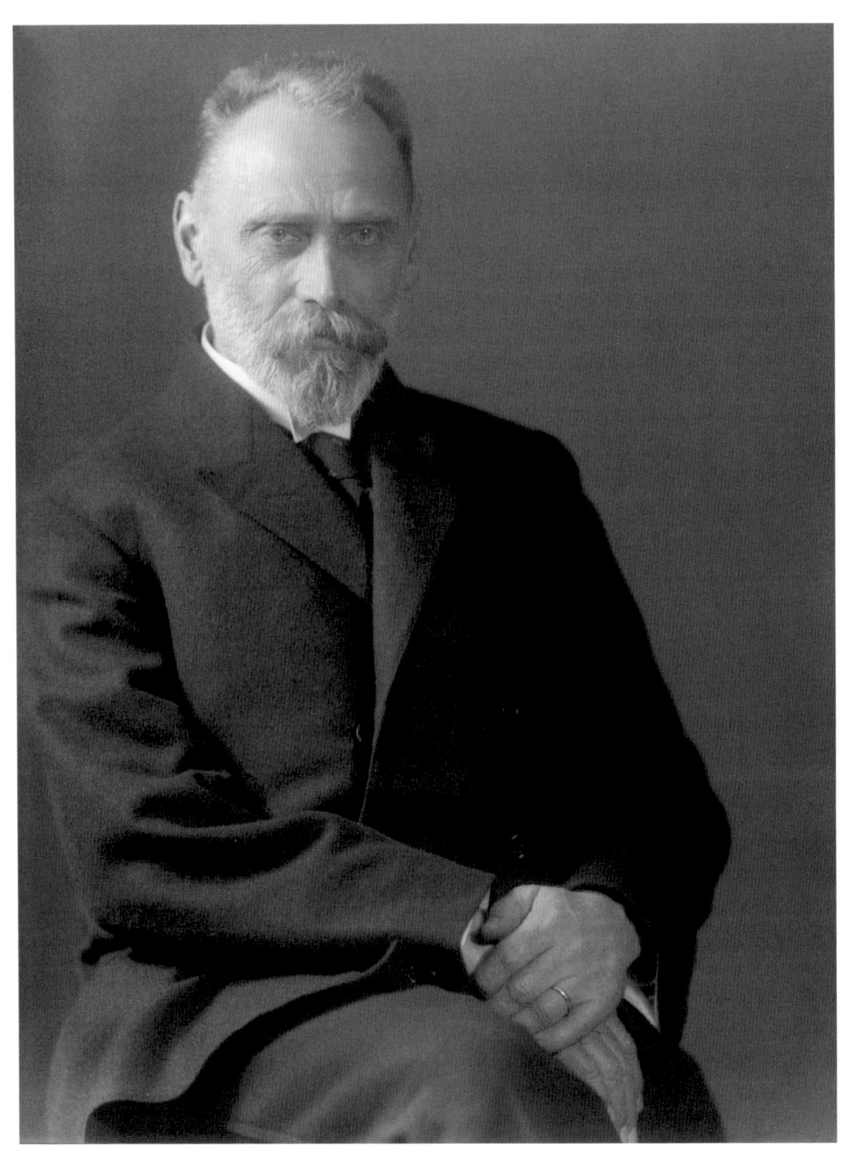

50 **Jan Laichter** c. 1922

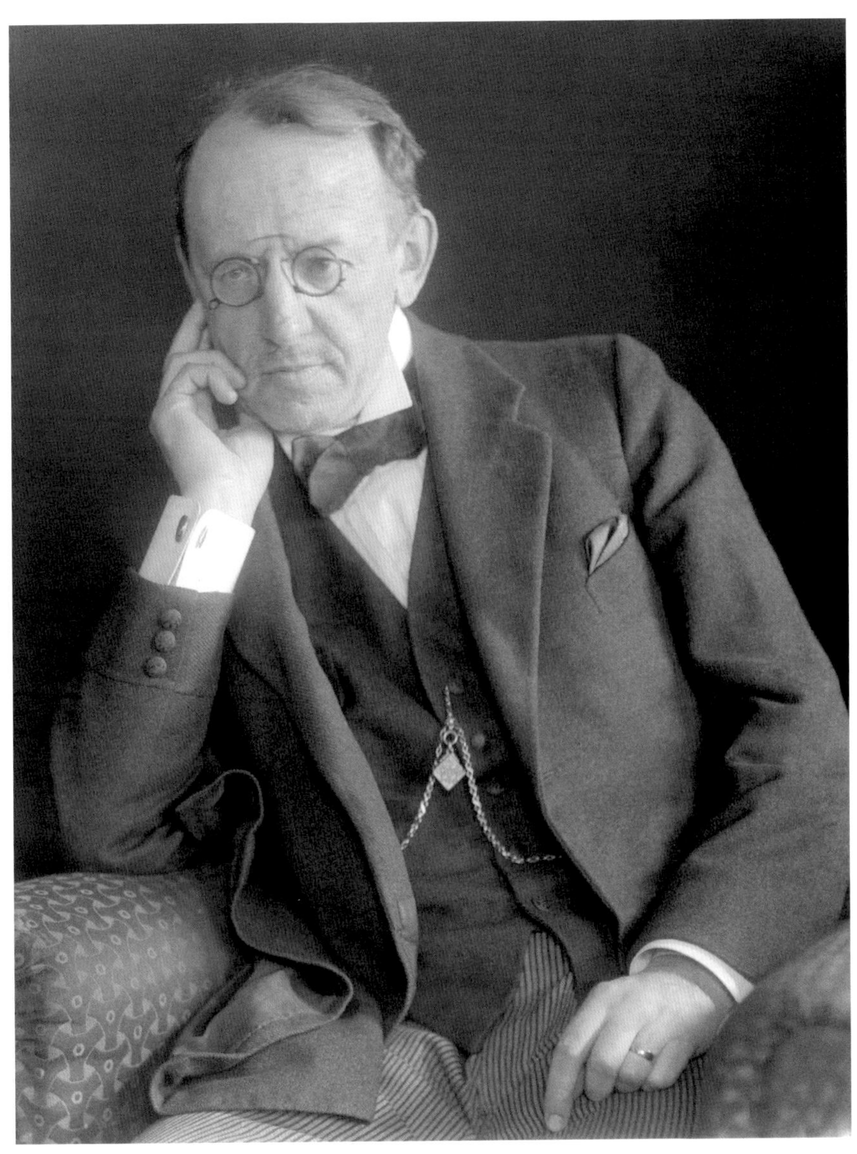

51 **Vítězslav Novák** 1920

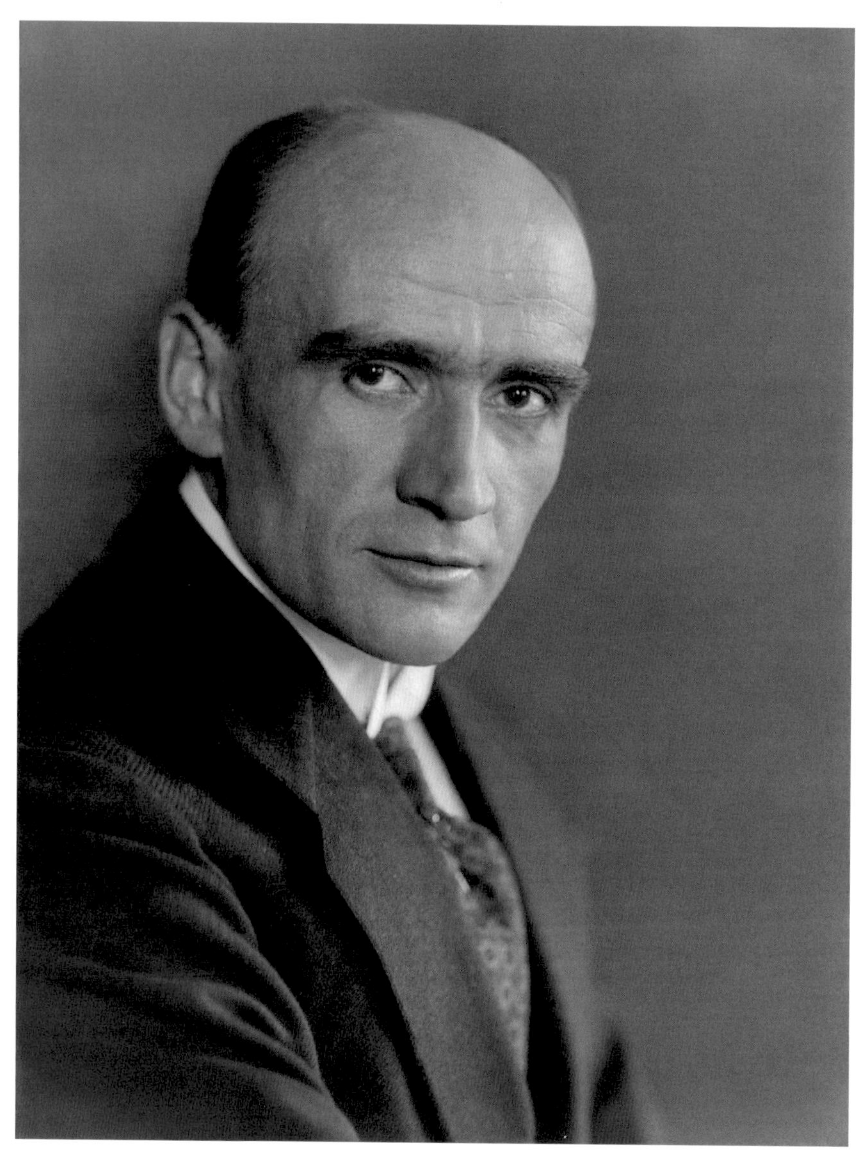

52 **Karel Hašler** c. 1925

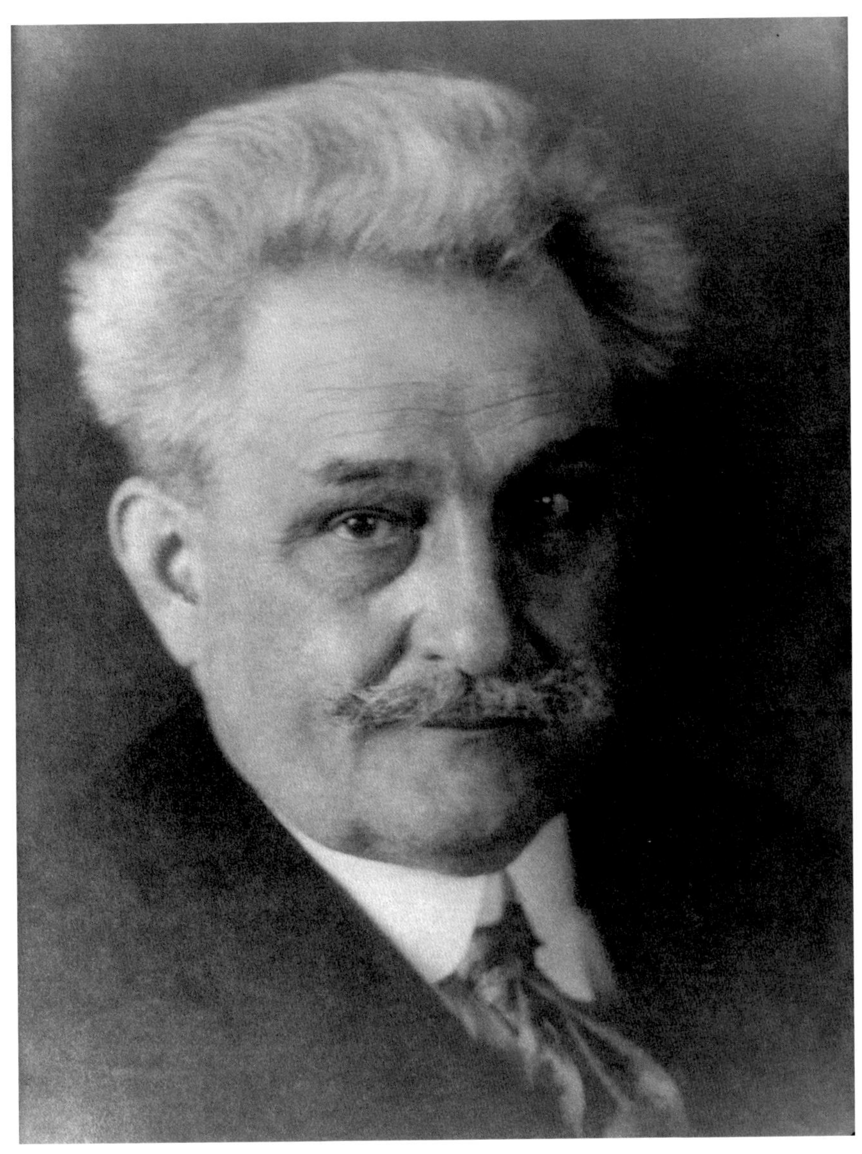

53 **Leoš Janáček** c. 1920

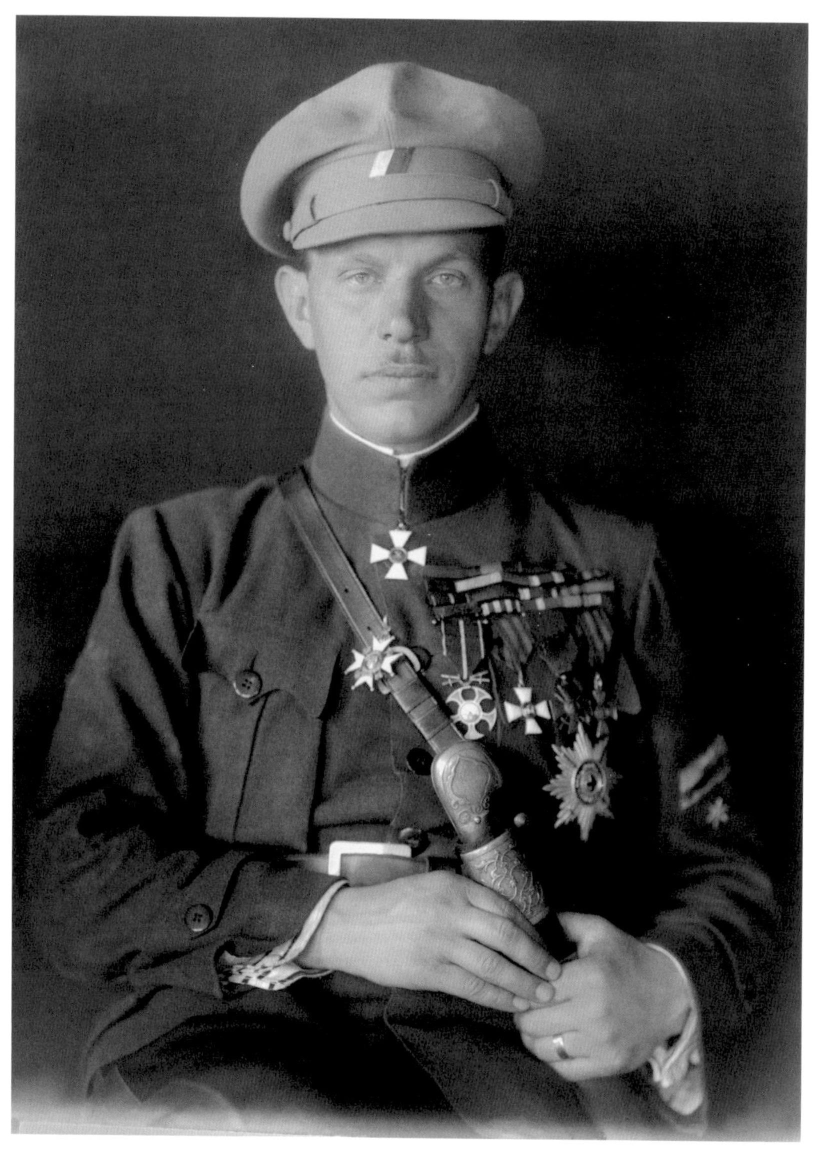

54 **Radola Gajda** c. 1925

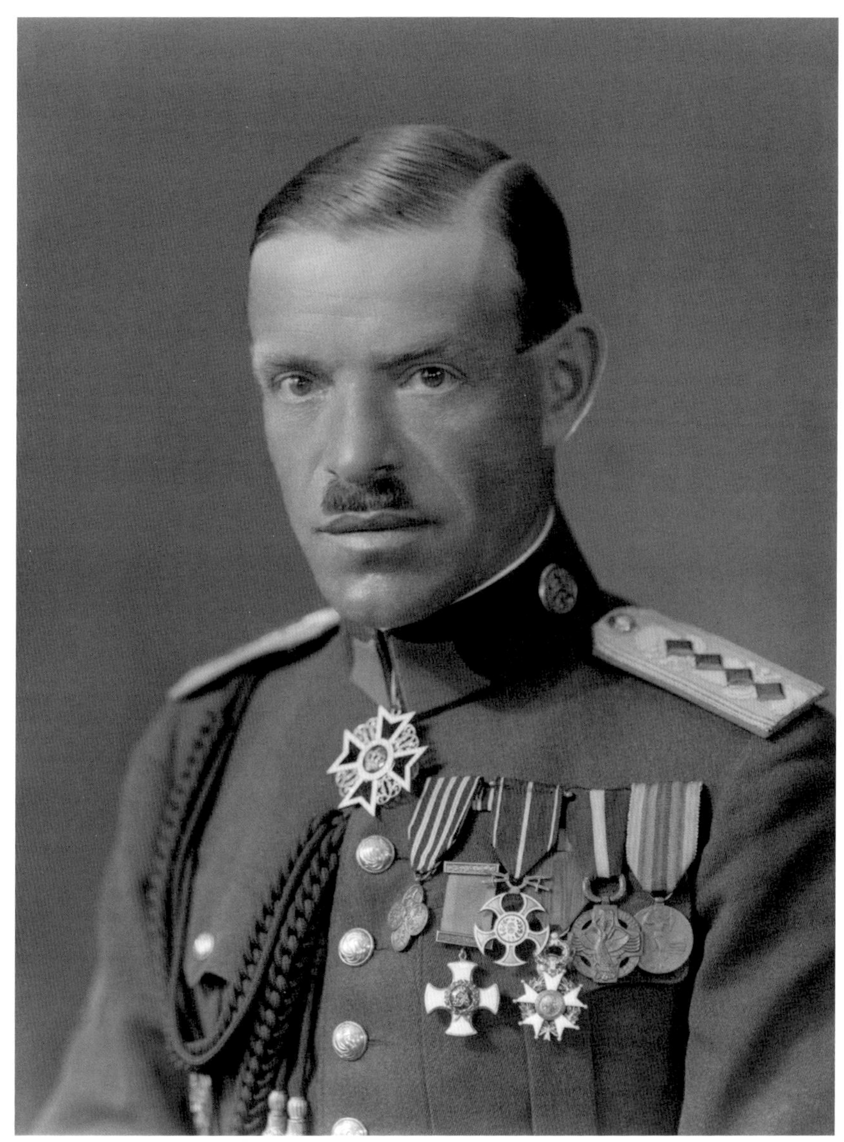

55 **František Hrabčík** c. 1932

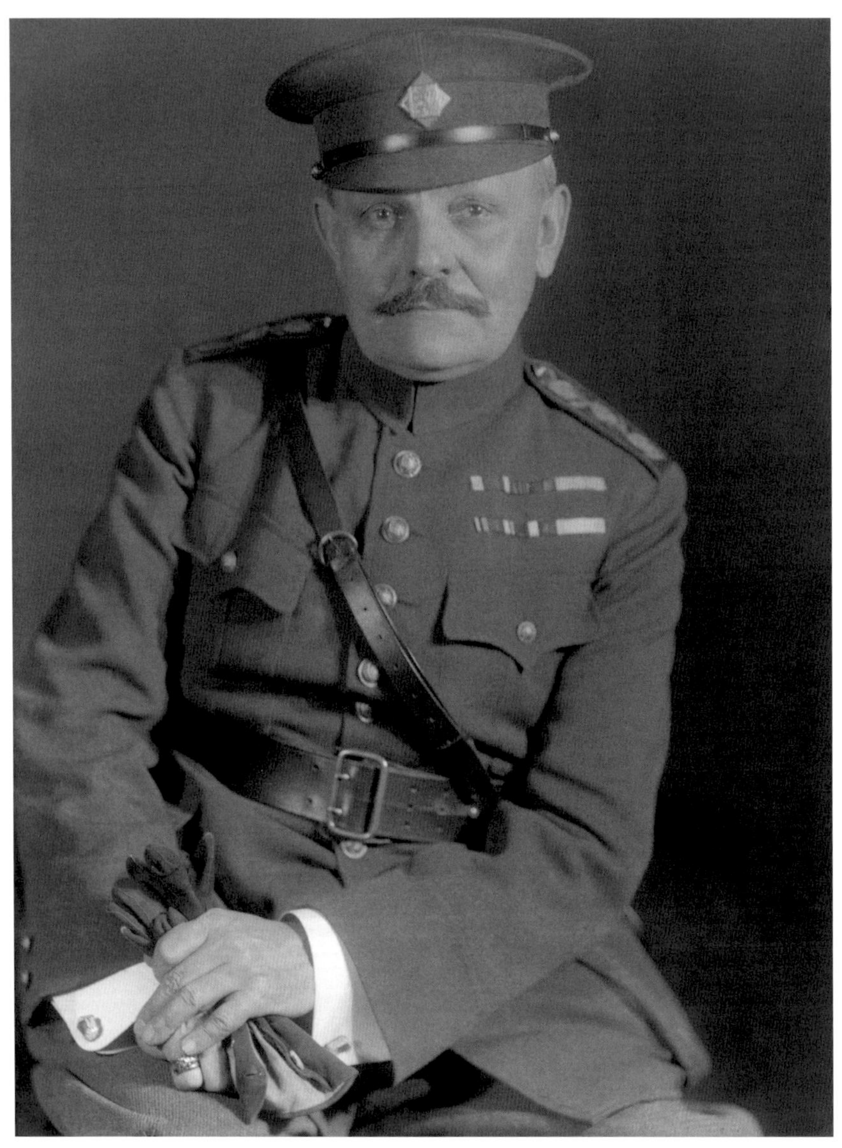

56 Josef Svatopluk Machar 1921

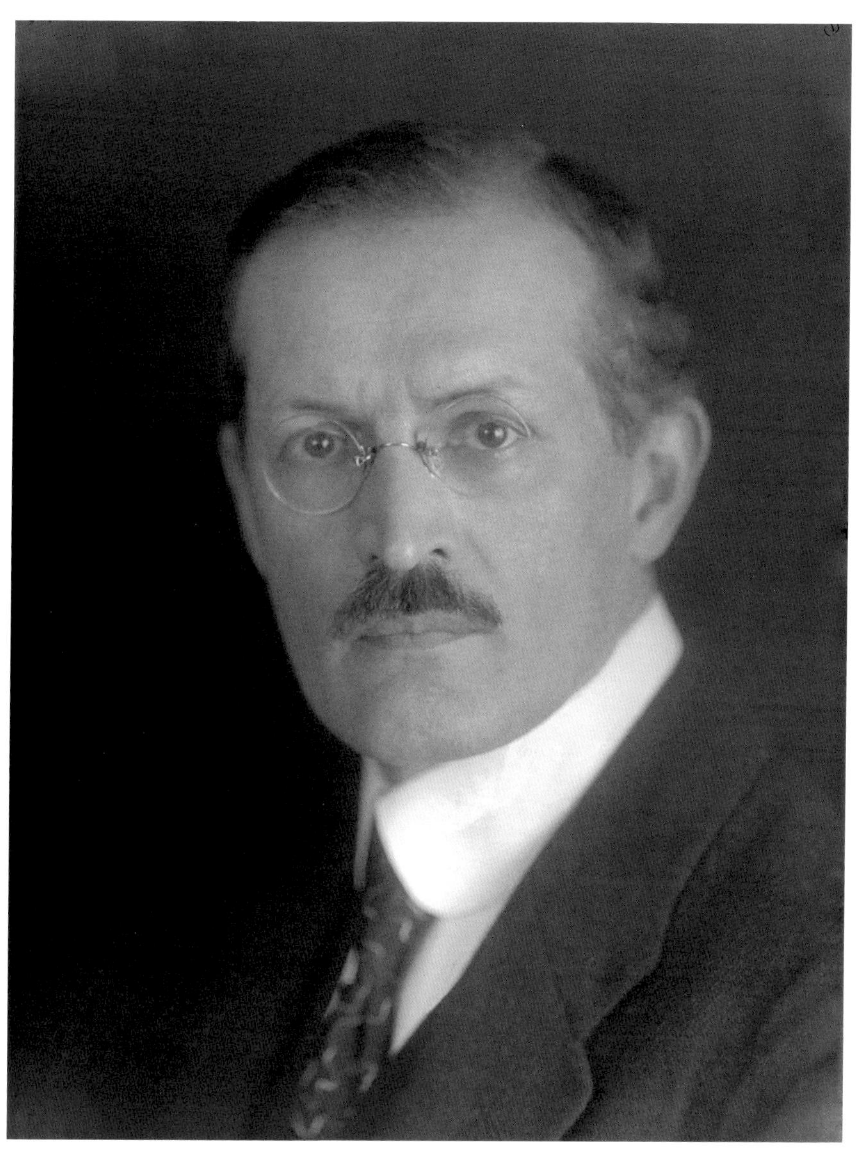

57 **Otakar Ostrčil** 1924

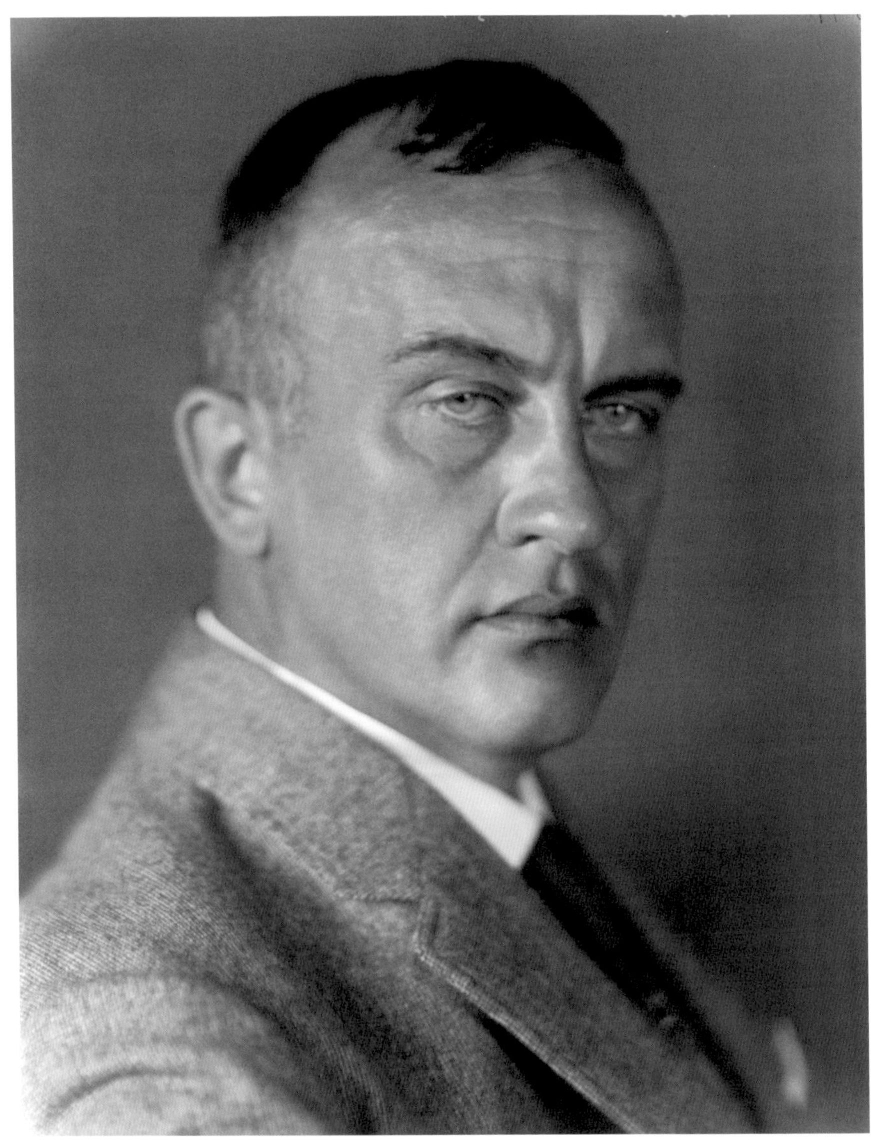

58 **Jan Kotěra** c. 1921

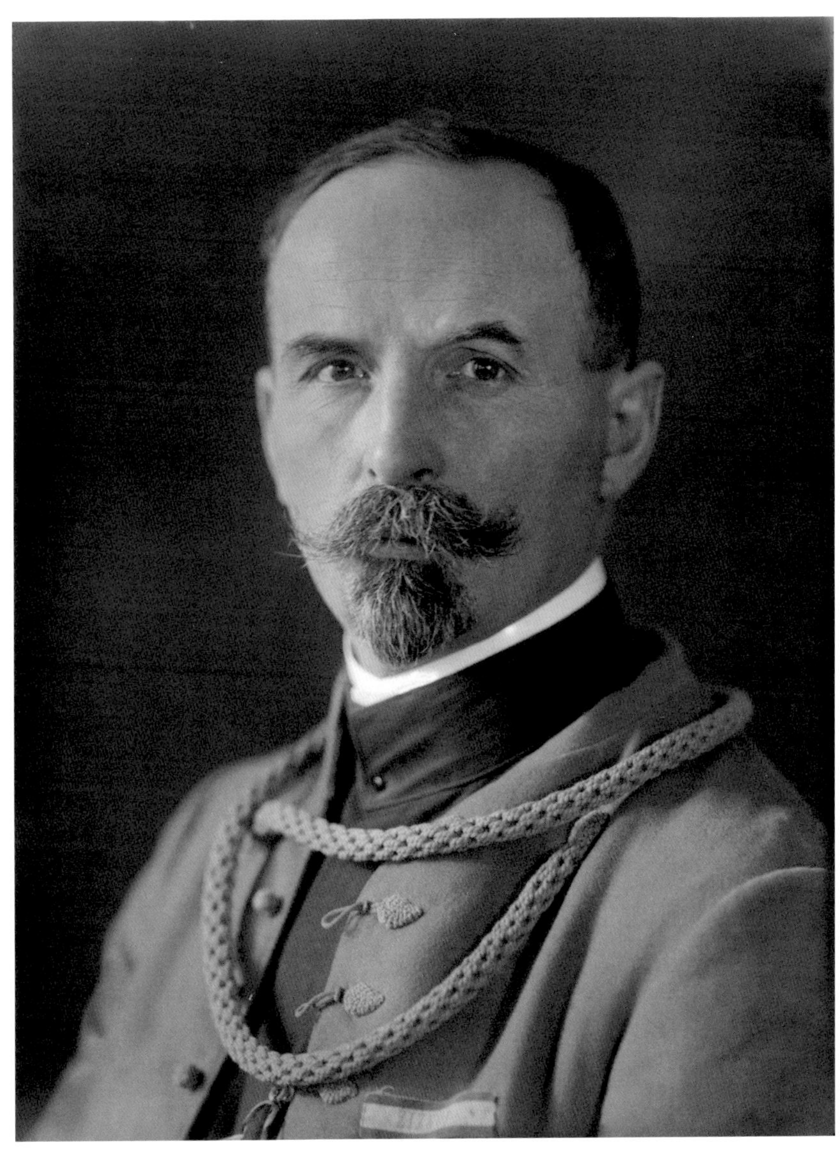

59 **Josef Scheiner** c. 1920

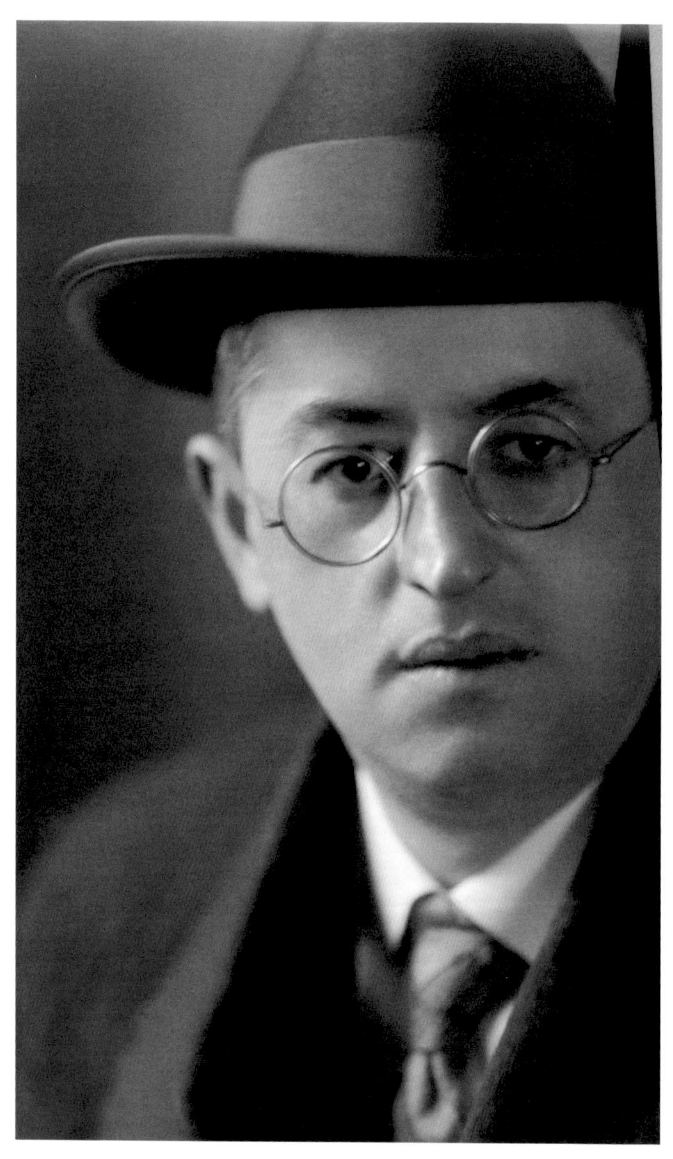

60 **Josef Čapek** c. 1922

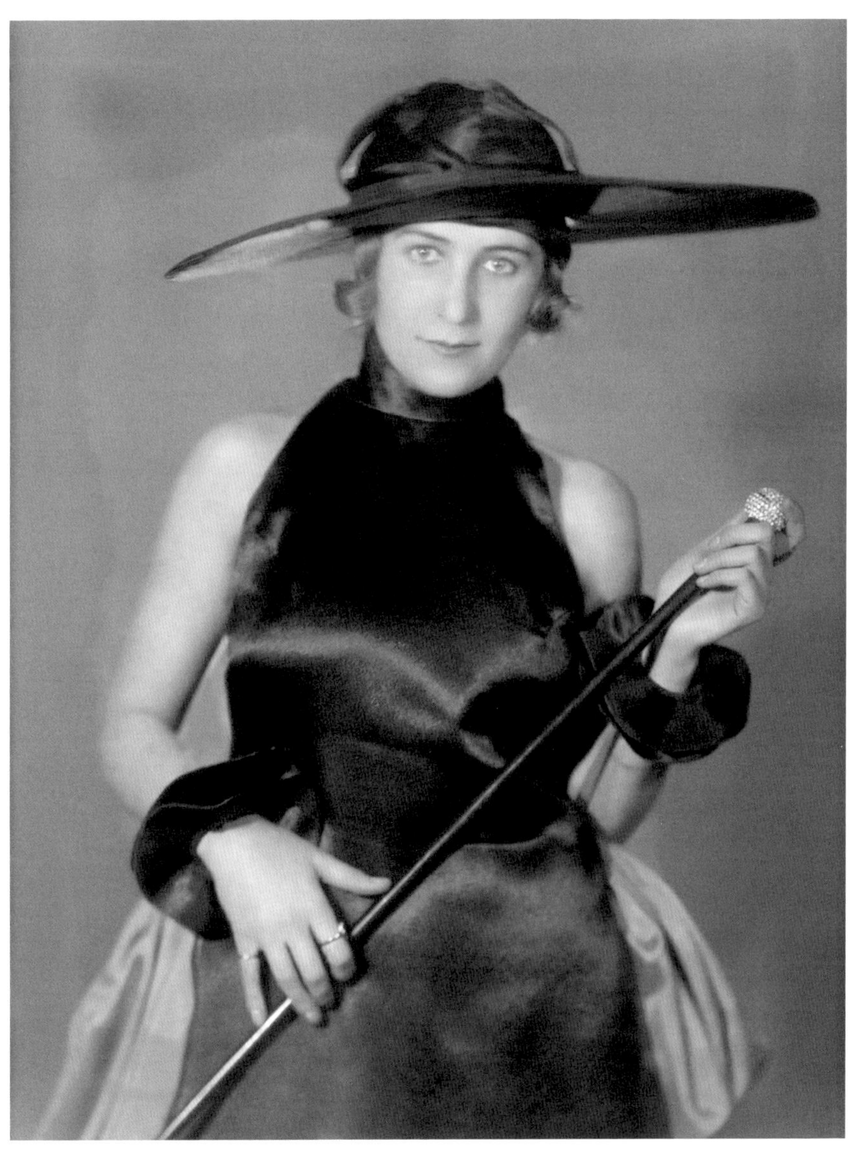

61 **Marie Grossová** c. 1925

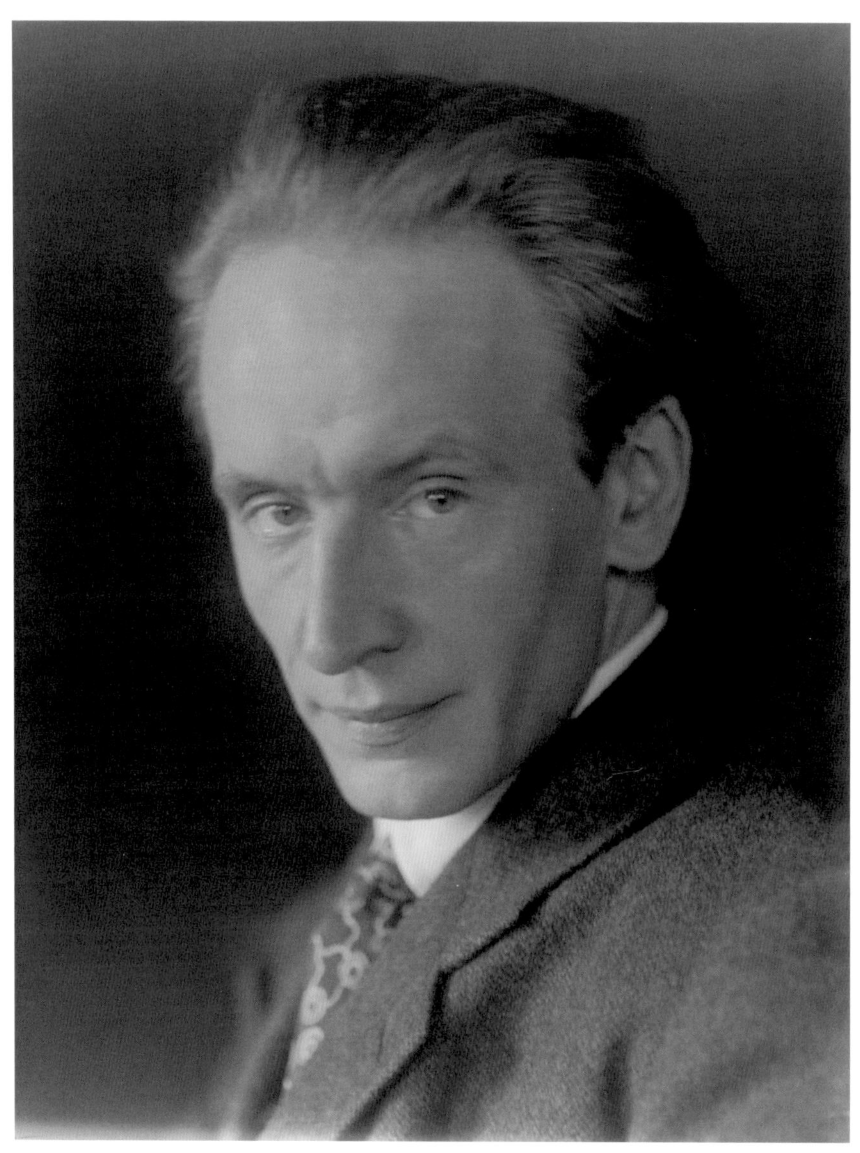

62 **Vratislav Nechleba** c. 1930

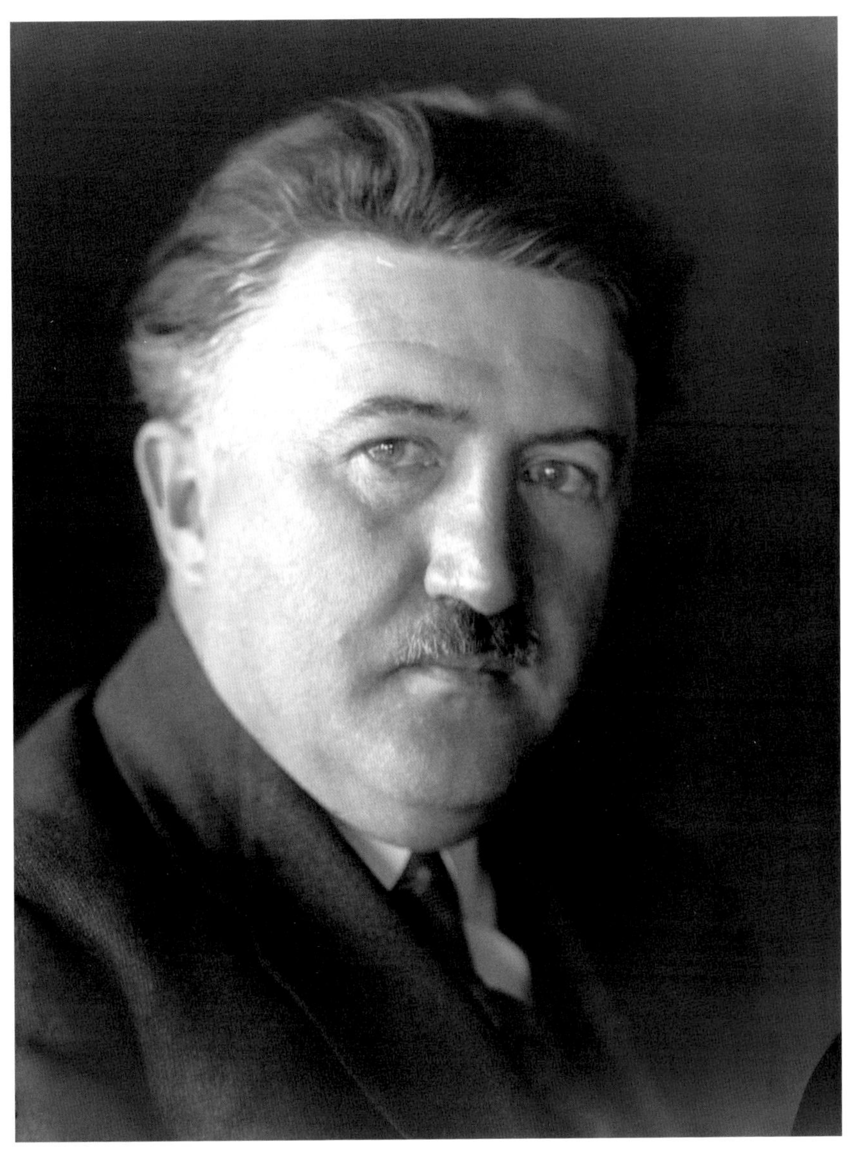

63 **Josef Suk** c. 1926

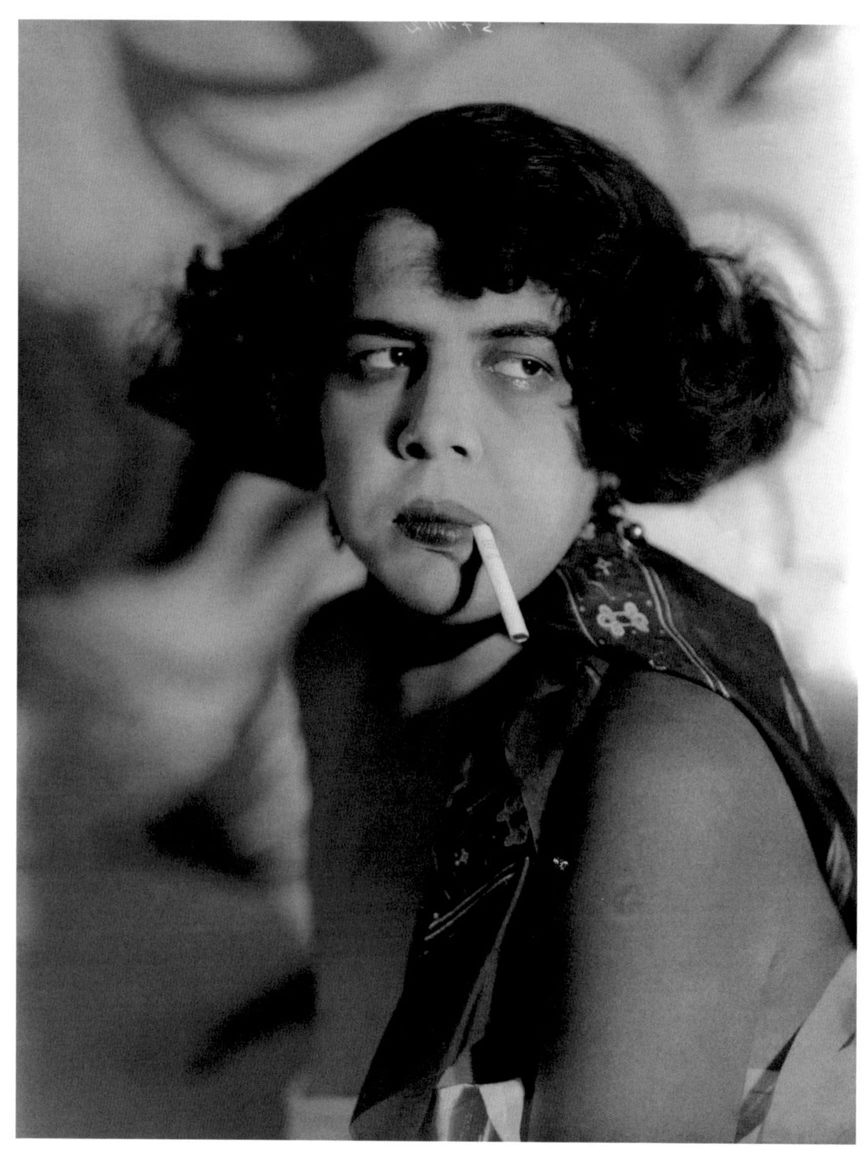

64 **Ervina Kupferová** 1921

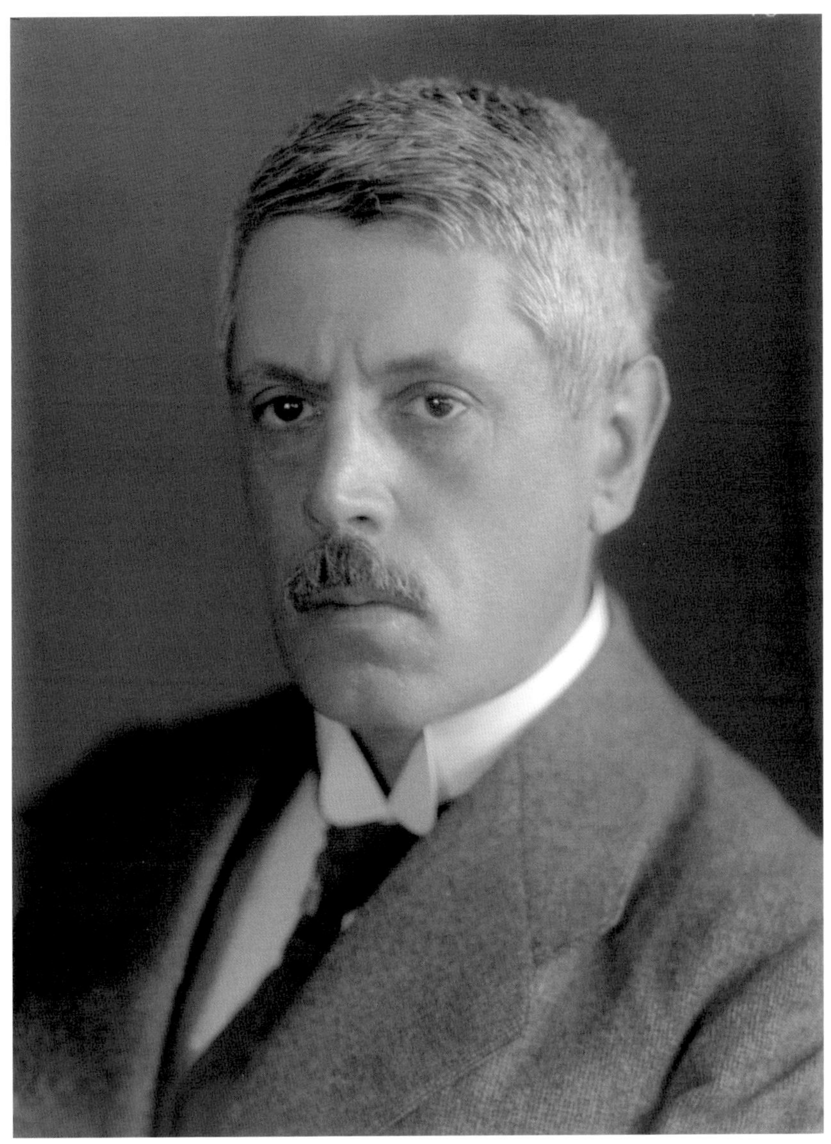

65 **Emanuel z Lešehradu** 1921

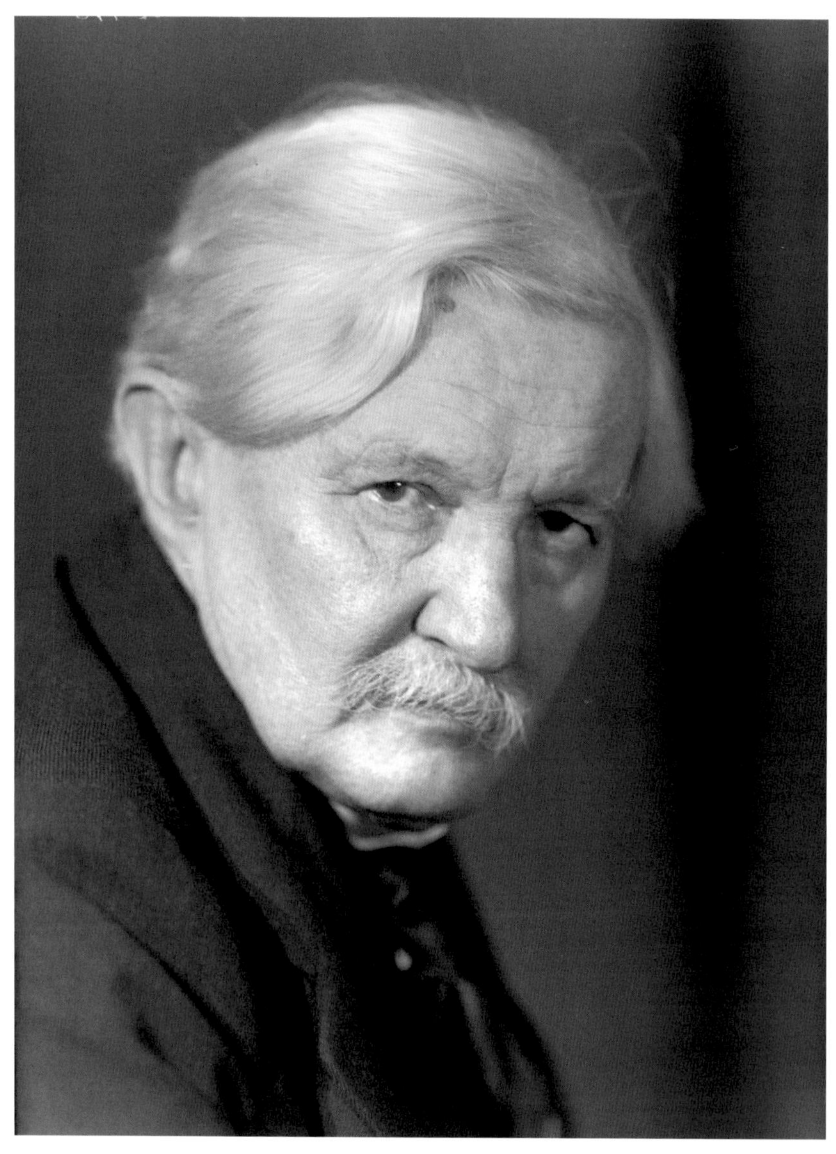

66 **Enrique Stanko Vráz** c. 1933

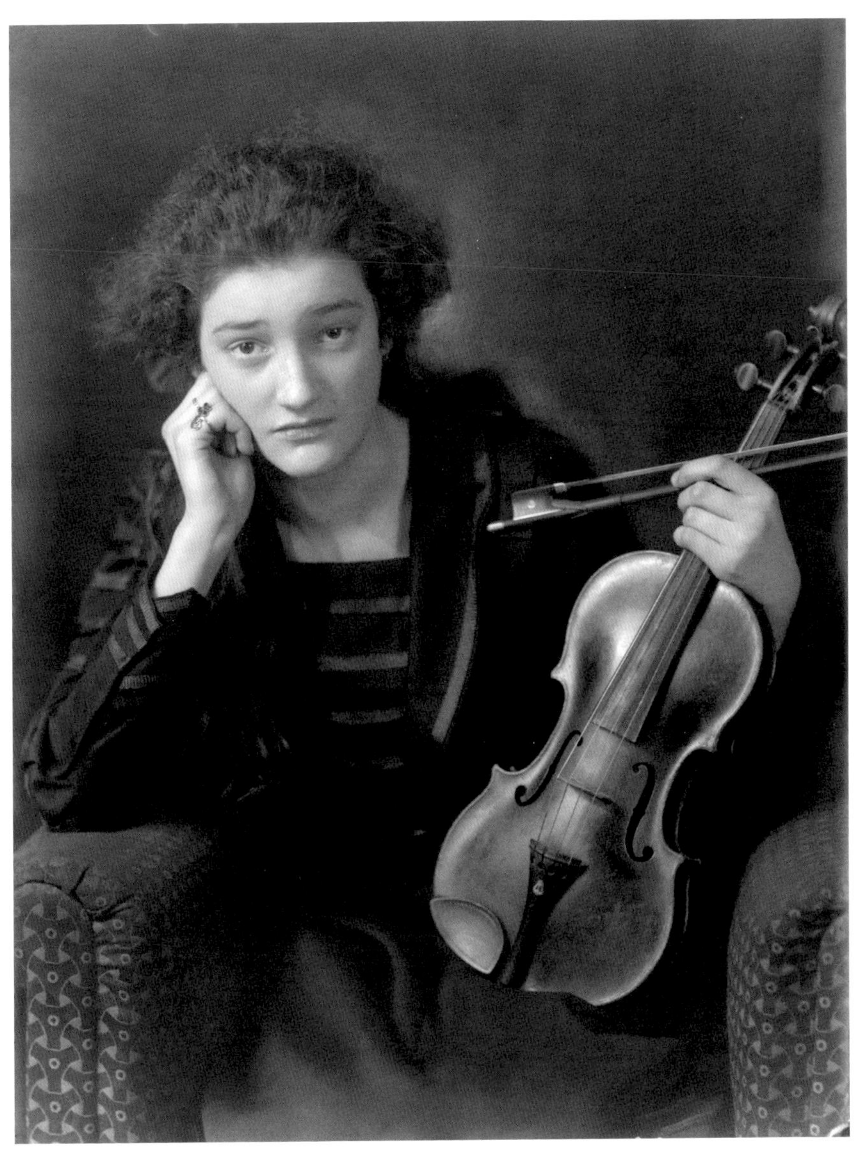

67 Kitty Červenková c. 1925

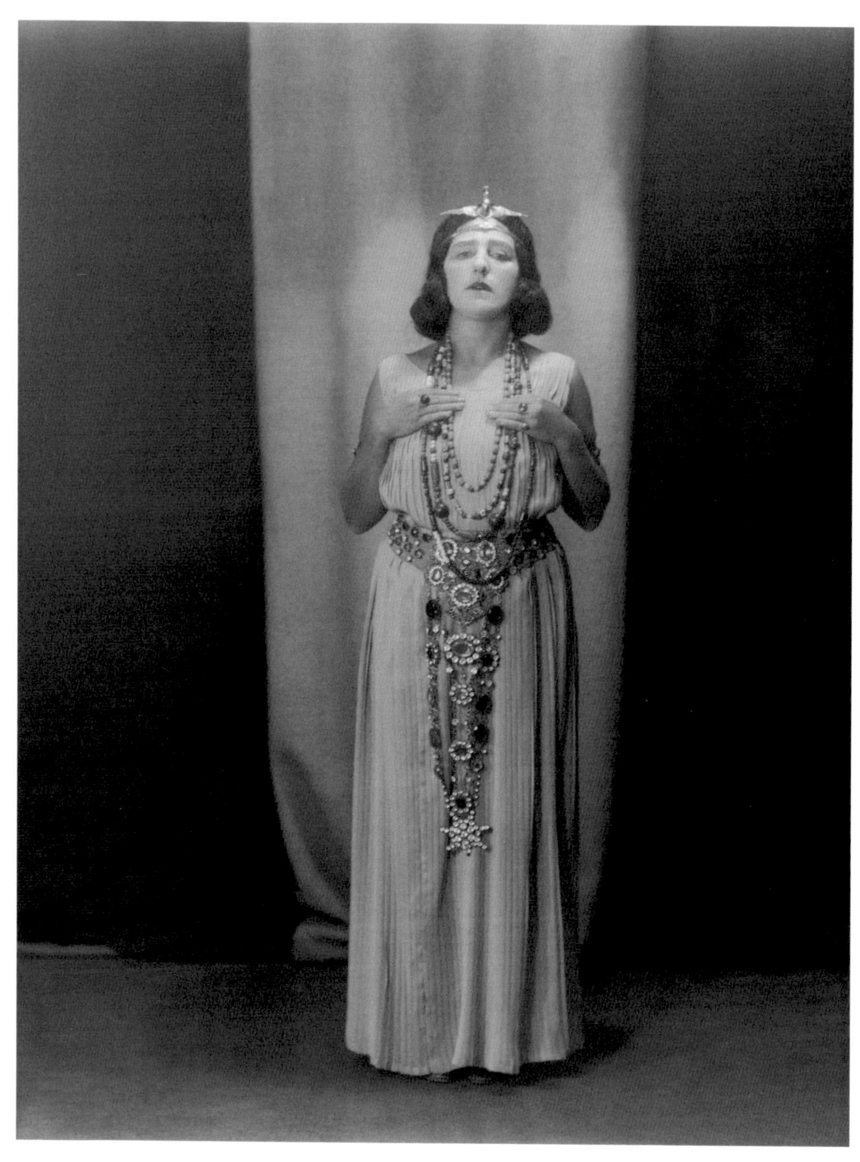

68 **Jelena Ježićová-Hanáková** c. 1925

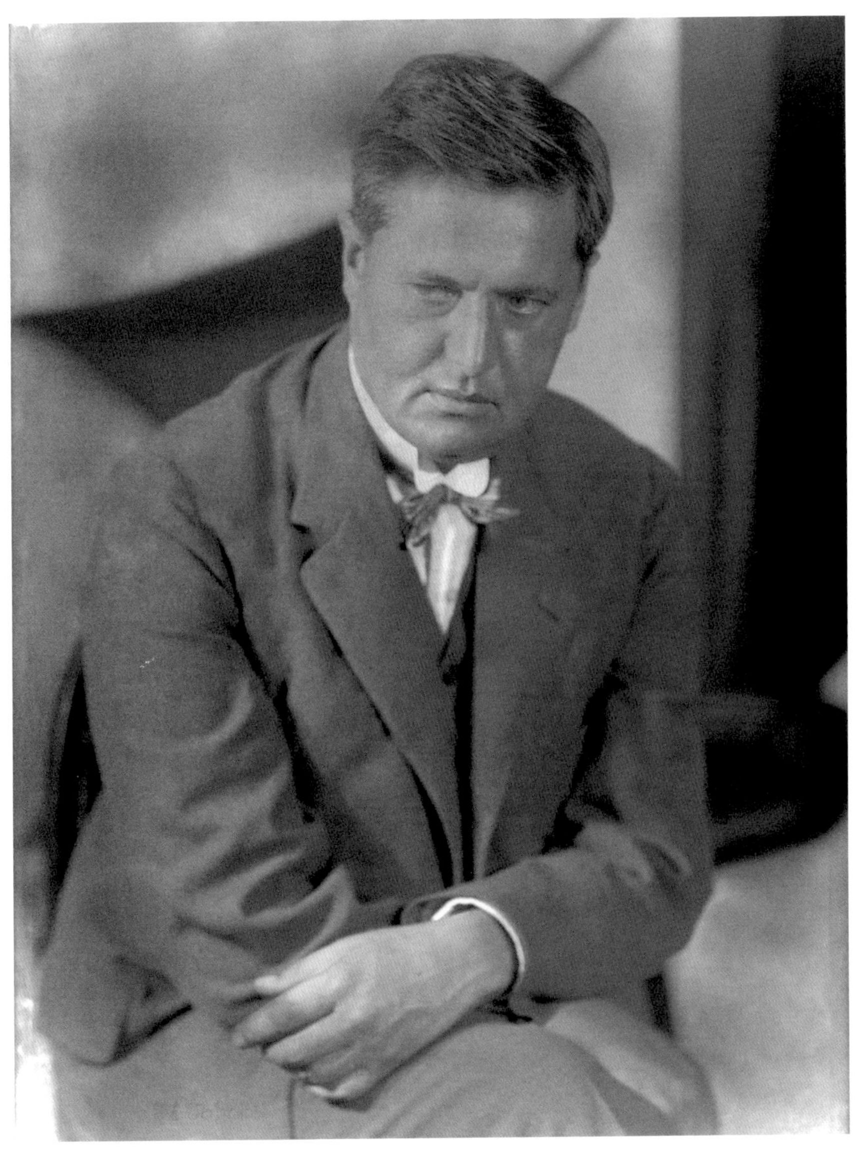

69 **Václav Talich** c. 1926

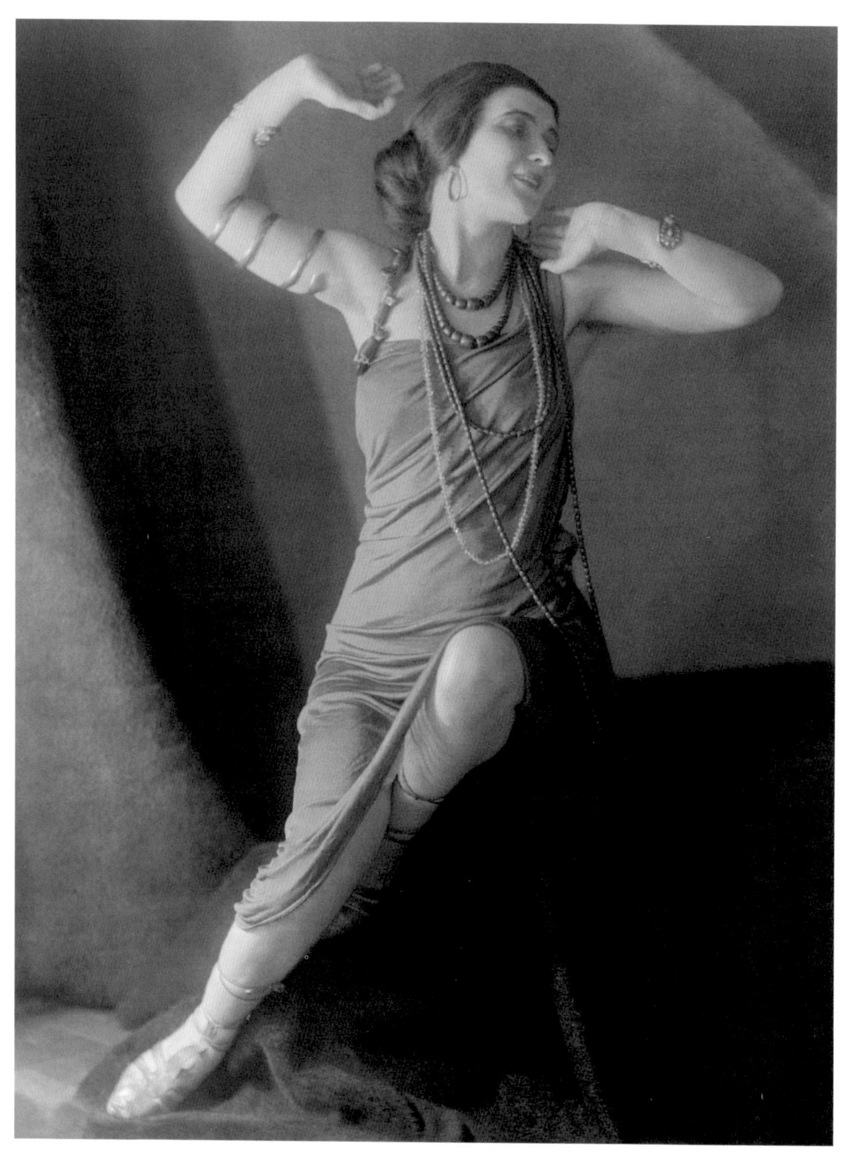

70 **Jarmila Kronbauerová** 1922

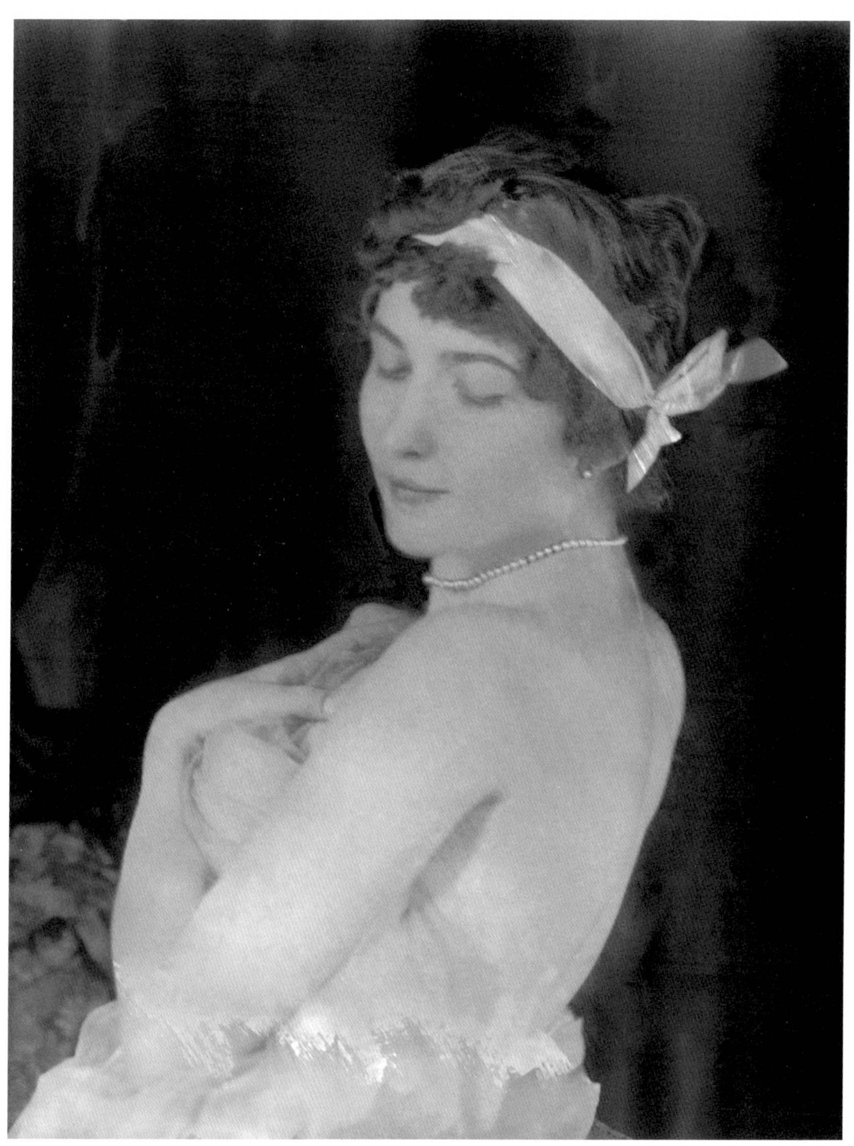

71 **Jarmila Kronbauerová** 1922

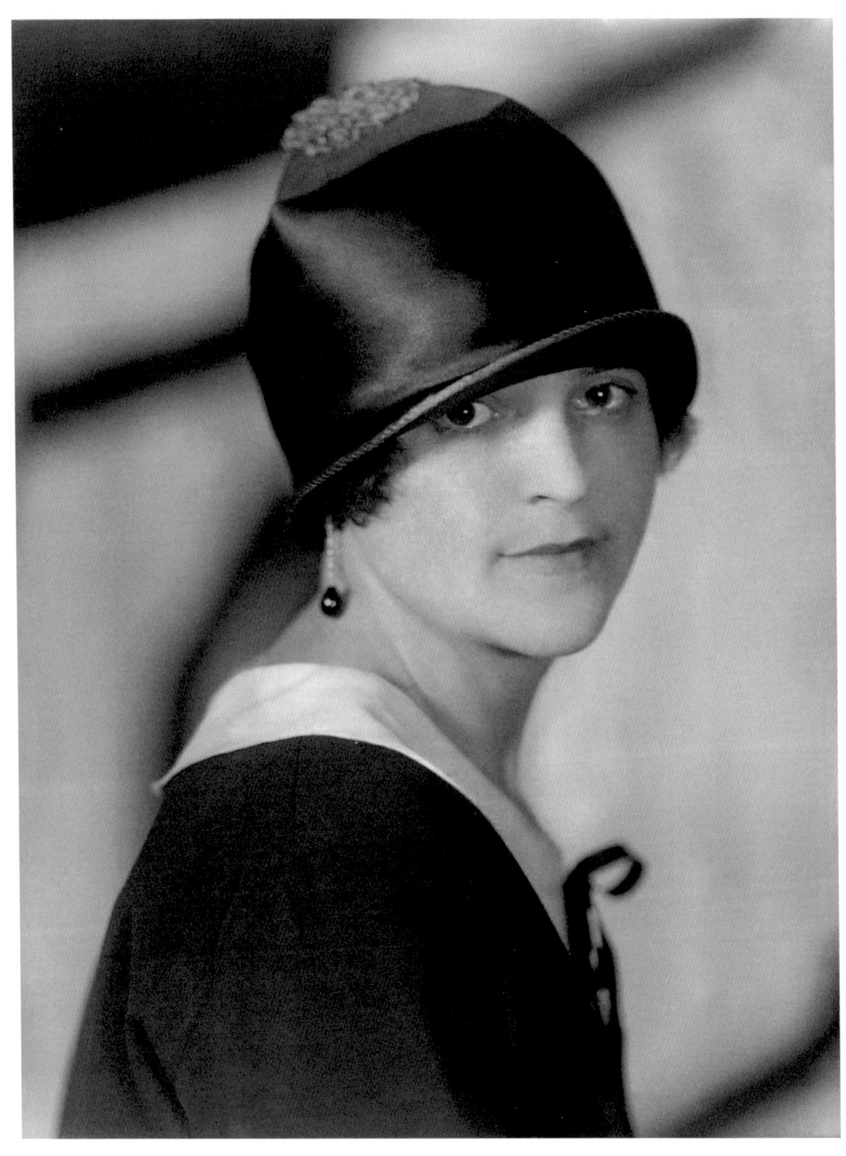

72 Lída Klímová-Grossmannová c. 1922

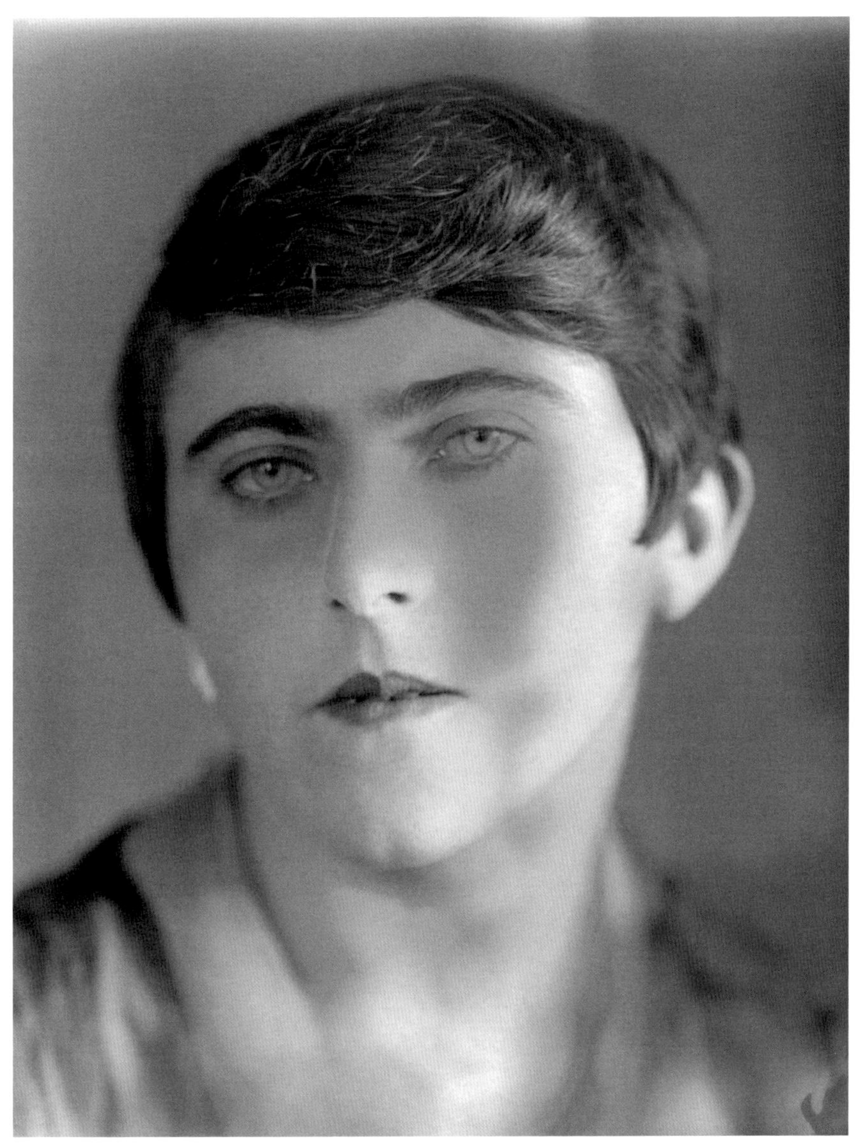

73 **Míla Mellanová** c. 1925

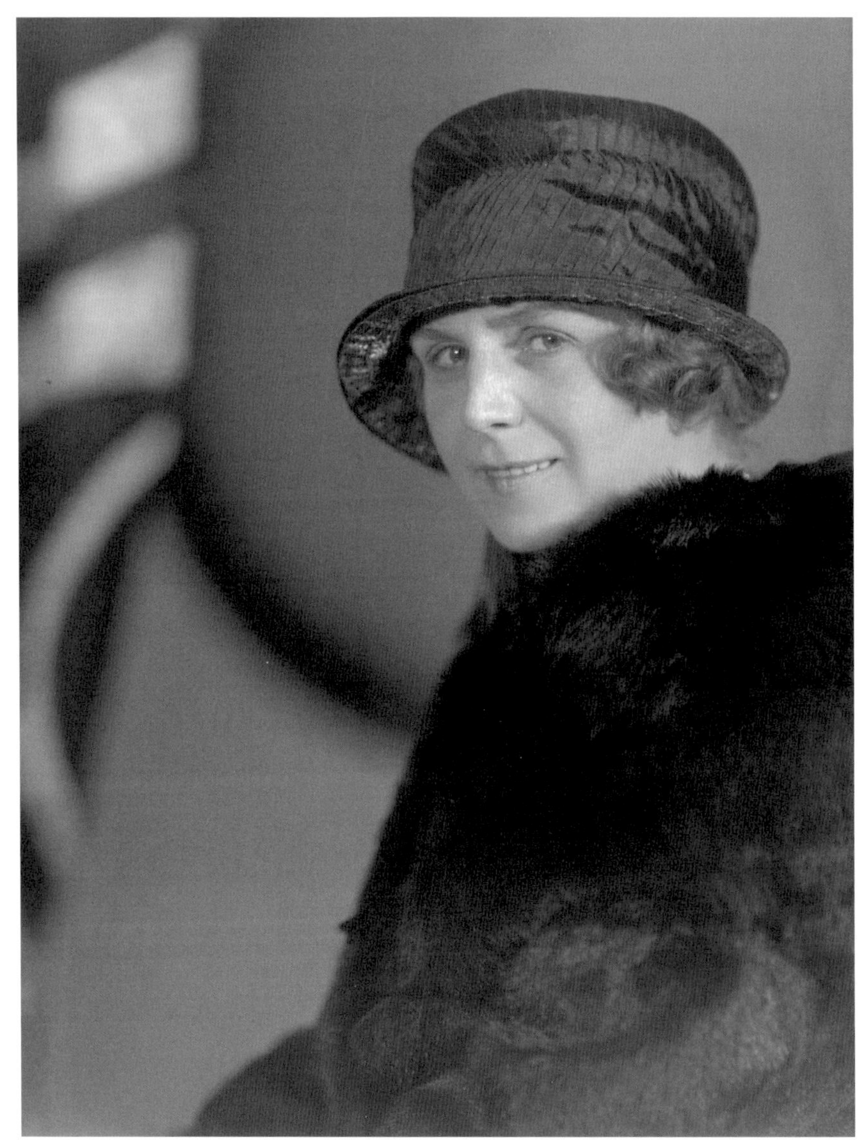

74 **Helena Friedlová** 1925

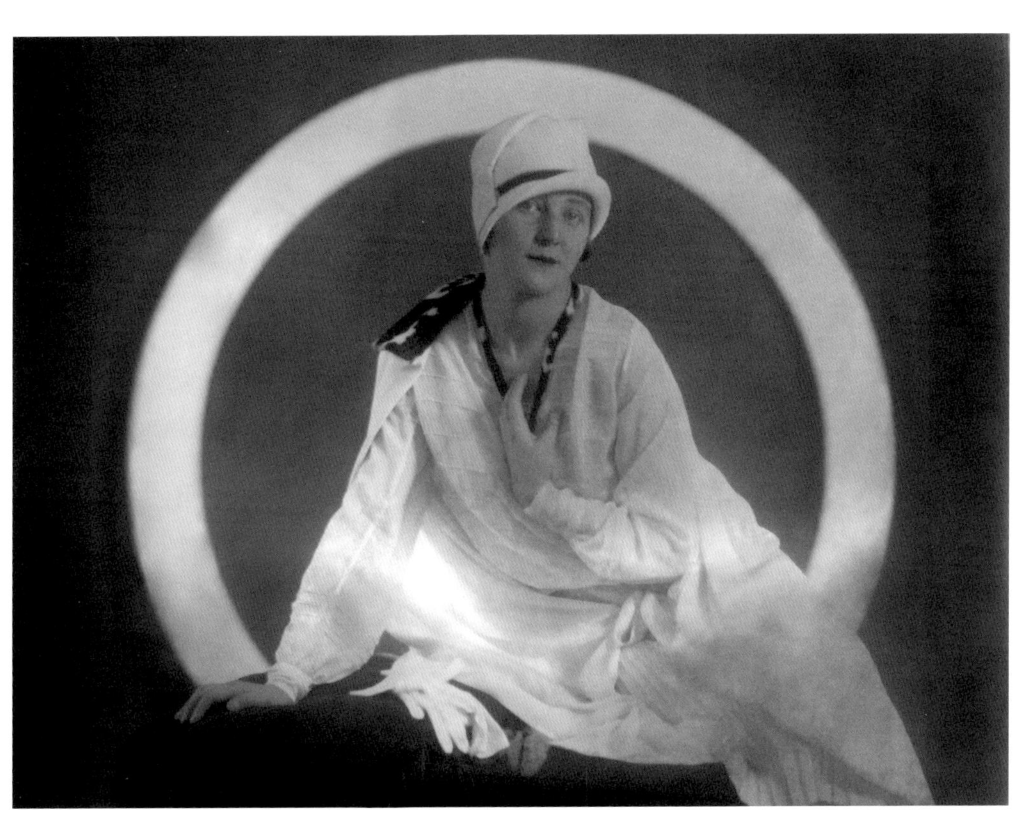

75 **Jarmila Horáková** c. 1925

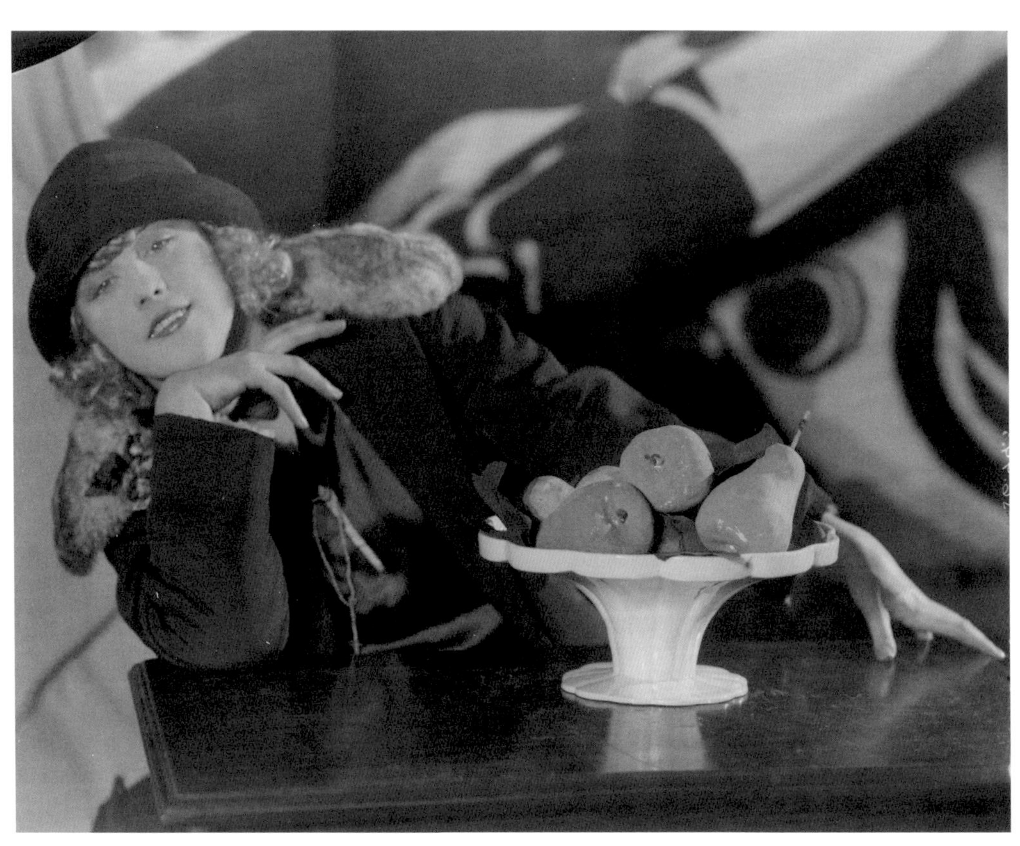

76 **Anny Ondráková** c. 1925

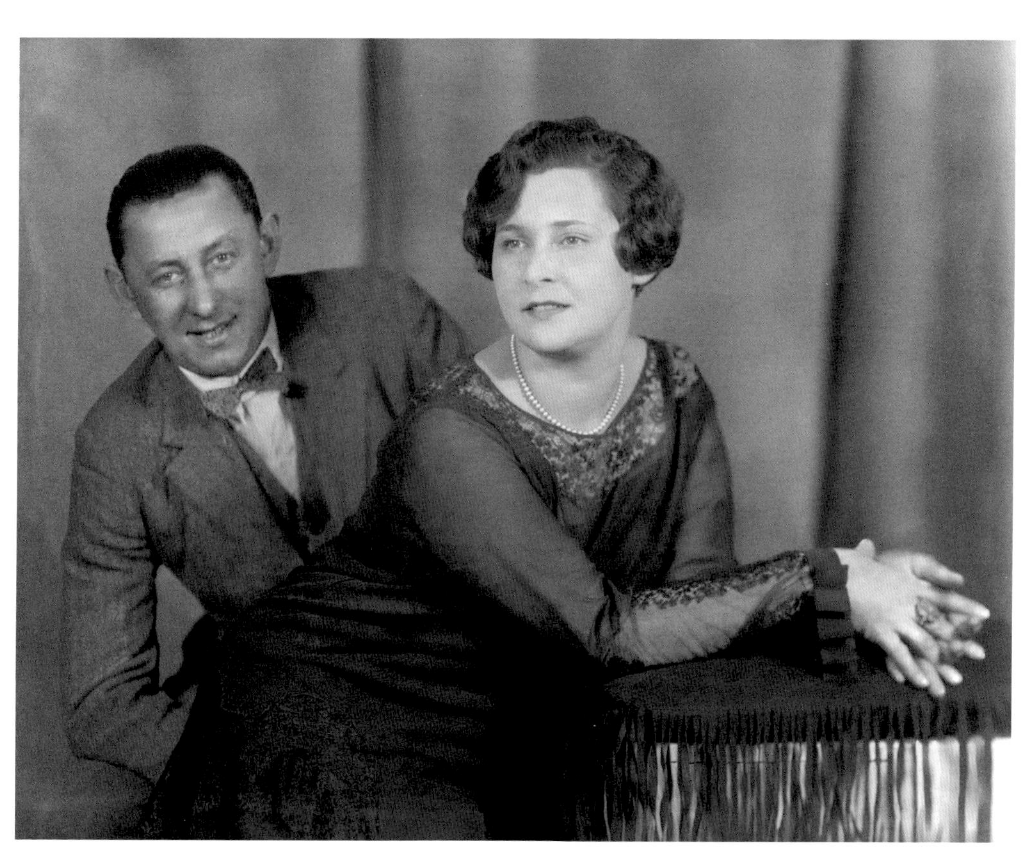

77 **Vlasta Burian with his wife Nina / s chotí Ninou** c. 1933

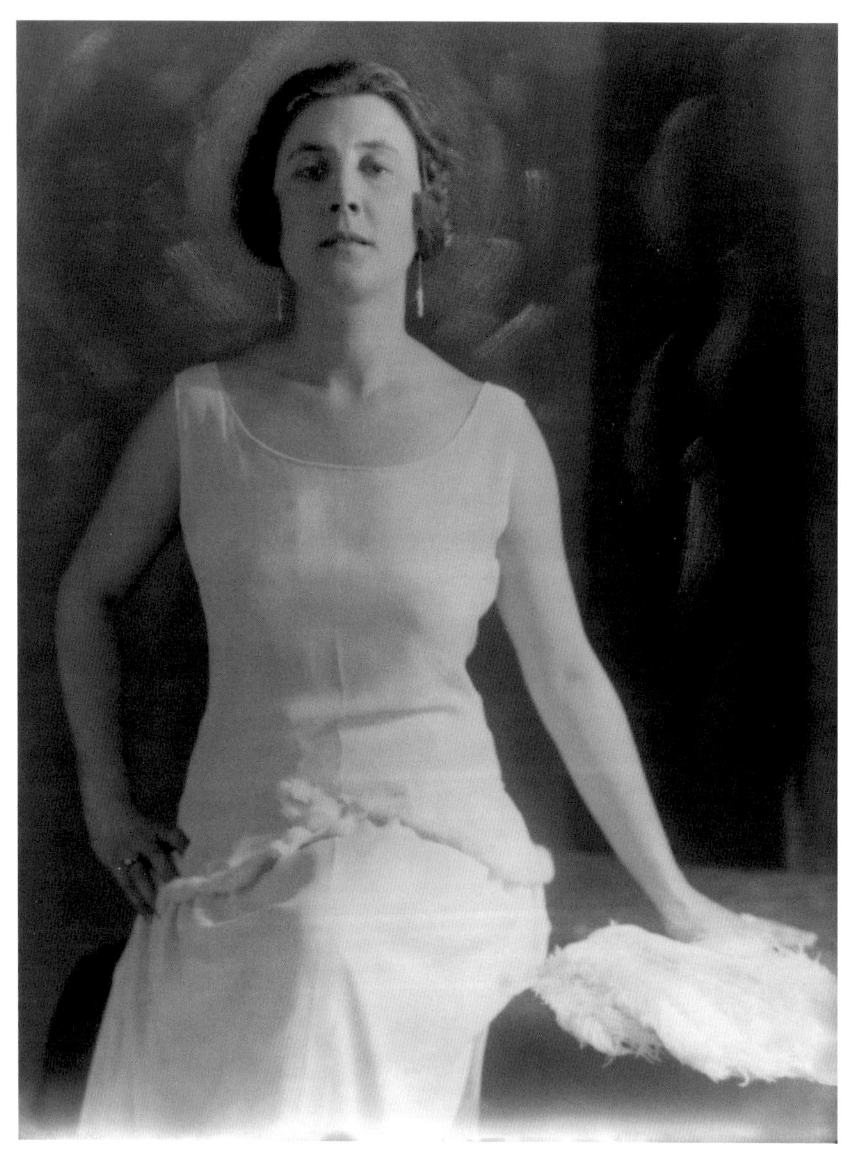

78 **Maria Molinari** c. 1923

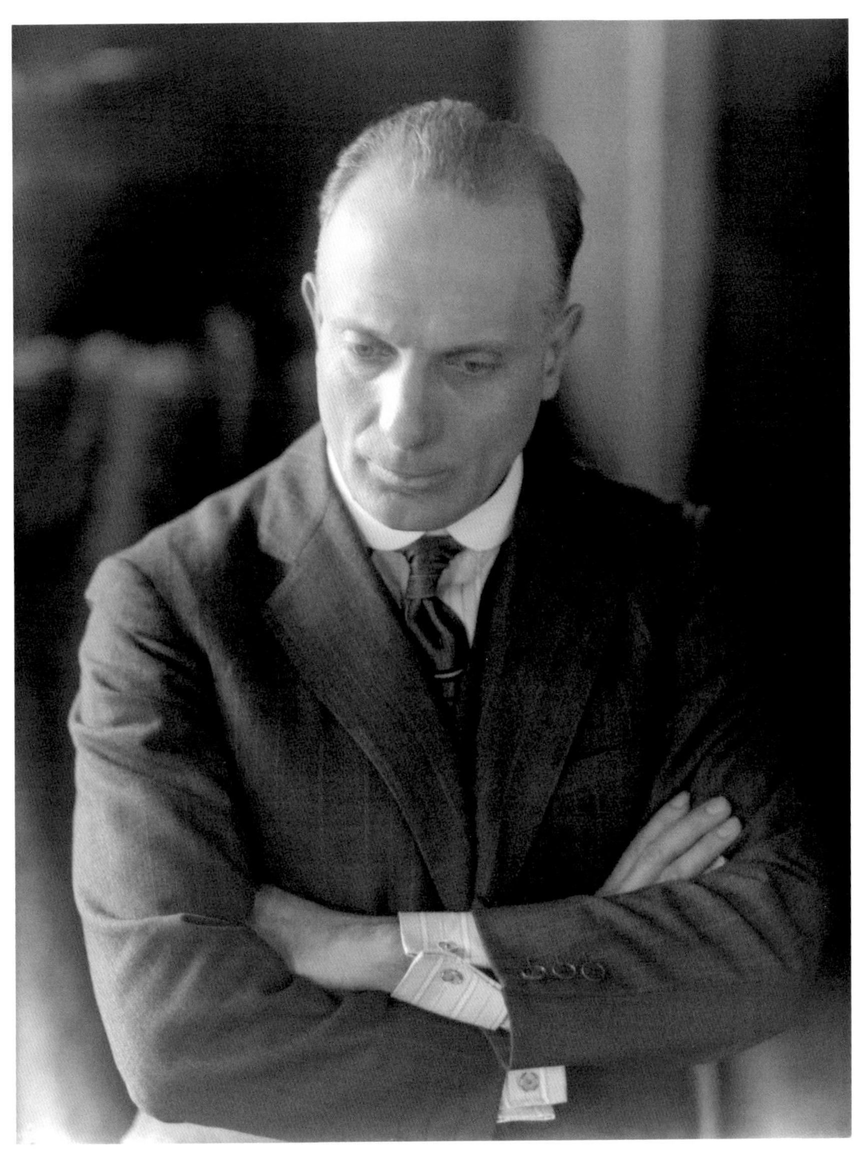

79 **Bernardino Molinari** c. 1923

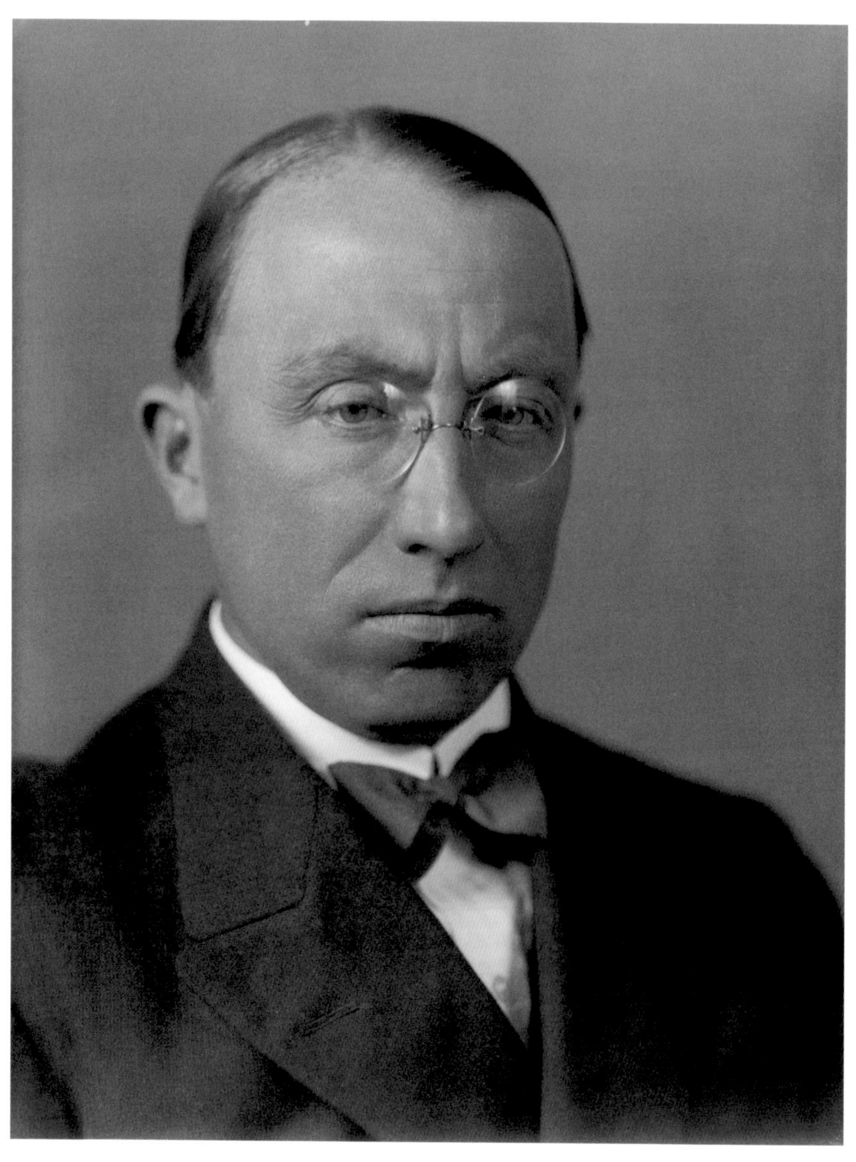

80 **Arnold Jirásek** c. 1934

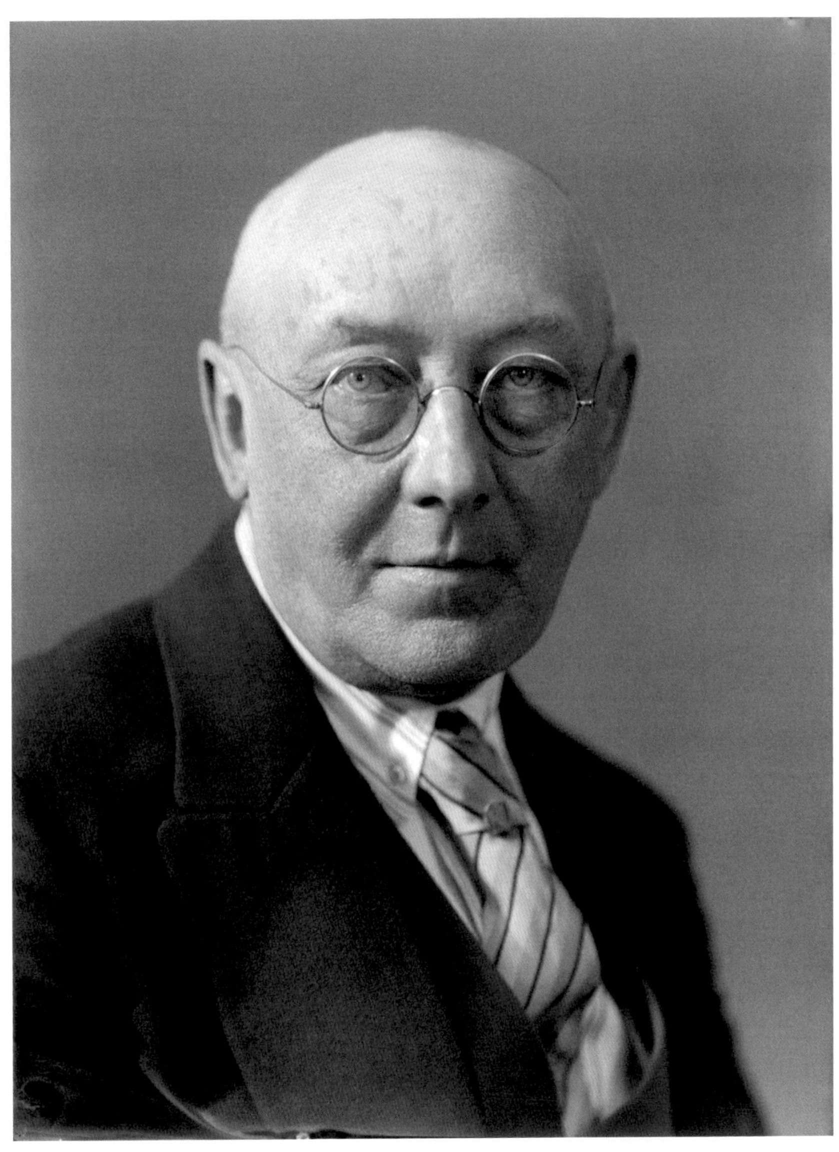

81 **Karel Weinfurter** c. 1929

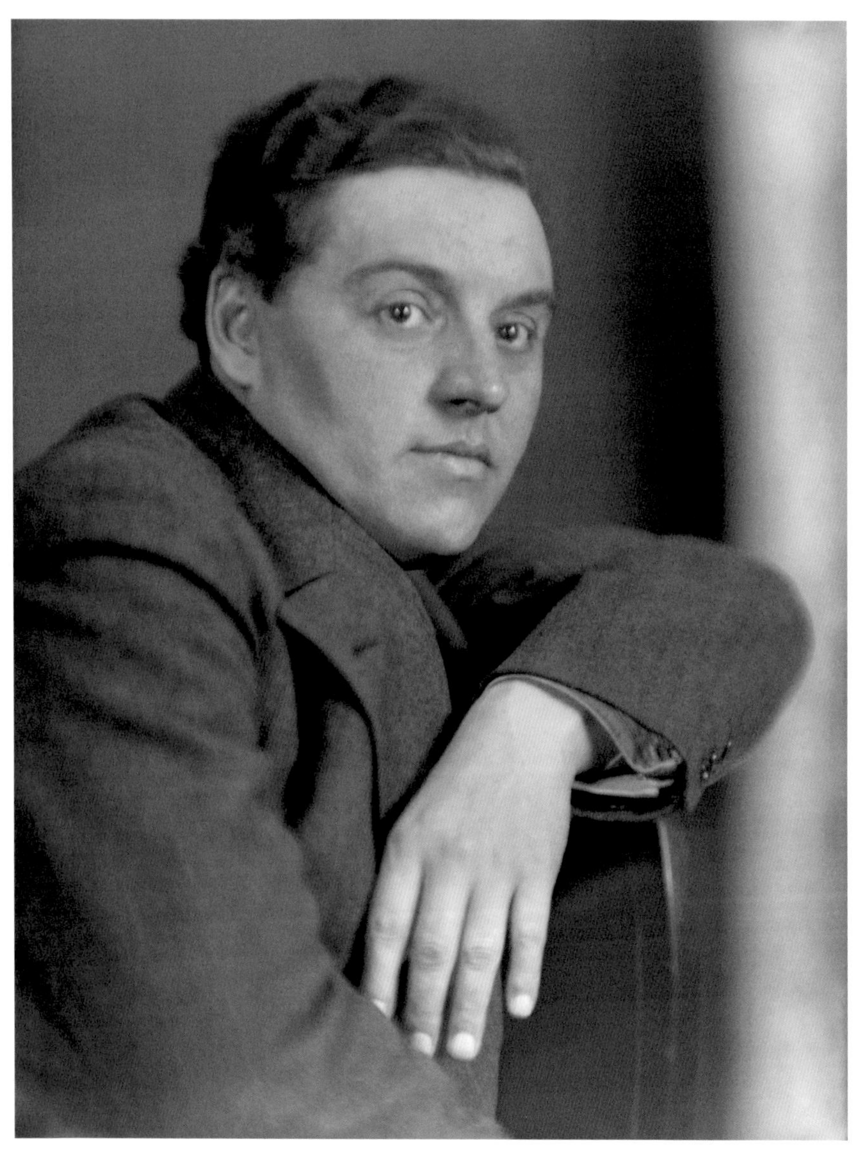

82 **Karel Hugo Hilar** c. 1930

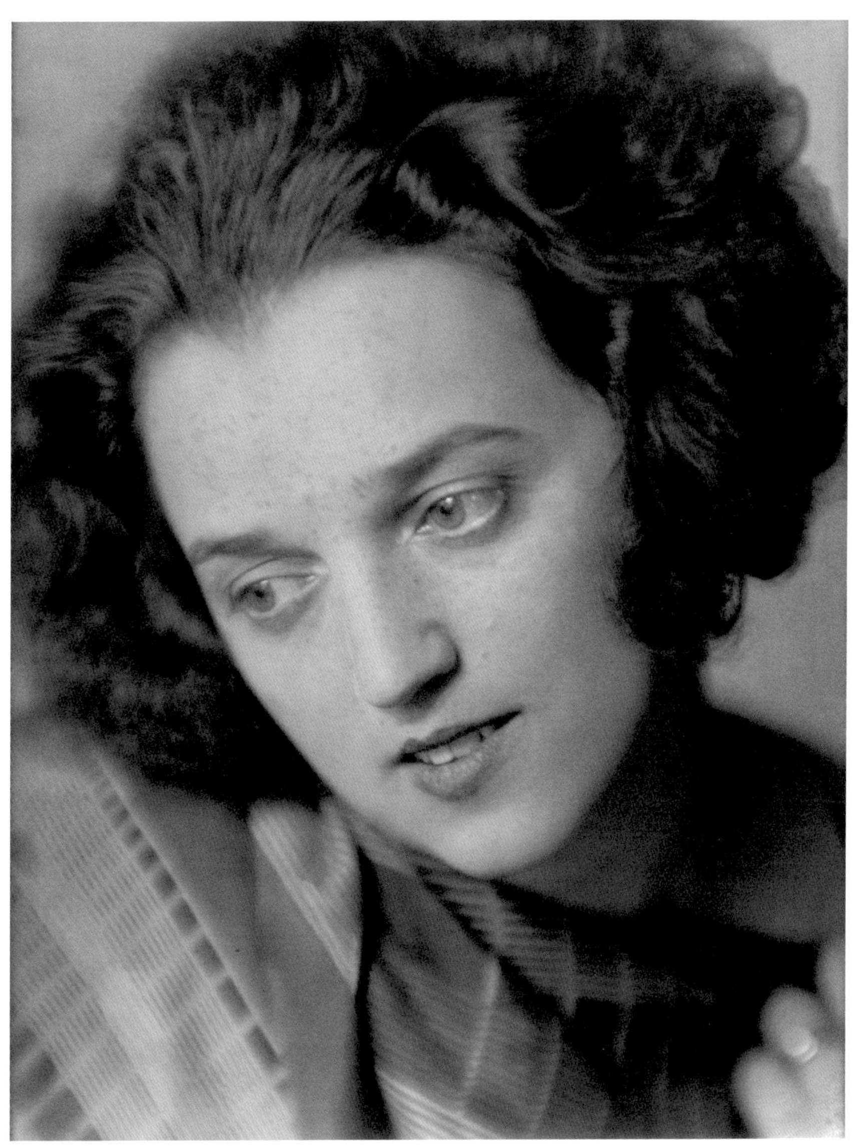

83 **Zuzka Zguriška** c. 1925

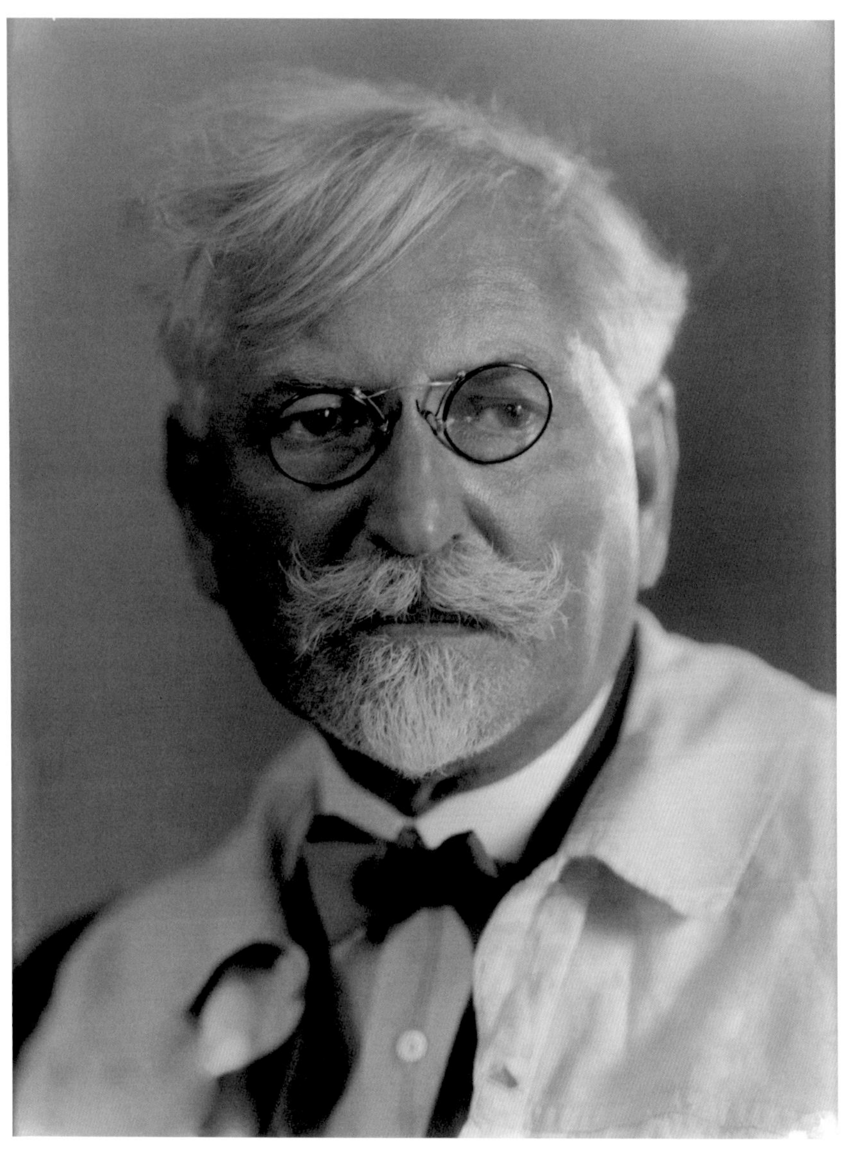

84 **Alfons Mucha** 1927

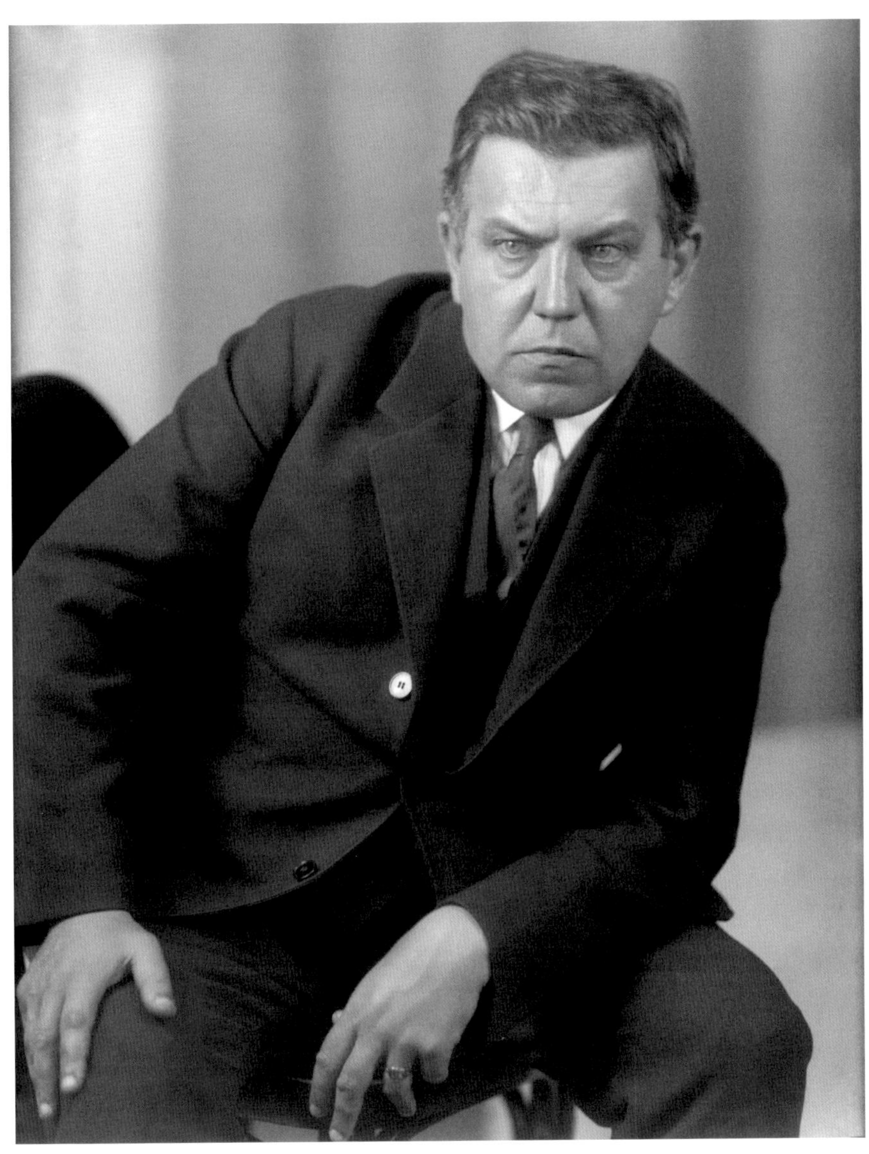

85 **Jan Konůpek** c. 1928

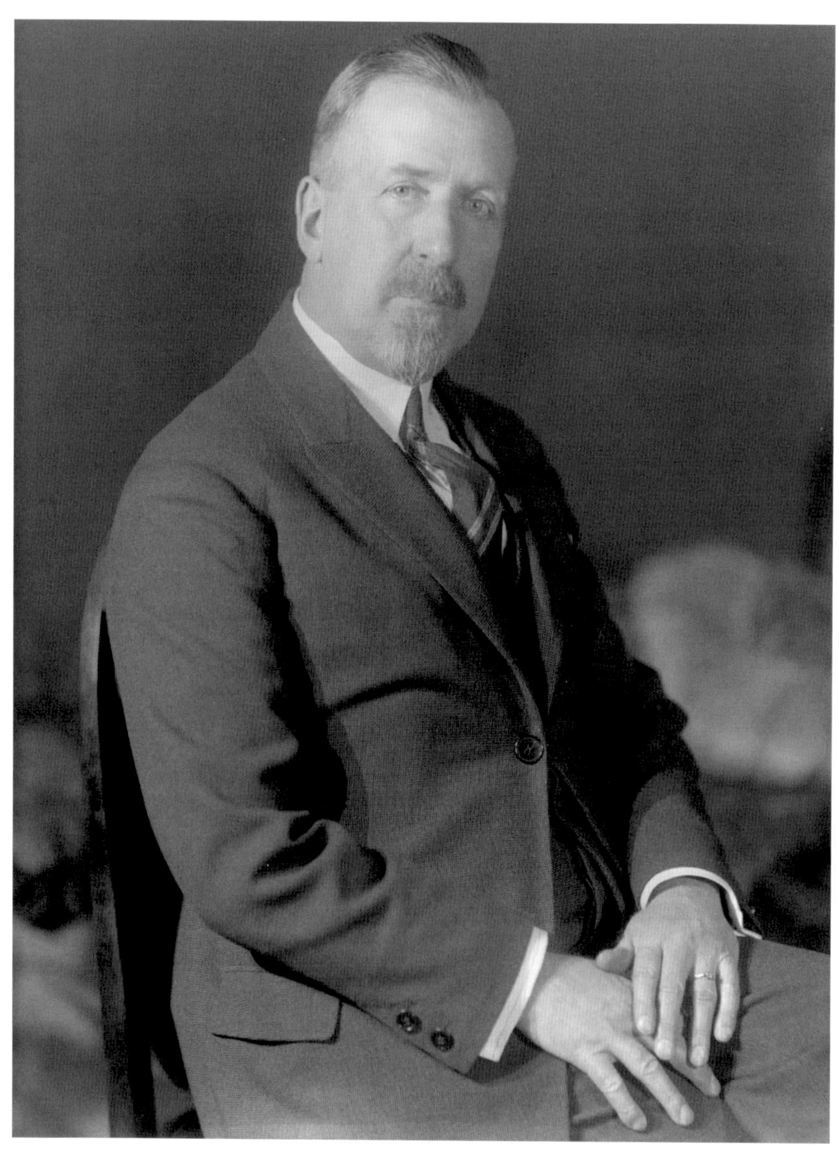

86 Heinrich Mann 1934

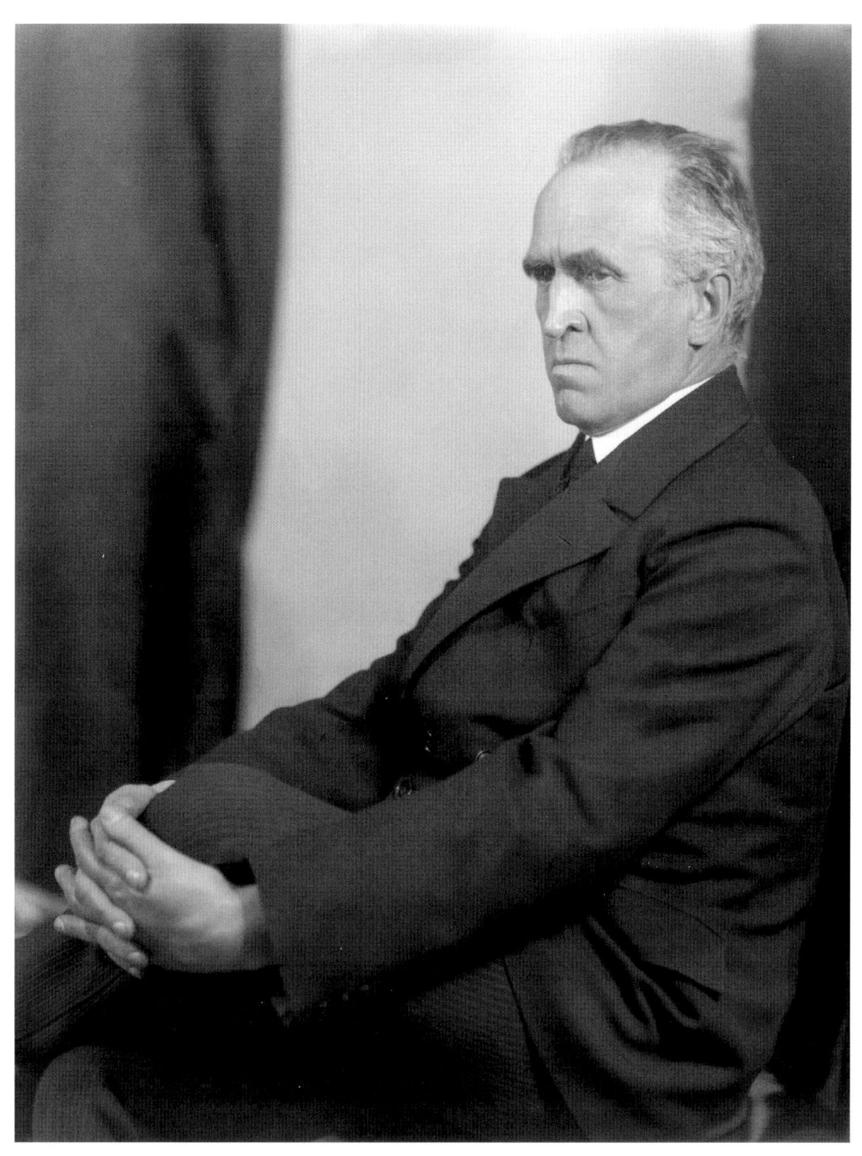

87 **Alois Musil** c. 1930

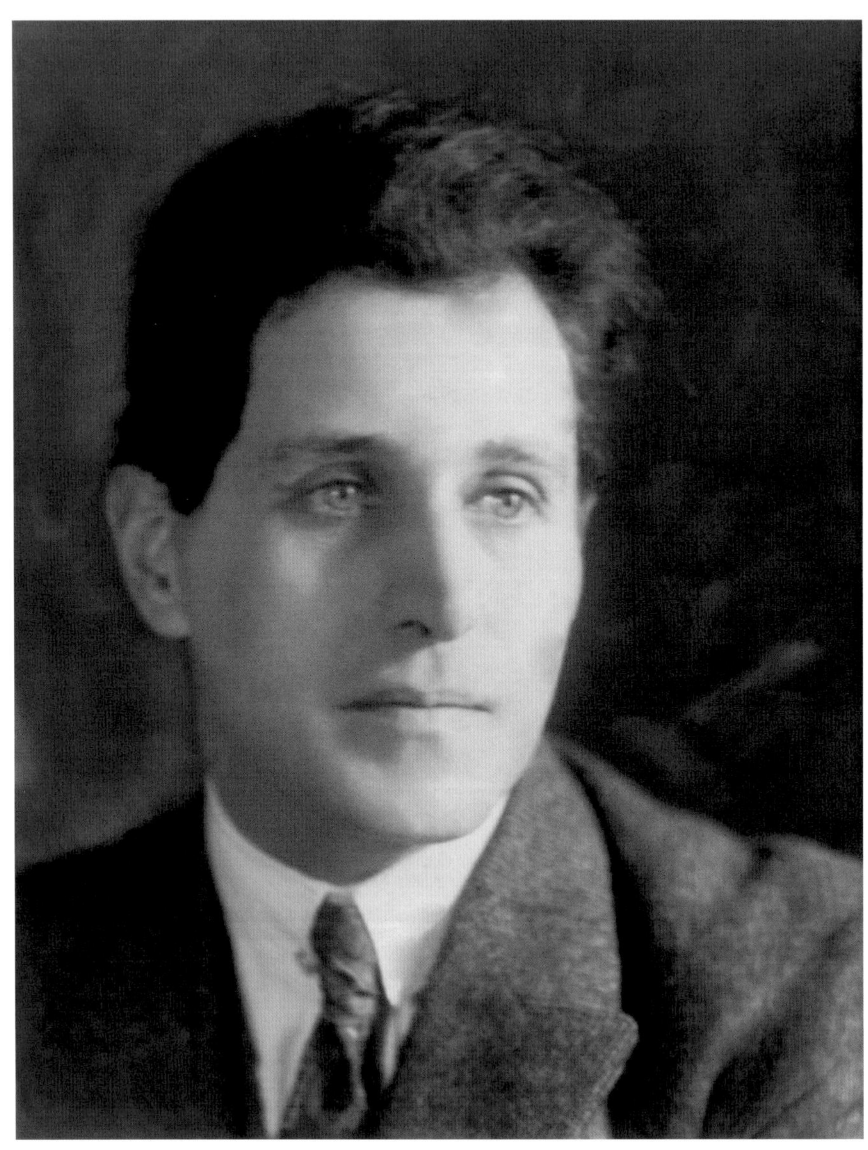

88 **Karel Dostal** c. 1931

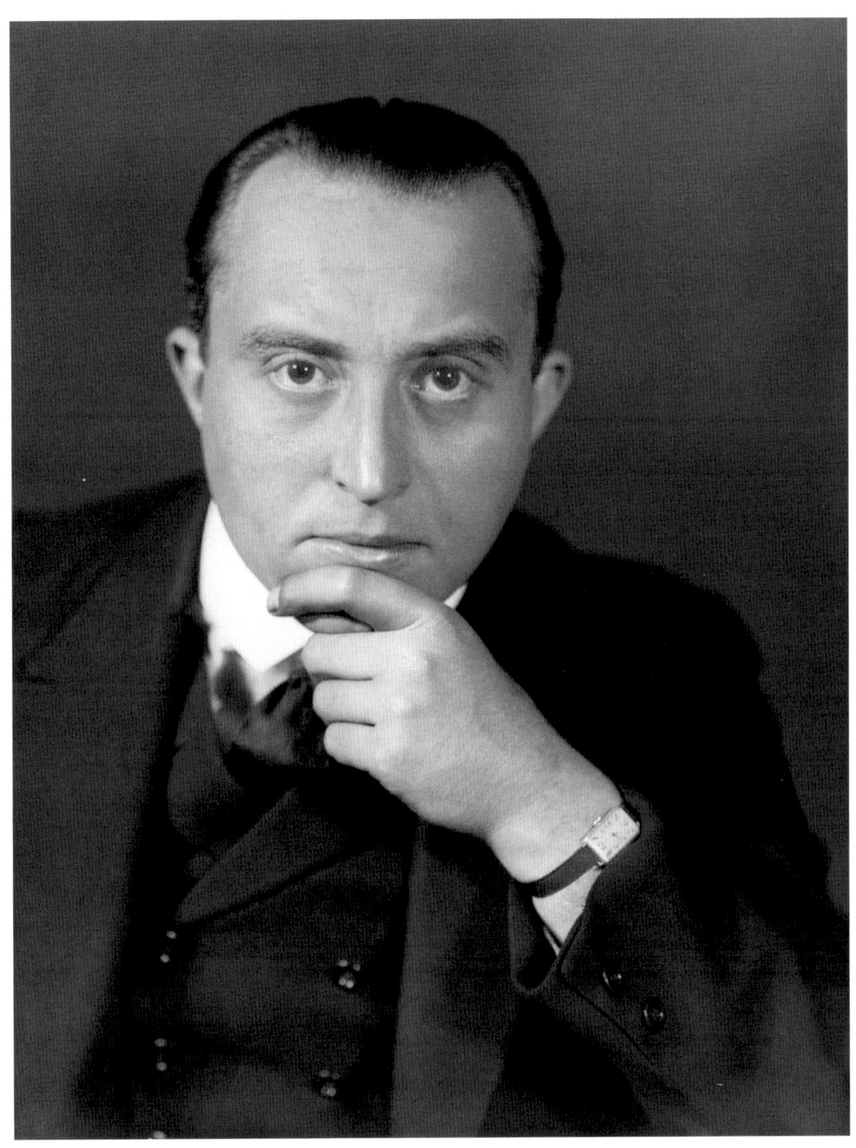

89 **Oldřich Nový** c. 1929

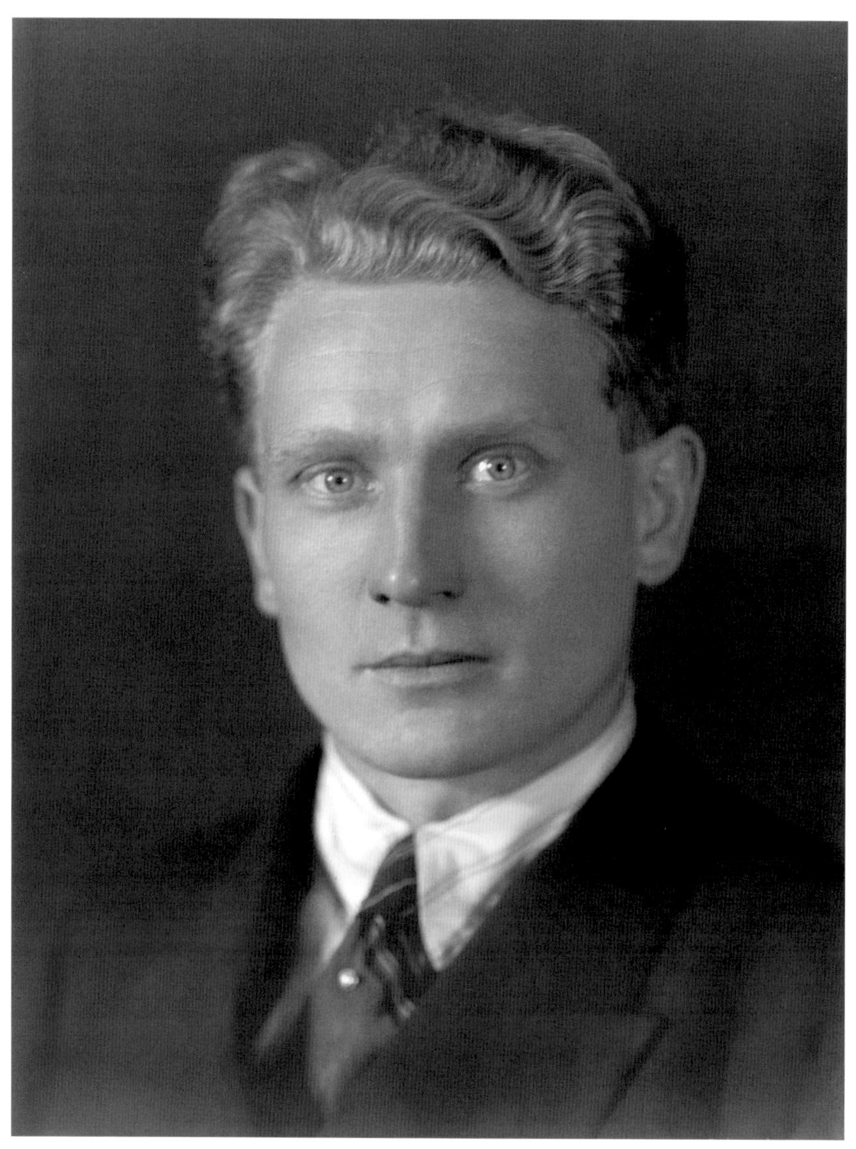

90 **Káďa Pešek** 1923

Biographical Chronology

1883   On 3 March, František Ferdinand Drtikol was born in house no. 275, Příbram, to Marie Drtikolová (née Opplová) and František Drtikol, a well-read merchant, altruist, and eventually town councillor. His elder sisters were Emilie and Marie. His paternal grandfather was František Drtikol, a veterinarian in Dobříš, and his grandmother was Terezie (née Seidlerová) from Cheb. His maternal grandparents were Vít Oppl, an innkeeper in Příbram, and Anastasie (née Fialová) also from Příbram, who was, in addition, the baby's godmother. He was given his middle name after his godfather Ferdinand Oppl of Příbram. Drtikol is listed in the register of births as a Roman Catholic. From childhood he showed himself to be artistically gifted.

1888   At the age of five and half, began primary school.

1895   Began secondary school. Liked to draw, paint, and read, for example the Czech translation of *History of the Conflict between Religion and Science* (1874) by John William Draper. Neglected his studies at the strongly clerical school, and, instead, "despite it being forbidden," used to go to the Sokol, the Czech nationalist physical-education organization. "What did you expect?" he said "It was at the foot of Svatá Hora, and the priests had a decisive influence on every aspect of life in Příbram."

1898   On 1 October, began an apprenticeship with the Příbram photographer Antonín Mattas. Drtikol was obsessed with painting, but he developed, printed, and tinted other peoples' photos without being permitted to assist in actually taking any himself. In the studio, which had no electricity, there were more tasks than could be managed even when working from sunrise to sunset everyday of the week, including Sunday morning.

1901   On 30 September, finished three years of apprenticeship (for which his father paid 200 guldens), and received his certificate. In autumn, began to attend the Lehr- und Versuchsanstalt für Photographie in the Rennbahnstrasse, Munich, having passed the entrance exams in summer. An interest in painting, a grounding in Art Nouveau, and the ideas of Symbolism determined Drtikol's views on photography for the next thirty years, though with time the pictures became simpler in terms of form. Even in his non-photographic period from the mid-1930s onward, he would remain true to the main impulse from his youth as the painter's canvas became the medium for his coded symbols.

1903   On 15 July, graduated from the school in Munich. Was considered an outstanding artist, which is confirmed by the school certificate, the jury's having awarded him First Prize, and, on 9 July, a review of the graduates' exhibition, which was published in the *Münchner neueste Nachrichten*. This was followed by a brief period of employment in the studio of the "Hofphotograph" Theodor Schuhmann & Sohn, Amalienstrasse 57, Karlsruhe, Germany (16 July–31 August). In the small Swiss town of Chur, was employed for three months in the Atelier für Photographie und Malerei Albert Bösch (often mispelt as Böse or Bos).

1904   On 21 April, the mayor of the royal mining town of Příbram issued Drtikol a time-book recording his previous jobs. According to its description of him, he had blue eyes, an angular mouth, an elongated, symmetrical face, brown hair, and was of medium height.

Continued to work as a "photographer's assistant" in the studios of Emanuel Grán in Turnov (17 April–30 May) and Josef Faix in Ječná ulice, Prague (1June–14 September). On 6 October, enlisted for three years' service in the 102nd Infantry in Benešov, Bohemia. Was also diligently drawing and painting small watercolors. "And because I knew German and was adroit and quick-witted, I worked my way up to the rank of sergeant. In the last year, I even served as a leader."

1905   His father could no longer keep the general store, since he used to forgive customers their debts: "Eventually Dad got into debt, and sold the business. He rented the space to a pharmacy. Later he sold the house for very little money."

1907   With the help of his father, Drtikol opened up Atelier F. Drtikol, Příbram. The entrance was at no. 144/II Wenceslas Square, in the garden of the house where he was born – it had a different house number in 1883. He placed advertisements for modern photography, portraits, and enlargements of all kinds. The small-town environment was not conducive to making nudes, Drtikol's future specialization, but the area around Příbram did provide him with opportunities to make a number of landscape photographs and photographs of ore mines, which remain unique documents.

1910   A children's group portrait in the collection of the František Drtikol Gallery, Příbram, is evidence that Drtikol was still working in his home town in 1910. After 22 October the Artěl shop accepted his offer of photographs: the exhibited items were on sale for between 40 and 60 silver crowns. Whereas Drtikol's first creative period is marked by Art Nouveau, when he moved to Prague it was Modern art that had an increasingly strong influence on him.

1911   On 26 January, he registered a business in the Old Town, Prague (at no. 920-I V kolkovně street, where he also lived). At that time there were 83 photography studios in Prague. He published picture postcards of miners, the photographs for which he had taken in previous years using artificial magnesium light in the Příbram mines. From 2 March onwards, was a contributing member of the Czech Amateur Photographic Club, Prague (with membership card no. 400), and showed nudes at one of its exhibitions. Was the first to publish nudes in a Czech photography book or periodical (*Fotografický obzor* 19 [1911], no. 7, p. 107). With Augustin Škarda, a photography hobbyist, clerk, and future editor of the *Fotografický obzor* monthly and the *Československá fotografie* annual, he published a portfolio of 50 oil-pigment prints called *Dvory a dvorečky staré Prahy* (Large and Little Courtyards of Old Prague).

1912   As of 1 February, Drtikol's studio was located in a new Prague apartment building, no. 730/II, at the intersection of Vodičkova ulice and Jungmannova ulice, a minute's walk from Wenceslas Square. The house was built by Eduard Hulicius. From the company records it is clear that Drtikol also lived there. That is confirmed as well by the bilingual *Úřední list Pražských novin / Amtsblatt zur Prager Zeitung* of Sunday, 4 January 1914 (no. 3), p. 6. His having a solid base is manifested in his commercial and art photography, which have backgrounds painted on the negatives and painstakingly produced prints. The last step was to mount the work like an engraving or lithograph. On the facade of the now demolished Urbánek House near the National Theatre, he set up a showcase to exhibit new photographs of the Russian dancer and actress Olga Vladimirovna Gzovskaya: "When I was photographing Olga Gzovskaya," he said in the mid-1950s, "[Josef] Mařatka, the sculptor, kept telling me what to do. He saw her as a sculptor would, but I saw her as a non-sculptor, and so I told him to go into the next room, and I made my photograph of Gzovskaya without Mařatka, in daylight, solely as I envisioned her." He was trying to get his viewers to think about the pictures, and so he gave the works names like *Music and Dance* (1912), *Before the Ball* (1913), *Nocturne* (c. 1913), *Sphinx* (1913), *Salome* (1914), and *Christ* (1914). On 10 October, the Czech Sokol Organization thanked him for a portfolio of foreign visitors to the VIth All-Sokol Rally: "Your art photographs will be deposited in our Sokol archive and future museum."

1913   For his self-portrait, Drtikol, now 30 years old, styled himself crucified. In August, received permission to set up showcases with examples of his work on the front of the apartment building where he had a photography studio on the fourth floor (fifth in America) and a printing room as well as storage space for his negatives on the floor above. In periodicals, particularly the weekly *Český svět* (which he would work with till the end of the 1920s), began to publish portraits as well as scenes of dancers and actors. On 28 March, he and Škarda announced the establishment of Drtikol a spol. (Drtikol & Co.), which had opened for business 1 January. The initial investment of each of the partners was 3,500 crowns. Each of the partners was authorized to represent the business separately. The internal revenue service set the income tax for their company at 128 crowns on 1 April. On 15 December, the Chamber of Trade and Commerce, Prague, informed the Imperial and Royal Commercial Court that the company Drtikol a spol. had "in a relatively short period soared to one of the leading positions in this district; and was in fifth place here in terms of the general income tax rate. The company has many employees, and the Chamber therefore believes [...] that the company must enter its name in the commercial register." This was duly performed on 19 December. The blindstamp and handwritten signature "Drtikol a spol." is also preserved on photographs from before 1913.

1914   On 28 February, to mark the fiftieth birthday of the Czech writer Josef Svatopluk Machar, Drtikol published "the latest true-to-life portrait of the writer in original photographs." The leaflet, a copy of which is now in the Museum of Decorative Arts, Prague, gives us an idea of Drtikol's prices: simple 24 × 18 cm or 38 × 26 cm prints were available for three crowns each, and seven crowns and 50 hellers if framed; mounted oil-pigment prints or platinum prints cost 15 crowns. The National Archives, Prague, has the negatives of 16 photos of Machar. In summer, Drtikol was invited to an "Awakening of Greece" celebration by Emanuel Siblík, the organizer. It was held in Riegr Gardens, and Drtikol was presented as the "best Prague photographer of the time." He photographed the meeting barefoot and in a short, light, sleeveless, ancient Greek robe. Siblík, an earlier theorist of dance and author of a book about Isadora Duncan, describes the event in his *Tyrš a rytmika: Zdraví-krása-umění* (Miroslav Tyrš and Rhythmics: Health, Beauty, and Art, 1933): "An unforgettable July morning, when, on the sunlit floral-patterned carpet, in the magnificently articulated scenery of shrubs and trees, in the dreaminess of the morning mists, teenage girls appeared with their hair down, tied with Greek ribbons.

144

The occasional morning pedestrians who stopped to look couldn't believe their eyes, as if it were only a mirage."

On 22 July a partnership agreement was signed by the owners of Drtikol a spol., which before the war broke out put Škarda in charge.

On 30 July, Austria-Hungary and Russia ordered general mobilizations of their armies, and within a few days war began. In August, Drtikol enlisted to serve in the military administration in Benešov, Bohemia, from where he wrote a long declaration of platonic love for Eliška Janská. This shocking essay full of self-reflection by one of a million infantry men manipulated by the state machinery is written in a raw language. No matter how much Drtikol did not want to admit it ("they loaded people in like cattle"), he was one of those sending others off to the front. Right away, two men of the first regiment shot themselves dead while the train was leaving. The art historian Anna Fárová describes the manuscript: "The first of his diaries was accompanied by illustrations, but the others were not. Drtikol probably found another place for his drawings. The frequency of the notes is interesting. They were written in intensive waves. The first notebook contains 136 pages and 18 drawings, but a mere 12 notes made between 22 August and 16 September. The beginning of the war was undoubtedly a shock, and Drtikol needed to express that. Army life and all the strange surroundings elicited a violent reaction from him. His love for Miss Janská, for whom he wrote the diaries, was just beginning, but was suddenly cut short by mobilization. Another, shorter diary was made during 8 days, from 21 to 29 November. It consists of 51 pages. Next, there are 58 pages from two days (4 and 6 December). That is the third notebook, provided of course I have them all."

After Drtikol's partner also enlisted, Škarda's brother-in-law Jiří Šourek, a teacher at a polytechnic, would manage the studio. He hired František Svoboda as a photographer.

1914–15	From 20 December 1914 to 31 January 1915 the Museum of Decorative Arts, Prague, organized a show of commercial studios in the Rudolfinum to mark the 75th anniversary of the announcement of the invention of photography. To accompany the exhibition, it published a small catalog by F. X. Jiřík, the Museum curator, who was systematically comparing miniature paintings and portrait photographs. The last of the 344 items in this catalog without illustrations is a "set of photographs from the studio of Drtikol and Škarda." The portrait collection of the partners is presented in another place, and it is reasonable to assume that it was the *Large and Little Courtyards of Old Prague* portfolio of oil-pigment prints.
1915	Sent Christmas greetings to his parents from the Hungarian town of Békés Csaba. The Czech Press Agency offered two outdoor photos by Drtikol from the war years, one of which is a group portrait of soldiers, with the title "A Souvenir of the Day They Went Off to War, 2 January 1915."
1917	On 1 September, Jaroslav Rössler, the most distinctive artist ever to work in Drtikol's studio, began his apprenticeship at Drtikol a spol. On 22 December, the Drtikols sold the house at no. 144/II Wenceslas Square, Příbram.
1918	In May, Rudolf Špillar, in the town of Krč near Prague, wrote the introduction to the first volume of the series *Nauky o fotografii* (Photography: Theory and Techniques): "As soon as

circumstances permit, two other works will be published, of which we would first mention the following: František Drtikol, *Portretování* (Portraiture), in a large format. Illustrated with many carefully selected photos by the author, it will be an excellent guide to photography and a paragon of various kinds of lighting and poses. František Drtikol, *Olejotisk (S uměleckými obrazy.)* (The Oil-pigment Print: With Artistic Pictures) (Cited after Jindra Imlauf, *Vyvíjení pozvolné a časové*, Prague: Josef Rašín, 1918, p. III.) These titles were never catalogued at the National Library. On 6 August, from Hartberg, Upper Austria, Drtikol wrote to Miss Janská: "Do you know I haven't taken any photographs since the war? Do you know that I'm now ashamed of the photographic trash I used to do? [...] The war really purged me." Despite what is said in this letter, several extant Drtikol photographs bear dates while the war was still on. In late August, Drtikol returned to Prague by way of Příbram, and pretended that he was in the hospital until the Czechoslovak declaration of independence on 28 October, though he was already working hard in the studio. In November, the Allies and the Central Powers signed armistices. After four years of battle, the Bohemian Lands were exhausted and shaken by hunger. Drtikol recalls this period in his autobiography from the late 1940s: "All the eminent people went to have their photographs taken and it had to be done right away. I also had to photograph all the official visitors that came to the country. There was no profit in that. It was done free of charge. No one wanted to pay." Upon his return, Drtikol destroyed the negatives of photographs taken in his absence. On 24 November he completed the syllabuses for four semesters of photography.

1919 Organized a course on portrait photography for the Czech Amateur Photographic Club, Prague. Except when aiming to evoke the theatre, his studio remained simple for portraiture. In other respects, he did not hesitate to go with current trends. As the photography historian Jan Mlčoch writes, "In 1919 he made several works on mythological subject matter in response to the current demands of society (for example, *Libuše Prophesying the Glory of Prague*), but the result was only nationalistic propaganda, working with archaic stereotypes. [...] A separate chapter, which has never been taken into account either at exhibitions or in publications, comprises the series of female nudes evoking odalisques. They were all buxom women, lounging on divans bedecked with luxuriously decorated coverlets, in front of heavy drapery." (Jan Mlčoch, "Fotografie," in Jana Horneková (ed.), *České art deco 1918–1938*, Prague: Obecní dům, 1998, pp. 216–17.)

1920 On 23 March the personal secretary of President Tomáš G. Masaryk thanked Drtikol for the portraits of members of the secret wartime organization for Czechoslovak independence (nicknamed the "Mafia"), which Drtikol had given Masaryk for his seventieth birthday: "The President accepts your present with great interest." On 19 June, Drtikol married the dancer Ervina Kupferová (who kept this name). From 1919 onwards, he had made dozens of photographs of her, writing to her and sending his apprentice Rössler to her with notes and bouquets of roses every day. To fetch modeling clay for Drtikol, Rössler used to go to Křižovnická ulice, and later used to take the master's allegoric sculptures to be cast in plaster. Some of his recollections are recorded in a letter of 6 February 1987, addressed to the art historian Kateřina Klaricová. From this letter one learns that Drtikol continued to live in his studio in Vodičkova ulice: "He always lived in the studio, even when he was married. [...]

When he got married, I had to move into the print room, which was upstairs." On 23 June, Drtikol, with the help of his brother-in-law Václav Šaman, a lawyer, managed to get from the District Commercial Court the first decision supporting his loss of trust in his partner Škarda, an official on the Bohemian Committee. The judgment was confirmed on 16 September at the appeals trial at the Commercial Court, Prague, and on 23 October Škarda lost the right to act on behalf of Drtikol a spol. On 16 November, the Supreme Court, Brno, decided to liquidate Drtikol and Škarda's company.

1921   On 31 May, "Augustin Škarda ceased to be a partner of the company [Drtikol a spol.]. The sole owner is now František Drtikol, who will run the business under the name of the existing company." (From the *Úřední list Republiky Československé* [Official Gazette of the Czechoslovak Republic], 29 June, no. 146, p. 2791.) On 12 June Drtikol's daughter Ervina was born. (She died 18 April 2005, at the age of almost 84.)

1922   As the financial situation of the studio became stable, the number of employees rose. Drtikol had his first solo exhibition at the Museum of Decorative Arts, Prague. On 21 June the museum director thanked Drtikol for the art photographs he had donated. (In the annual report of the museum the following year, the board of trustees called Drtikol's works the basis of a collection of "new photography in this country." On 16 November, the Amateur Photographic Club in the Prague district of Královské Vinohrady expressed its thanks to Drtikol for his talk on his "experiences in artistic portrait photography" with examples of pictures and "practical portraiture in our studio."

1922–23   Was inspired by the stage designs of the Futurists Enrico Prampolini and De Pistoris (Federico Pfister), as well as those of Aleksander Yakovlevich Tairov (Aleksandr Kornblit), moving from quasi-Cubist backdrops using brushwork to define the picture field with shadow and light in geometric scenes, which were built to his designs by the National Theatre workshops.

1923   On 19 July, the lawyer Václav Šaman applied on Drtikol's behalf for a patent for the invention of grey-scale photolithography: "It is a combination of oil-pigment printing and lithography. The essence of the process is that an oil-pigment picture is transferred to a lithographic stone. The purpose is to break down shadows into half tones and quarter tones. The prints have the velvety depth of photogravure printmaking and the fine grain of lithography." Drtikol used this original method to print a series of earlier portraits of President Tomáš Garrigue Masaryk, which he then gave to the President. On 4 October the President's personal secretary, Vasil Škrach, thanked Drtikol and ordered one print of each of the Masaryk photos for the President's personal use. The National Archives, Prague, has 17 of these negatives. This is the beginning of Drtikol's best period. In the 1920s he began to turn less to *belles-lettres* for inspiration and also manipulated the negatives less, yet he continued to employ symbolism, for example in *The Dancing of Dolls* (1925), *Meditation* (1927) and *Reflection* (1927). Some works, like *Desire, Curtain, Theatre, Lighting Effect* and *Figure Composition*, are undated.

1924   The Minister of Education appointed Drtikol to the Department of Portrait Photography and Cinematography attached to the Board of Trustees of the State School of Graphic Arts for 1924–27.

1925	On 28 July, Drtikol was granted a patent for photolithography (patent no. 16640), a "method of lithographic grey-scale printing from plates by transferring oil-pigment photographs onto stone, zinc, aluminum, and the like," which, according to his memoirs, he had been experimenting with back in the early 1920s. This is the beginning of his most fruitful period in the Art Deco style: his dynamic expressive nudes of the 1920s are the best of his career as a photographer. As an artistic device he also used out-of-focus shots and motion blurs. (By 1930 he had entered work in more than 150 photo exhibitions.) He considered becoming a member of the Umělecká beseda (Art Society), and talked about it with the chairman of the society, Václav Rabas. It was perhaps this year or the next that the photographer Jaromír Funke formulated a joint request for the acceptance of four photographers as members in the society, but only he and Drtikol signed it. (The type-written document is amongst Drtikol's papers at the Museum of Decorative Arts, Prague.)
1926	On 8 November, he divorced Ervina Kupferová.
1927	Began an exhibition tour of the USA. (By 1930, his works had been shown in eleven places.) On 28 October the publisher and photographer Antoine Calavas spotted Drtikol's collection at the Salon international de photographie, Paris, and soon began plans to publish a volume of his photographs.
1928	Was made an Associate Member of the Camera Pictorialists of Los Angeles. At the age of 45, posed as Buddha for a self-portrait. Began to record his observations, which are compiled in "Moje myšlenky 1928–1945" (My Thoughts, 1928–45), published many years later as a chapter of *Duchovní cesta* (A Spiritual Journey, 2004).
1929	*Les nus de Drtikol* was published in Paris by the Librairie des Arts Décoratifs in a print-run of 500 copies. The book did not earn him the money he hoped it would. On 4 July, wrote to the První občanská záložna, a savings bank in Prague: "I am willing to pay only as much rent as you are entitled to by law. Because I have so far paid higher rent, I kindly ask, please, to be told the exact amount of rent you may charge by law." On 20 October he made a note of a dream, which took place in Svatá Hora, where he used to wander as a boy: he was levitating in the dream, longing to be crucified, and increasingly feeling the stigmata; and then before a plain, unplastered wall he triumphantly declared that was where he would hang for ever, "as if sprayed into the stone." He donated examples of his work to the museum in his native Příbram. The crash on Wall Street in late October, followed by the Great Depression, meant the end of Drtikol's company. But he also stopped making photographs because a period style had ended. Whereas the fashion of the 1920s was the unnaturalness of Art Deco, a style which Drtikol continued to offer masterful work in, the vogue of the 1930s was austere Functionalism. In his drafts of a letter to the art historian Kateřina Klaricová, of 6 February 1987, Rössler mentions that in Paris, as early as 1929, he had received news from home that Drtikol's studio was up for sale.
1930	Drtikol concentrated on making photographs in a mystical mood. To that end he had begun in 1929 to make figures out of plywood. The work he did strictly for himself is not within the dominant trends; it is inwardly aimed at hermetic levels of meaning. Apart from the usual titles he gave his photographs, like *Image* (1930), *Girls* (1930), and *Photopurism* (1934), others are called *Soul* (1931), *Mother–Earth* (1931), *The World of the Soul* (1934), *Fairy,*

from *The World of the Soul* series (1935), *Liberated Woman* (1930s), and *Release* (n.d.). His choice of the nude as his genre may be explained by one of his notes: "Nature is God made manifest. It is woman." In his "photopurism" period he used the sepia pigment process, but he also made many as simple contact prints on bromide paper. His pastels from the early 1930s are also important. In the first half of the decade he offered photography courses with a focus on the portrait, the nude, and the still life, also orienting his pupils to lighting, characterization of the model, and staging. The course was given to groups of several people, who paid the models. The photography was done either in Drtikol's studio or at the Czech Amateur Photographic Club, No. 3 Nekázanka street, Prague.

At the end of his career in photography, Drtikol was teaching to try to keep his business afloat. He received offers to give similar courses outside Prague. In the late 1920s or early 1930s he began to complete the manuscript of his lessons, called *Oči široce otevřené* (Eyes Wide Open). In an undated leaflet, he recommends *Drtikolovy ozdobné předměty* (Drtikol's Decorative Objects) for lighting and decor.

1932	On 15 October, drafted a reply to a classified ad that had been published that day in *Foto-noviny* (Photo News): "I am taking the liberty of offering you a chance to buy my acclaimed studio in the centre of Prague at a price of 90,000 [Czechoslovak crowns]. I am doing this purely for personal reasons. The business comprises a studio, two waiting rooms, a workroom, laboratory, kitchen, and two storage rooms. It owns many rare negatives, like those of President [Tomáš] Masaryk, [Foreign] Minister [Edvard] Beneš, Dr [Karel] Kramář, Dr [Alois] Rašín, the whole "Mafia" [Czechs who worked clandestinely for Czechoslovak independence] and the leading politicians, artists from all fields, and other eminent people. The turnover from last year was 100,000 Czechoslovak crowns, which would certainly be increased if the business began to look after amateur work and taking photographs outside the studio, since I have so far been involved only with portrait photography."
1933	In a self-portrait the 50-year-old artist stylized himself as a Taoist pilgrim. At the prompting of the Friends of Photography Association (Sdružení přátel fotografie), Olomouc, he exhibited about 200 of his works in the Friends of Art Club (Klub přátel umění), Olomouc. Pavel Altschul, the publisher of a weekly called *Světozor* (Illustrated News of the World or World View) wrote in the periodical: "Drtikol can actually be considered our only great photographer, who has already gone through a period of experimenting and searching, and has achieved his own distinctive artistic style. The other Czech photographers are either still experimenting or are too dependent on their subject matter." The overall decline in Czechoslovak productivity in the late 1920s had terrible consequences: the economy was far worse than what it had been when Drtikol was struggling to make ends meet in the Bohemian metropolis before the First World War. In a letter of 17 December 1947 he recalls the situation in the 1930s: "Creditors and executors followed each other in rapid succession – and yet I was getting work and had to keep it going somehow. And that's the way we muddled through all those years. When it all finally pissed me off, I sold everything, paid my bills, and was left without a penny in my pocket. That was in 1935."
1935	On 14 March, the Director of the State School of Graphic Arts (Státní grafická škola), Prague, thanked Drtikol for having donated periodicals and other publications, and announced

that Professor Karel Novák would be visiting the closed-down studio in the coming days to say what "things could be bought for the school." From 12 April, he lived in part of the house left to him by a woman called Marie Malečková (no. 1018, Jihozápadní V) in Spořilov, a garden community of Prague. Here he made his last photographs: *Visions, Wood Nymphs*, and *Fairy* from *The World of the Soul* series. From then on, he would devote himself to meditation, concentration exercises, spiritual teaching in an informal group of pupils, and painting. The spiritual pictures also reveal the inspiration of visions from meditation. Auras are a frequent motif of Drtikol's late, non-photographic period, and their radiation can have resonance even with the uninitiated.

1938   On 8 February, requested that his business be struck off the register of companies: "I, the undersigned, František Drtikol, painter, currently of house no. 1018, in the Prague district of Spořilov, am the sole owner of the registered company 'Drtikol & spol.', at Vodičkova street, no. 7, Prague. Owing to the unfavorable financial and economic situation, I have decided to wind up this company, and I no longer operate it. I therefore ask that it be removed from the register of companies. I am making a corresponding announcement to the Businesses Office and the Internal Revenue Service in District II of Prague."
The Regional Commercial Court, Prague, removed the company, 30 June. Eduard Beaufort, Prague, published the portfolio *Žena ve světle* (Woman in Light) with a commentary by the artist and critic Josef Richard Marek (1883–1951). This selection of 46 nudes reveals an attempt to appeal to contemporary tastes. Even some questionable works were printed, and some earlier photographs have new titles.

1939   On 15 March the German occupation of Bohemia and Moravia began. In the late spring or early summer, Drtikol donated some of his finished photographic works to the Museum of Decorative Arts, Prague, following on from the donation of 1922.

1939   On 3 September, Great Britain and France declared war on Germany.
Drtikol's last exhibition in his lifetime was also held in this museum; called "A Hundred Years of Czech Photography, 1839–1939", and running from 26 October to 31 December 1939, it presented in the "Commercial Photography" section only his early works (from 1910–22). Of the 27 exhibited photographs eleven were portraits.

1940   In June, gave the Czech Press Agency a selection of his negatives. (On 30 July 1980 the Czech Press Agency would offer these to the Central State Archive, today called the National Archives.) The list of photographs, which was presented "in keeping with a records-disposal guideline relating to pre-archival care of photographic information in the Picture Archive of the Czech Press Agency," comprises 2,113 undated items, some of which it calls 'missing'." Since 31 October 1980 the archive has only 1,872 negatives (and slides, of which by no means all are of the original destroyed plates). In addition to portraits, there are series of dance-pose images made in the studio rather than capturing the fleeting moments of real dance performances.

1941   In June, Germany attacked the Soviet Union.

1942   On 25 February, Drtikol gave a substantial number of his photographs as well as some drawings and written documents to the Museum of Decorative Arts, Prague. (Despite the losses, more than 5,000 items were preserved as State property.) In April, married the photographer

Jarmila Rambousková, who since 1921 had been an employee of Drtikol a spol., and had lived with Drtikol in Spořilov after the studio had been sold. In early June, Reichsprotektor Reinhard Heydrich died after being ambushed in Prague. The Germans unleashed furious reprisals against the Czechs. On 21 November, Drtikol was made an honorary member at the annual meeting of the Czech Photographic Society, Prague. (Established in 1882, this was the oldest professional photographic association.)

1945   Was actively involved in the Prague Uprising against the German Occupation in early May. On 1 June, František and Jarmila Drtikol joined the Czechoslovak Communist Party.

1945–46   Worked part-time as a teacher at the State School of Graphic Arts, Prague (Státní grafická škola). On 20 February 1946, drafted the last of a series of syllabuses for a photography course, which he hoped would be an impetus to establish a professional school of art photography in Prague. The school was intended to be a four or five-year institution of higher learning, which might expand to include cinematography. Drtikol had been dissatisfied with the State School of Graphic Arts: "The curriculum includes some utterly useless subjects, whereas its lacks others – drawing and anatomy – which should be taught." After two years of the rudiments, the students should, Drtikol proposed, choose from three areas of specialization: technical, advertising, and art photography. "The whole curriculum of this school would aim to raise the artistic level of photography."

1946   Left the Roman Catholic Church at the parish church in the Prague district of Michle, Prague, 26 January (file no. IV C 572/46). This was also recorded in the register of births and deaths, 25 January 1947.

1947   The dust-jacket of the first edition of Jaroslav Kulhánek's *Černobílá fotografie* (Black-and-white Photography), published by Eduard Beaufort, carries Drtikol's recommendation, which ends: "I shall try to ensure that this publication becomes an official textbook for professional photographers at the Czechoslovak [*sic*] State School of Graphic Arts."

1948   After the Communists took power in late February, Drtikol was a watchman in the Party office in Spořilov, sometimes spending the night there. Put together his curriculum vitae when required. (A four-page CV for the Czechoslovak Communist Party and a single-page CV for the Association of Czechoslovak Fine Artists – SČSVU – are now deposited in the Museum of Decorative Arts, Prague.) On 17 December, was made a member of the Association of Czechoslovak Fine Artists. (His application for membership had previously been turned down; in a rejection letter of 29 October, the Arts Council wrote that it "could not, on the basis of the works presented by you, recommend that you be made a member of the Association.")

1955   The one and only known interview with Drtikol, conducted by Jiří Jeníček, was published as "Na besedě u Františka Drtikola," *Československá fotografie* 6 (1955) no. 2.

1956   Stopped painting, and expressed a desire to go into an old people's home, so as not to be a burden to his family and friends.

1959   On 9 January, Drtikol's wife Jarmila died of injuries suffered in a car accident. Owing to old age, Drtikol became bedridden, dependent on the care of Anna Soukupová, a family friend.

1960   Wrote Christmas and New Year's greetings as always with an energetic hand revealing mental alertness.

1961   František Drtikol died of natural causes in Prague on 13 January. His ashes were sent to
        a cemetery in his native Příbram. In November a commission of the Museum of Decorative
        Arts in Prague classified roughly 5,500 photographs of his bequest as items of no value for
        the collections.

1968   21 August, the Soviet-led military occupation put an end to the Czechoslovak hopes of
        reform.

1970   The curator of the Photography Collection at the Museum of Decorative Arts in Prague,
        Anna Fárová, began to ensure that Drtikol's photographs would be given the care and
        respect they merit.

Životopisná data

1883	Františka Ferdinanda Drtikola přivádí na svět 3. března v Příbrami (č. p. 275) matka Marie, rozená Opplová. Otcem je sečtělý kupec, altruista a časem radní František Drtikol. Starší sestry se jmenují Emilie a Marie. Prarodiči z otcovy strany jsou František Drtikol, zvěrolékař na Dobříši a Terezie, narozená v Chebu jako Seidlerová. Druhým dědem je Vít Oppl, hostinský v Příbrami; jeho žena Anastasie, pocházející z příbramské rodiny Fialových, se stává novorozenci kmotrou. Dům těchto prarodičů je od jara následujícího roku přes zahradu (Dlouhá ulice 159). Po kmotrovi Ferdinandovi Opplovi, příbramském měšťanovi, získává František druhé jméno. Zapsán je jako katolík. Výtvarné nadání se u něj projeví od dětství.
1888	Jako pětiapůlletý vstupuje do první třídy obecné školy.
1895	Začíná studovat na reálném gymnáziu. Kreslí, maluje a čte – například *Dějiny konfliktů mezi náboženstvím a vědou* od Johna Williama Drapera. Silně klerikální školu zanedbává: „*Vzdor tomu, že bylo zakázáno chodit do Sokola, tak jsem do Sokola chodil. Holt, jo, bylo to pod Svatou Horou a páni páteři měli rozhodující vliv na celý příbramský život.*"
1898	1. října nastupuje k příbramskému fotografovi Antonínu Mattasovi jako učedník. Je posedlý malováním, ale vyvolává, kopíruje a tónuje cizí práce, aniž by směl asistovat při fotografování. Úkolů je víc, než se dá v ateliéru bez elektřiny od slunka do slunka stihnout (při dennodenním nasazení včetně nedělních dopoledn í).
1901	30. září končí tři učební léta (za která otec zaplatil 200 zlatých) a získává doporučující vysvědčení. S podzimem odchází studovat do Mnichova na Lehr- und Versuchsanstalt für Photographie se sídlem v Rennbahnstrasse, kam v létě úspěšně složil přijímací zkoušky. Malířské zájmy, secesní průprava a myšlenky symbolismu předurčí Drtikolovo fotografické myšlení na dlouhé tři dekády, byť časem obrazy formálně zjednoduší. Dokonce i následující nefotografické období bude věrné základnímu impulzu umělcova mládí.
1903	15. července obdrží diplom mnichovské školy; je považován za vynikajícího umělce, což stvrzuje jak vysvědčení, tak porota udělením první ceny; 9. července pak i kritika absolventské výstavy v *Münchner neueste Nachrichten*. Následuje krátké angažmá v ateliéru Theodor Schuhmann & Sohn v německém Karlsruhe (Amalienstrasse 57, 16. 7.–31. 8.). V malém švýcarském městě Chur (Obergasse 182) zaměstnává Drtikola čtvrt roku Atelier für Photographie und Malerei Albert Bösch. (Veškerá drtikolovská literatura komolila jméno Bösch na Böse nebo Bos.)
1904	21. dubna vydává starosta královského horního města Příbrami Drtikolovi pracovní knížku. Podle ní je modrooký, špičatých úst, souměrného podlouhlého obličeje, hnědých vlasů a prostřední postavy. Praxe „*pomocníka fotografického*" pokračuje u firem Emanuela Grána v Turnově (Hruštická 464, 17. 4.–30. 5.) a Josefa Faixe (v Ječné ulici v Praze, 1. 6.–14. 9.). Dne 6. října rukuje k tříleté službě u 102. pěšího pluku v Benešově. Pilně kreslí a maluje drobné akvarely. „*A protože jsem uměl německy a protože jsem byl šikovný a bystrý, tak jsem to dotáh až na četaře. Dokonce jsem dělal poslední rok službu vedoucího.*"
1905	Otec dále neudrží obchod se smíšeným zbožím, neboť zákazníkům odpouštěl dluhy: „*Na konec se tatínek zadlužil a obchod prodal. Místnosti pronajal lékárně. Později prodal moc lacino i dům.*"

| 1907 | Fotograf otevírá za otcovy pomoci *Atelier F. Drtikol Příbram*, přístupný z Václavského náměstí 144/II. Je v zahradě rodného domu – do roku 1890 měl odlišné číslo popisné. Drtikol inzeruje moderní fotografii, portrétování a zvětšení každého druhu. Prostředí nevelkého města nepřeje fotografování aktů, autorově budoucí doméně, zato dá Příbramsko vzniknout řadě krajin a dokumentárně jedinečných záběrů rudných dolů. |

1907 — Fotograf otevírá za otcovy pomoci *Atelier F. Drtikol Příbram*, přístupný z Václavského náměstí 144/II. Je v zahradě rodného domu – do roku 1890 měl odlišné číslo popisné. Drtikol inzeruje moderní fotografii, portrétování a zvětšení každého druhu. Prostředí nevelkého města nepřeje fotografování aktů, autorově budoucí doméně, zato dá Příbramsko vzniknout řadě krajin a dokumentárně jedinečných záběrů rudných dolů.

1910 — Skupinový dětský portrét v majetku příbramské Galerie Františka Drtikola dokládá, že umělec působí ještě v roce 1910 v rodném městě. Po 22. říjnu akceptuje prodejna Artěl jeho nabídku fotografií: exponáty jsou ke koupi po 40 až 60 stříbrných korunách. Jestliže Drtikolovu první tvůrčí etapu poznamenala secese, v období přechodu do Prahy sílí vliv moderny.

1911 — Dne 26. ledna přihlašuje Drtikol podnik na Starém Městě pražském (sídlí V kolkovně č. p. 920–I, kde rovněž bydlí). V metropoli je tou dobou 83 fotografických ateliérů. Jako pohlednice publikuje snímky horníků, exponované v předchozích letech za umělého svitu magnézia, zažíhaného v příbramských štolách. Od 2. března je přispívajícím členem Českého klubu fotografů amatérů v Praze (s číslem legitimace 400), na jehož výstavě zveřejňuje akty. V domácí fotografické literatuře nemá předchůdce co do otištění původní české umělecké realizace v tomto žánru [*Fotografický obzor* 19, 1911, č. 7, s. 107]. S Augustinem Škardou, fotografem ze záliby, úředníkem a budoucím redaktorem *Fotografického obzoru* i ročenek *Československá fotografie* vydává portfolio padesáti olejotisků *Dvory a dvorečky staré Prahy.*

1912 — Od 1. února sídlí Drtikolův ateliér v novostavbě činžovního domu (č. p. 730/II). Zbudoval jej stavitel Eduard Hulicius na souběhu ulic Vodičkovy s Jungmannovou nedaleko pražského Václavského náměstí. Z obchodních spisů vyplývá, že fotografovo bydliště je shodné. Potvrzuje to i dvojjazyčný *Úřední list Pražských novin / Amtsblatt zur Prager Zeitung* z neděle 4. ledna 1914 [č. 3, s. 6]. Pevné zázemí se projeví v užité i volné tvorbě, při níž sahá k domalbám pozadí na negativy a k tvárnému zušlechťování pozitivů. Finále představuje adjustace exponátu na způsob grafického listu. Na již strženém Urbánkově domě v blízkosti Národního divadla zřizuje vitrínu a vystavuje v ní čerstvé fotografie ruské herečky a tanečnice Olgy Vladimirovny Gzovské: „*Když jsem Olgu Gzovskou fotografoval*", řekne v polovině 50. let, „*moc mně do toho chtěl mluvit sochař Mařatka. Viděl ji po sochařsku, já po nesochařsku, a tak jsem mu řekl, aby šel do vedlejší místnosti a udělal jsem Gzovskou bez Mařatky, při denním světle, cele podle své představy.*" Usiluje o diváckou kontemplaci, díla pojmenovává *Hudba a tanec* (1912), *Před plesem* (1913), *Nokturno* (c. 1913), *Sfinx* (1913), *Salome* (1914), *Kristus* (1914)... Dne 10. října mu děkuje Česká obec sokolská za darované album zahraničních hostí VI. všesokolského sletu: „*Umělecké fotografické snímky Vaše uloženy budou do našeho archivu všesokolského a do příštího musea našeho.*"

1913 — Třicetiletý umělec se pro vlastní podobiznu stylizuje do polohy ukřižovaného Krista. V srpnu obdrží povolení k zřízení vitrín s ukázkami prací na průčelí činžovního domu, kde má v čtvrtém podlaží fotografický ateliér a o patro výš kopírnu se skladem negativů. Začíná časopisecky publikovat portréty, taneční kreace a herecké etudy zejména v listu *Český svět*, s nímž bude spolupracovat do konce 20. let. K 28. březnu přihlašuje s Augustinem Škardou veřejnou obchodní společnost Drtikol a spol. s tím, že fotografickou činnost započala 1. ledna téhož roku. Vstupní kapitál každého z partnerů činí 3500 korun. K zastupování podniku jsou oprávněni oba veřejní společníci, každý samostatně.

Berní správa jejich firmě předepisuje 1. dubna daň výdělkovou 128 korun. Obchodní a živnostenská komora v Praze sděluje 15. prosince C. K. Obchodnímu soudu, že závod Drtikol a spol. *„během poměrně krátké doby vyšvihnul se na jedno z předních míst ve zdejším obvodu; co do sazby všeobecné daně výdělkové figuruje zde na pátém místě. Zaměstnává také větší počet pracovních sil, tak že komora soudí, [...] že firma jmenovaná povinnosti zápisu do obchodního rejstříku podléhá.“* K zápisu dochází 19. prosince. Slepotiskové razítko i ruční signování Drtikol a spol. je dochováno i na fotografiích předcházejících rok 1913.

1914 František Drtikol 28. února vydá k padesátinám Josefa Svatopluka Machara *„nejnovější životně věcný portrét básníkův v původních fotografiích“*. Leták, archivovaný Uměleckoprůmyslovým museem v Praze, dává představu o cenách: jednoduché pozitivní průměty 24 × 18 cm nebo 38 × 26 cm jsou k mání po 3 korunách, s rámem za 7, 50; paspartované olejotisky nebo platinotypie stojí 15 korun. Národní archiv vlastní negativy šestnácti macharovských záběrů. V létě je organizátorem probuzení Helady Emanuelem Siblíkem pozván do Riegrových sadů v úloze *„nejlepšího tehdy pražského fotografa“* k zachycení seance pořádané naboso v krátkém vzdušném starořeckém rouchu bez rukávů. Jmenovaný teoretik, mimo jiné autor knihy o Isadoře Duncanové, popsal scenérii roku 1933 v knize *Tyrš a rytmika:* *„Nezapomenutelné červencové jitro, kdy na sluncem zalitém květnatém koberci v rámci velkoryse členěných kulis křovin a stromů, v zasnění ranní páry, se objevily dorostenky s rozpuštěným vlasem, řeckou stužkou upevněným. Řídcí ranní chodci zastavující se nechtěli věřiti svým očím, jakoby přeludem šáleným.“* Dne 22. července je mezi majiteli podniku Drtikol a spol. uzavřena smlouva společenská, jež před vypuknutím války vkládá správu firmy na Augustina Škardu. V srpnu narukuje Drtikol k týlovému vojsku v Benešově, odkud adresuje obsáhlá vyznání platonické lásce Elišce Janské. Otřesné sebereflexe jednoho z miliónů státní mašinérií manipulovaných pěšáků píše nehledaným jazykem. Jakkoli si to nechce připustit (*„nakládali lidi jak dobytek“*), patří k těm, kteří odesílají ostatní na frontu. A hned dva z prvního regimentu se při odjezdu vlaku sami zastřelí. Anna Fárová přibližuje rukopisy takto: *„První z deníků doprovázely ilustrace, v dalších se neobjevují. Pravděpodobně si Drtikol pro kreslení našel jiný prostor. Zajímavá je frekvence zápisů, vznikajících v intenzívních návalech. Úvodní sešit čítá 136 stran a 18 kreseb. Ale jedná se o pouhých 12 záznamů. Vznikly během 26 dnů (22. 8.–16. 9.). Začátek války byl zřejmě šok, který ze sebe Drtikol potřeboval dostat. Celá situace v armádě a všechno to cizí prostředí vzbudily Drtikolovu prudkou reakci. Láska k Elišce Janské, pro níž deníky psal, byla ve fázi rozvíjení, mobilizací náhle přerušené. Další, kratší deník vznikl za 8 dnů v listopadu (21.–29. 11.). Má 51 stranu. Následuje 58 stran z 2 dnů (4. a 6. 12.). To je 3. sešit, pokud je mám ovšem všechny.“* Poté, co nastoupí vojenskou službu i Drtikolův společník, bude v pražském ateliéru hospodařit Škardův švagr inženýr Jiří Šourek, pedagog na vysokém učení technickém. Coby fotografa angažuje Františka Svobodu.

1914–15 Od 20. prosince 1914 do 31. ledna 1915 pořádá pražské Umělecko-průmyslové museum Obchodní a živnostenské komory v Rudolfinu přehlídku komerčních ateliérů k 75. výročí zveřejnění vynálezu fotografie s útlým katalogem F. X. Jiříka, který se jakožto muzejní kustod soustavně zabýval srovnáváním malířských miniatur a fotografických podobizen; neilustrovaný katalog uvádí coby poslední položku (344) *Soubor fotografií ateliéru Drtikol a Škarda*. Portrétní kolekce společníků je uvedena na jiném místě a lze tudíž dovodit, že se jednalo o portfolio olejotisků *Dvory a dvorečky staré Prahy*.

1915   Přání k Vánocům posílá rodičům z maďarské Békés Csaby. Česká tisková kancelář nabízí
        z válečné doby dva Drtikolovy exteriérové záběry, z nichž jeden je skupinovým portrétem
        vojáků s nápisem „*Upomínka na den odjezdu do války 2. 1. 1915.*“

1917   1. září nastupuje do učení u filmy Drtikol a spol. Jaroslav Rössler, nejosobitější z umělců
        se zkušeností z Drtikolova ateliéru. 22. prosince prodávají manželé Drtikolovi dům na
        příbramském Václavském náměstí 144/II.

1918   V květnu píše v Krči u Prahy Rudolf Špillar úvodem prvního svazku knižnice *Nauk o foto-*
        grafii: „*Jakmile tomu jen poněkud tiskové poměry dovolí, vyjdou další díla, z nichž pro začátek uvádíme:*
        Ve velkém formátu: Fr. Drtikol: Portretování. Vyzdobeno množstvím vybraných snímků autorových,
        které fotografujícím bude výborným vodítkem a vzorem různých osvětlení i posic. Fr. Drtikol: Olejotisk.
        (S uměleckými obrazy.)“ [Cit. dle: Jindra Imlauf: *Vyvíjení pozvolné a časové.* Praha, Ústřední nakla-
        datelství, knihkupectví a papírnictví učitelstva českoslovanského Josef Rašín 1918, s. III.]
        Ve fondu Národní knihovny nebyly ohlášené tituly nikdy registrovány. Dne 6. srpna sděluje
        František Drtikol z Hartbergu slečně Janské: „*Víte, že co je vojna, že jsem nefotografoval? – Víte,*
        že se teď stydím za ty svoje vejplody fotografické, co jsem kdysi dělával? [...] Ta válka mě silně očistila.“
        Navzdory citovanému dopisu je válečnými roky datováno několik dochovaných fotografií.
        Koncem srpna se přes Příbram vrací do Prahy a do vyhlášení republiky 28. října simuluje
        nemocniční péči, ačkoli již vehementně pracuje v ateliéru. Dne 3. listopadu kapituluje Ra-
        kousko-Uhersko, 11. listopadu Německo a 14. listopadu je na první schůzi Národního shro-
        máždění vyhlášena Československá republika, sestavena vláda a prezidentem zvolen Tomáš
        Garrigue Masaryk. Po čtyřech letech bojových konfliktů jsou české země vyčerpány a zmítá
        jimi hlad. Fotograf na tu dobu ve vlastním životopise z konce 40. let vzpomíná: „*Dávaly se*
        fotografovat všechny významné osobnosti a muselo se to ihned zpracovat. Rovněž všechny mise, které se
        v naší republice objevily, musel jsem fotografovat. Zisk z toho nebyl žádný, protože se to dělalo zadarmo.
        Platit nechtěl žádný.“ Negativy exponované v době své válečné nepřítomnosti dá zlikvidovat.
        S datem 24. listopadu završuje osnovy pro čtyřsemestrální studium fotografie.

1919   Pořádá kurz portrétní fotografie pro Český klub fotografů amatérů v Praze. Pokud neevoku-
        je divadelní prostor, zůstává scéna ateliéru při portrétování civilní. Jinak neváhá vycházet
        vstříc dobovým náladám: „*V roce 1919 vytvořil několik prací s mytologickou tematikou, které reagovaly*
        na aktuální společenskou objednávku (Libuše věstí slávu Prahy), ale výsledkem byla pouze nacionalistická
        agitka, pracující s archaickými stereotypy. [...] Samostatnou kapitolou, která nebyla dosud ani výstavně,
        ani publikačně připomínána, je řada ženských aktů, evokujících harémové odalisky. Byly to vesměs kypré
        akty, polehávajících na divanech, pokrytých bohatě zdobenými přehozy, doplněných těžkými závěsy.“
        [Jan Mlčoch: *Fotografie.* In: Jana Horneková (ed.): *České art deco 1918–1938,* Praha, Obecní dům
        1998, s. 216–217.]

1920   23. března děkuje soukromý tajemník Tomáše G. Masaryka za podobizny členů tajné
        organizace československého odboje za světové války, Maffie, věnované hlavě státu
        u příležitosti sedmdesátin: „*pan president přijal Váš dar s velikým zájmem*“. Na 19. června připadá
        sňatek s Ervinou Kupferovou. Od roku 1919 pořizuje desítky jejích záběrů, denně jí píše
        a list s kyticí růží posílá po učni Jaroslavu Rösslerovi. Ten chodíval Drtikolovi také pro
        modelářskou hlínu do Křižovnické ulice a poté nosíval mistrovy alegorické plastiky k odlití
        do sádry. Vzpomínky zachytil koncepty ke korespondenci z 6. února 1987, adresované

Kateřině Klaricové. Vyplývá z nich, že Drtikol ateliér ve Vodičkově ulici i nadále obýval:
„Bydlil vždy v ateliéru, i když byl ženat. [...] Když se oženil, musel jsem se přestěhovat do kopírny, která byla o patro výše." Dne 23. června Drtikol s pomocí švagra JUDr. Václava Šamana dociluje u Okresního soudu pro věci obchodní prvního výnosu o oprávněnosti ztráty důvěry ve společníka Augustina Škardu, úředníka Zemského výboru. Rozsudek potvrzuje 16. září odvolací přelíčení u Obchodního soudu v Praze a 23. října je pozastaveno Škardovo právo jednat za firmu Drtikol a spol. Nejvyšší soud v Brně rozhoduje 16. listopadu o zrušení společnosti uzavřené mezi Františkem Drtikolem a Augustinem Škardou.

1921   31. května z firmy Drtikol a spol. *„vystoupil veřejný společník Augustin Škarda. Nyní jediný majitel: František Drtikol, který závod pod dosavadní firmou povede."* [*Úřední list Republiky Československé* z 29. června, č. 146, s. 2791.] Dne 12. června se stává otcem dcery Erviny, která se dožije požehnaného věku (dnem jejího úmrtí bude 18. duben 2005).

1922   S hospodářskou stabilizací ateliéru vzrůstá počet zaměstnanců. V Umělecko-průmyslovém museu Obchodní a živnostenské komory v Praze má Drtikol první samostatnou výstavu; 21. června mu ředitel muzea děkuje za dar *uměleckých fotografií*; Drtikolovy práce budou následujícího roku výroční zprávou muzejního kuratoria označeny jako základ sbírky *„nové domácí fotografie"*. Dne 16. listopadu kvituje Klub fotografů amatérů na pražských Královských Vinohradech s povděkem Drtikolovu přednášku o *„zkušenostech z umělecké portrétní fotografie"* s ukázkami obrazů *„a praktickým portrétováním v našem atelieru"*.

1922–23   Inspirován scénickými výpravami italských futuristů Enrico Prampoliniho a De Pistorise, jakož i scénografií Alexandra Jakovleviče Tairova přechází od kubizujících pozadí utvářených štětcem k vymezování obrazového prostoru světly a stíny v geometrických kulisách, které podle jeho návrhů vyrábějí dílny Národního divadla.

1923   Dne 19. července podává prostřednictvím advokáta Václava Šamana přihlášku o udělení patentu *Vynálezu půltónové fotolitografií: „Je to kombinace olejotisku s litografií. Podstata tohoto tisku je v tom, že se olejotiskový obraz přenese na litografický kámen. Smyslem způsobu je rozložit stíny v polostíny a čtvrtstíny. Tisky mají sametovou hloubku hlubotisku, lehkost zrnění litografie."* Touto metodou rozmnožuje sérii starších podobizen Tomáše G. Masaryka, jemuž obrazy zasílá darem. Dne 4. října osobní tajemník prezidenta republiky Vasil Škrach děkuje a objednává po jednom pozitivu všech záběrů T. G. Masaryka pro prezidentovu soukromou potřebu. V Národním archivu je uloženo 17 doličných negativů. Nadchází vrcholná fáze tvorby. V umělecké práci 20. let polevují literární inspirace a tvárné procesy, symbolika ovšem nemizí úplně: *The Dancing of Dolls* (1925), *Meditace* (1927), *Reflection* (1927). Nedatované jsou práce jako *Desire, Opona, Divadlo, Světelný efekt, Figurální komposice.*

1924   Ministr školství a národní osvěty jmenuje Františka Drtikola na funkční období 1924–27 členem Sekce portrétní fotografie a kinematografie při kuratoriu Státní grafické školy.

1925   Dne 28. července je Drtikolovi přiznán patent fotolitografie (listinou č. 16640), neboli vynález *„způsobu litografického půltónového tisku z matric získaných přenešením olejových fotografických obrazů na kámen, zinek, hliník a pod."*, s nímž dle vlastních vzpomínek experimentoval již začátkem 20. let. Začíná nejplodnější období stylu art deco: dynamické expresivní akty 20. let představují maximy umělcovy fotografické dráhy. Jako výtvarného prostředku využívá i afokalizace a pohybové neostrosti. Do roku 1930 obešle přes sto padesát fotosalonů.

Uvažuje o členství v Umělecké besedě a hovoří o tom s jejím předsedou Václavem Rabasem; Jaromír Funke formuluje snad tohoto nebo následujícího roku společnou žádost o přijetí pro čtyři fotografy, podepíše ji však pouze on a Drtikol, v jehož fondu strojopis archivuje Uměleckoprůmyslové museum v Praze.

1926 8. listopadu dochází k závěrečnému dějství rozvodu s Ervinou Kupferovou.

1927 Začíná série výstav ve Spojených státech amerických; do roku 1930 bude instalována na jedenácti místech. Dne 28. října spatří nakladatel Antoine Calavas na mezinárodním salonu fotografií v Paříži Drtikolovu kolekci a záhy plánuje sběratelské vydání jeho fotografií.

1928 Jmenován čestným členem The Camera Pictorialists of Los Angeles. Jako pětačtyřicetiletý se stylizuje k autoportrétu do pozice Buddhy. Začíná si zapisovat postřehy, shrnuté kapitolou *Moje myšlenky 1928–1945* v knize *Duchovní cesta*.

1929 V Paříži vychází péčí Librairie des Arts Décoratifs v nákladu 500 exemplářů titul *Les nus de Drtikol*. Finanční efekt se nedostavuje. Dne 4. července píše První občanské záložně v Praze: *„jsem ochoten platiti pouze činži takovou, na kterou máte podle zákona právo. Ježto jsem platil dosud činži vyšší, prosím, aby mi byla sdělena přesná výše činže zákonu odpovídající."* K 20. říjnu si poznamená sen, odehrávající se ve scenérii Svaté Hory, kam v mládí rád chodíval: levituje v něm, touží po ukřižování a pociťuje stále silněji stigmata, aby před holou, neomítnutou stěnou vítězně uzavřel, že tam bude věčně viset, *„jako v kámen nastříkán"*. Ukázky své práce věnuje muzeu v rodné Příbrami. Říjnový krach na newyorské burze a následující hospodářská krize přivodí úpadek Drtikolovy firmy. S fotografováním však končí nejen v důsledku ekonomického, nýbrž i kulturního zlomu. Jestliže 20. léta slyšela na vypjatost art deco, jehož mistrovské podání umělec dál nabízí, 30. léta už měla vidět prioritu v strohém funkcionalismu. Jaroslav Rössler v konceptech dopisu Kateřině Klaricové z 6. února 1987 uvádí, že již roku 1929 dostal z domova do Paříže zprávu, že je Drtikolův ateliér na prodej.

1930 Drtikol se orientuje na fotografování v mystickém rázu. K tomu začal v předchozím roce vyřezávat stolní modely postav z překližky. Volné práce tvoří mimo hlavní dobový proud, vnitřně zaměřen k hermetickým významovým vrstvám. Vedle obvykle zpřístupňovaných názvů jako *Obraz* (1930), *Girls* (1930) či *Fotopurismus* (1934) označuje fotografie tituly *Duše* (1931), *Matka – Země* (1931), *Svět duše* (1934), *Svět duše – Víla* (1935), *Osvobozená* (30. léta), *Odpoutání*. Vysvětlení volby žánru aktu nabízí jedna z Drtikolových poznámek: *„Příroda je projevený Bůh, je žena."* Z ušlechtilých technik se v údobí takzvaného fotopurismu uplatňují hnědavé pigmenty. Nicméně hojně vznikají i pozitivy prostým kontaktním průmětem na bromostříbrný papír. Význačnými díly jsou rovněž pastely z rozběhu 30. let. V první polovině dekády nabízí fotokurzy portrétu, aktu a zátiší, přičemž pozornost zájemců zaměřuje k osvětlení, charakteristice modelu a jeho režii. Školení se odehrává ve skupinkách několika účastníků, mezi něž se rozpočítají náklady na honorář modelkám. Fotografuje se buď v Drtikolově ateliéru, nebo v sídle Českého klubu fotografů amatérů v Praze (Nekázanka 3). Drtikol se tak v závěru fotografické kariéry snaží udržet rentabilitu firmy. Dostává i mimopražská pozvání k podobným školením. Na konec 20. nebo na začátek 30. let bývá situováno ucelení strojopisu souboru pouček *Oči široce otevřené*. Navrhuje osvětlovadla a figurální *Drtikolovy ozdobné předměty* (jak uvádí nedatovaným letákem); podobají se předlohám pro souběžně vznikající aranžované fotografie.

1932 15. října koncipuje odpověď na inzerát zveřejněný toho dne *Foto-novinami:* „*dovoluji si Vám nabídnouti ke koupi můj renomovaný ateliér, který se nalézá v centru Prahy, za cenu 90 tisíc. Důvody, proč tak činím, jsou rázu čistě osobního. Závod pozůstává z ateliéru, 2 čekáren, pracovny, laboratoře, kuchyně a 2 magazinů. Vlastní bohatý a vzácný negativní materiál, jako negativy presidenta Masaryka, min. Beneše, Dra Kramáře, Dra Rašína, celou Maffii a veličiny politic. světa, umělce všech oborů a osobnosti známé. Obrat za minulý rok obnášel Kč 100.000, kterýžto obnos by se jistě zvětšil zavedením se pro práci amatérskou a fotografování mimo ateliér, ježto sám jsem se dosud výlučně zabýval fotografií pouze portrétní.*"

1933 Padesátiletý umělec se autoportrétem stylizuje do postavení taoistického poutníka.
Z podnětu Sdružení přátel fotografie v Olomouci vystavuje v tamním Klubu přátel umění na dvě stě děl. Majitel a vydavatel *Světozoru* Pavel Altschul píše do svého listu: „*Drtikola můžeme vlastně považovati za svého jediného fotografa velkého formátu, který si již odbyl období pokusů a hledání a dopracoval se svého osobitého výtvarného stylu, zatím co ostatní naši fotografové ještě buď experimentují, nebo jsou příliš závislí na svých námětech.*" Propad produktivity, který opanoval zemské hospodářství koncem 20. let, prodělává nejhorší důsledky: index výroby poklesl pod úroveň, za níž se Drtikol před první světovou válkou v metropoli Českého království těžko uchytil. Dne 17. prosince 1947 připomene situaci 30. let v korespondenci: „*Věřitelé a exekutoři si podávali kliku – a přitom ‚kšeft' jsem měl a musel jsem ho nějakým způsobem stále udržovat. A tak se to tlouklo celé ty roky. Až mě to všechno nasralo, všechno jsem prodal, zaplatil účty a v kapse nezbyla ani vindra. To bylo v roce 1935.*"

1935 14. března děkuje ředitel Státní grafické školy v Praze za darované časopisy i různé další publikace a oznamuje, že rušený ateliér v nejbližších dnech navštíví profesor Karel Novák, aby se dohodl „*o předmětech, které by bylo možno pro školu zakoupit*". V pražské zahradní čtvrti Spořilov, kde obývá od 12. dubna část Marií Malečkovou postoupeného domu (v ulici Jihozápadní V., č. p. 1018), vytváří poslední série fotografií: *Vize, Lesní nymfy* a *Svět duše.* Napříště se bude věnovat meditacím, cvičením koncentrace, duchovnímu působení na neformální okruh žáků a malbě. Spirituální obrazy mohou sloužit za ilustrace i roznětky meditačních vizí. Častými syžety Drtikolova pozdního, nefotografického období bývají aury, jejichž sálání je s to vyvolat rezonanci i u nezasvěcených.

1938 8. února žádá o úřední výmaz firmy: „*Podepsaný František Drtikol, malíř, nyní Praha – Spořilov, č. p. 1018 jest jediným majitelem protokolované firmy ‚Drtikol & spol.' Praha II, Vodičkova ul. č. 7. Pro nepříznivé finanční a hospodářské poměry rozhodl jsem se tuto firmu likvidovati a také ji již neprovozuji. Žádám proto, aby tato firma byla z obchodního rejstříku vymazána. Živnostenskému referátu a Berní správě v Praze II. činím o tom souhlasné oznámení.*" Krajský soud obchodní v Praze provádí výmaz 30. června. U pražského nakladatele Eduarda Beauforta vychází album *Žena ve světle* s textem malíře, grafika, ilustrátora a kritika Josefa Richarda Marka. Výběr 46 aktů poznamenala snaha o vstřícnost k publiku. Do tisku se dostaly i problematické projevy, změněny jsou některé dřívější názvy fotografií.

1939 15. března obsazují německá vojska zbytek Mnichovským diktátem okleštěných území Čech a Moravy, v září začíná druhá světová válka. Koncem jara nebo začátkem léta věnuje Umělecko-průmyslovému museu Obchodní a živnostenské komory v Praze část uzavřeného fotografického díla a naváže tak na dar z roku 1922. V témž muzeu naposledy za svého života vystavuje: přehlídka *Sto let české fotografie 1839–1939,* pořádaná od 26. října do 31. prosince, uvádí v oddílu *živnostenská fotografie* pouze jeho starší práce (1910–22); mezi sedmadvaceti exponáty je jedenáct portrétů.

1940   V červnu přijímá Česká tisková kancelář účelový výběr Drtikolových negativů. Agentura ČTK je nabídne 30. července 1980 Státnímu ústřednímu archivu (dnes Národní archiv). Soupis snímků předaný *„na základě skartační směrnice stanovující postup předarchivní péče o foto-informace v Redakci obrazového zpravodajství ČTK"* vykazuje 2113 nevročených položek, z nichž některé označuje jako chybějící. Archiv disponuje od 31. října 1980 toliko 1872 negativy (a diapozitivy, jimiž jsou zdaleka ne všechny rozbité desky nahrazeny). Vedle portrétů jde o série záběrů pohybových kreací: zachycují studiové pózování pro kameru a nikoli prchavé momenty reálných tanečních vystoupení.

1942   K 25. únoru věnuje Drtikol podstatnou část fotografického díla i s některými kresbami a s písemnou dokumentací Umělecko-průmyslovému museu Obchodní a živnostenské komory v Praze. (Přes veškeré ztráty se v majetku státu dochová více než pět tisíc položek.) Druhou jeho chotí se v dubnu stává fotografka Jarmila Rambousková, od roku 1921 zaměstnankyně firmy Drtikol a spol., s níž po výprodeji ateliéru vedl spořilovskou domácnost. 21. listopadu přijímá Františka Drtikola za čestného člena valná hromada Českého fotografického spolku v Praze, tehdy nejstarší odborné organizace českých fotografů (založené roku 1882).

1945   Aktivně se účastní Pražského povstání. K 1. červnu vstupují manželé Drtikolovi do Komunistické strany Československa.

1945–46   Působí jako externí pedagog Státní grafické školy v Praze. Z 20. února 1946 pochází poslední z řady návrhů osnov studia fotografie, vypracovaný jako podnět ke zřízení odborné školy umělecké fotografie v Praze, zamýšlené jako čtyř až pětileté vyšší vzdělání s výhledem k rozšíření o kinematografii. Vede ho k tomu nespokojenost se stavem Státní grafické školy: *„Osnova učebná je taková, že některé předměty jsou úplně zbytečné a některé, které by se měly vyučovat, jako kreslení, anatomie, vůbec nejsou."* Po všeobecném dvouletém základu navrhuje tři specializace: technickou, reklamní a uměleckou fotografii. *„Celá učební osnova této školy by byla usměrněna na povznesení umělecké úrovně fotografie."*

1946   U farního úřadu v Praze-Michli vystupuje 26. ledna z katolické církve (č. j. IV C 572/46), což od 25. ledna 1947 eviduje i matrika.

1947   Na záložce přebalu prvního vydání knihy *Černobílá fotografie* od Jaroslava Kulhánka (zveřejněné nakladatelem Eduardem Beaufortem) je vysazeno Drtikolovo doporučení, končící slovy: *„Budu usilovat, aby se stala oficiení učebnicí Československé státní grafické školy pro fotografy z povolání."*

1948   Za únorového uchopení moci komunisty hlídkuje ve stranickém sekretariátu na Spořilově, někdy přes noc. Vypracovává příležitostné životopisy, uložené v Uměleckoprůmyslovém museu v Praze (čtyřstránkový pro KSČ, jednostránkový pro SČSVU). Dne 17. prosince je přijat do Svazu československých výtvarných umělců (když předtím obdržel zamítavou zprávu z 29. října od umělecké rady, která *„nemohla na základě Vámi předložených prací doporučit výboru SČSVU, abyste byl přijat za člena"*).

1955   Jiří Jeníček zveřejňuje jediný známý rozhovor s umělcem *Na besedě u Františka Drtikola.*

1956   Přestává malovat a projevuje přání uchýlit se do domova důchodců, aby nebyl přítěží svým blízkým.

1959   9. ledna podléhá manželka Jarmila následkům zranění, utrpěných při automobilové ne-
       hodě. Pro sešlost věkem je František Drtikol upoután na lůžko a odkázán na péči rodinné
       přítelkyně Anny Soukupové.

1960   Blahopřání k Vánocům a k nadcházejícímu roku píše jako vždy energickými tahy, prokazu-
       jícími duševní svěžest.

1961   František Drtikol umírá přirozenou smrtí 13. ledna v Praze. Jeho popel je uložen na měst-
       ském pohřebišti v rodné Příbrami. V listopadu klasifikuje revizní komise na 5500 položek
       jeho odkazu pražskému Uměleckoprůmyslovému museu jako předměty bez sbírkové
       hodnoty.

1970   Kurátorka obnovené fotografické sbírky Uměleckoprůmyslového musea Anna Fárová při-
       stupuje k rehabilitaci Drtikolova odkazu.

Solo Exhibitions / Samostatné výstavy

1922 Umělecko-průmyslové museum Obchodní a živnostenské komory, Praha
1925 *Exposition Internationale des Arts Décoratifs et Industriels Modernes*, Paris
1927 Camera Club of Syracuse, Syracuse
1927 Schenectady Photographic Society, Schenectady
1927 Milwaukee Art Institute, Milwaukee
1927 The Photo Club of Baltimore City, Baltimore
1927 The Photographic Society of Philadelphia, Philadelphia
1928 Chicago Camera Club, Chicago
1928 Cleveland Photographic Society, Cleveland
1928 Portage Camera Club, Akron, Ohio
1929 The Museum of Fine Arts, Houston
1929 Salon Polskiego Towarzystwa Miłośników Fotografii, Warszawa
1930 Kodak Camera Club, Rochester
1931 Brooklyn Institute of Arts and Sciences, New York
1933 The Royal Photographic Society of Great Britain, London
1933 Cambridge University Camera Club, Cambridge
1933 *Výstava fotografických obrazů Františka Drtikola a ing. Aloise Zycha*, Klub přátel umění, Olomouc
1934 Ústav pro zvelebování živností, České Budějovice
1936 City Art Gallery, Durban
1936 Arts Hall, Port Elizabeth
1967 *Fotografie Františka Drtikola*, Výstavní dům U Hybernů, Praha
1967 Dům kultury, Kroměříž
1972 Uměleckoprůmyslové museum v Praze, Praha
1973 Dům umění města Brna
1973 *František Drtikol dalla collezione del museo d'Arti decorative di Praga*, Salone internationale
     cine – foto – ottica, Milano
1974 The Photographers' Gallery, London
1974 The Royal Photographic Society of Great Britain, London
1974 Komorná galéria fotografie Profil, Bratislava
1976 Photographies Galerie Houyoux, Bibliothèque royale de Belgique, Bruxelles
1977 Secession Gallery, Victoria (& Adolf de Meyer)
1983 Rudolf Kicken Galerie, Köln
1984 Miller Gallery, New York
1984 Nieuwe Kerk, Amsterdam
1987 Robert Koch Gallery, San Francisco (& Josef Ehm)
1988 *František Drtikol Fotografie*, Galerie Jaroslava Gruse, Pardubice
1989 *František Drtikol Fotografie*, Malá výstavní síň, Liberec
1989 *František Drtikol Fotografie*, Galerie 4, Cheb
1989 Výstavní síň Odeon, Praha

1989   Dům kultury, České Budějovice
1990   Galerie municipale du Château d'Eau, Toulouse
1990   Galerie de la Société française de photographie, Paris
1990   *Femme séductrice. Femme Fatale*, Rencontres Internationales de la Photographie, Palais de l'Archevêché, Arles (& Jan Saudek)
1990   Galerie Robert Heitz, Palais Rohan, Strasbourg
1990   Státní zámek Kozel
1990   Malovaný dům, Třebíč
1991   Museet for Fotokunst, Odense
1991   Det kongelige Bibliothek, København
1991   Fotoforum, Bremen
1991   Fotografie Forum, Frankfurt am Main
1991   *The Other Side of František Drtikol*, Jacques Baruch Gallery, Chicago
1991   Howard Greenberg Gallery, New York
1992   Musée de la Photographie de Charleroi
1994   *František Drtikol*, Pražský dům fotografie
1997   *Frantisek Drtikol – Modernist Nudes*, Robert Koch Gallery, San Francisco
1997   Howard Greenberg Gallery, New York
1997   Galerie Zur Stockeregg, Zürich
1998   *František Drtikol fotograf, malíř, mystik*, Galerie Rudolfinum, Praha
1998   *František Drtikol fotograf, malíř, mystik*, Moravská galerie v Brně, Brno
1998   *František Drtikol photographe, peintre, mystique*, Palais des Beaux-Arts, Charleroi
1999   *František Drtikol. Photographs from the period between 1901–1914 and the album From Large and Little Courtyards of Old Prague*, Fondation Neumann, Gingis
2000   *František Drtikol. Fotografie z let 1901–1914 a album Z dvorů a dvorečků staré Prahy*, Uměleckoprůmyslové museum v Praze
2000   *Fotograf František Drtikol*, Galerie Františka Drtikola, Příbram
2001   *František Drtikol*, Ateliér Josefa Sudka, Praha
2003   *František Drtikol. Photographs from the Years 1918–1935*, The Moscow House of Photography
2004   *František Drtikol. Photographs from the Years 1918–1935 in the Collections of the Museum of Decorative Arts in Prague. Fotografie z let 1918–1935 ze sbírek Uměleckoprůmyslového musea v Praze*, Uměleckoprůmyslové museum v Praze
2004   *Eyes Wide Open*, Hungarian House of Photography, Budapest
2004   *František Drtikol: Oči široce otevřené*, Galerie Františka Drtikola, Příbram

1902–03 Die Ausstellungen der Lehr- und Versuchsanstalt für Photographie, München
1903 *Internationale Ausstellung für Photographie und Graphische Künste*, Mainz
1911 *Výstava Českého klubu fotografů amatérů*, Lucerna, Praha
1913 *International Exhibition of the London Salon of Photography*, London
1914 *Výstava fotografií*, Rudolfinum, Praha
1922–32 *Annual Exhibition of the Royal Photographic Society of Great Britain*, London
1923 *I° Esposizione Internazionale di Fotografia, Otticae, Cinematografia*, Torino
1924–30 *7th–13th Annual Salon of Pictorial Photography*, Los Angeles
1924–34 19ème–29ème *Salon International de Photographie*, Société française de Photographie, Paris
1924–35 *International Exhibition of the London Salon of Photography*, London
1925 *International Exhibition of Professional Photography*, London
1925 *Mostra internazionale delle Arti Decorative*, Monza
1927 *Mostra internazionale delle Arti Decorative*, Monza
1927 *Hundert Jahre Lichtbild*, Geverbemuseum Basel
1928 *International Exhibition of Photographic Art*, Preston Scientific Society
1928 Výstava soudobé kultury ČSR, Zemské výstaviště, Brno
1930 *International Exhibition of Photographic Art*, Preston Scientific Society
1930 *Internationale Ausstellung, Das Lichtbild, Lehr- und Versuchsanstalt für Photographie*, Vereinigung Münchener Absolventen, München
1932 *The Modern Spirit in Photography*, Royal Photographic Society of Great Britain, London
1932 *První celostátní výstava fotografů z povolání*, Zemské výstaviště, Brno
1932 *15th Annual Salon of Pictorial Photography*, Los Angeles
1933 *Premier Salon International du Nu*, Paris
1934 *International Exhibition of Photographic Art*, Preston Scientific Society
1934 *Internationale Lichtbild Ausstellung*, Berlin
1936 *Exposition Internationale de la Photographie Contemporaine*, Paris
1936 *Tanec v čsl. umění výtvarném a ve fotografii*, Mánes, Praha
1939 *Sto let české fotografie 1839–1939*, Umělecko-průmyslové museum Obchodní a živnostenské komory v Praze
1967 *Československá fotografie mezi dvěma světovými válkami*, Obecní dům, Praha
1973–74 *Osobnosti české fotografie I / ze sbírek Uměleckoprůmyslového musea v Praze*, Oblastní galerie výtvarného umění, Roudnice nad Labem; Uměleckoprůmyslové museum v Praze; Dům umění města Brna
1977 *Česká medzivojnová fotografia (zo sbierok Moravskej galérie v Brne)*, Komorná galéria fotografie, Bratislava
1979 *Photographie als Kunst 1879–1979*, Tiroler Landesmuseum Ferdinandeum, Innsbruck
1981 *Česká fotografie 1918–1938*, Moravská galerie v Brně, Brno
1980 *Das imaginäre Photo-Museum*, Josef Haubrich Kunsthalle, Köln
1982 *Fotografie 1922–1982*, Josef Haubrich Kunsthalle, Köln

1983   *Photographes tchèques 1920–1950*, Musée national d'Art moderne, Centre Georges Pompidou, Paris

1988   *Linie / barva / tvar v českém výtvarném umění třicátých let*, GHMP – Dům U Kamenného zvonu

1989   *Transformations in Czech Documentary Photography 1839–1989 / Proměny české dokumentární fotografie (1839–1989)*, Galerie 4, Cheb

1989   *What is Photography. 150 Years of Photography / Co je fotografie. 150 let fotografie*, Mánes, Praha

1989   *Česká fotografická moderna (V. J. Bufka, F. Drtikol, K. Novák, J. A. Trčka)*, Uměleckoprůmyslové museum v Praze

1989–90   *Czech Modernism 1900–1945*, The Museum of Fine Arts, Houston

1990–91   *Photographie Progressive en Tchécoslovaquie 1920–1990*, Galerie Robert Doisneau, Vandoeuvre-lès-Nancy; Lorient; Saint Nazaire; Krefeld; Städtisches Museum Mülheim a/d Ruhr; L'Aubette, Strasbourg; Mulhouse; Renncs

1990   *Fotografija Češke moderne 1908–1926*, Cankarjev Dom Ljubljana; Muzej suvremene umjetnosti, CEFFT, Zagreb

1991   *Photographie der Moderne in Prag 1900–1925*, Neue Galerie der Stadt Linz; Österreichisches Fotoarchiv im Museum moderner Kunst, Wien

1992   *Mittel Europa, fin de siècles 1892–1992*, La Villette, Paris

1993   *El Arte de la Vanguardia en Checoslovaquia 1918–1938*, IVAM, Centre Julio González, Valencia

1993   *Za zrcadlem. Čeští sochaři ve fotografiích a dokumentech*, Národní galerie, Praha

1993   *Umění pro všechny smysly. Meziválečná avantgarda v Československu*, Národní galerie, Praha

1994   *Europa, Europa. Das Jahrhundert der Avantgarde in Mittel- und Osteuropa*, Kunst- und Ausstellunsghalle der Bundesrepublik Deutschland, Bonn

1997   *Prague 1900–1938. Capitale secrète des avant-gardes*, Musée des Beaux-Arts de Dijon

1998   *České art deco 1918–1938*, Praha, Obecní dům

1998–99   *Modern Beauty. Czech Photographic Avant-garde 1918–1948 / Moderní krása. Česká fotografická avantgarda 1918-1948*, Museu Nacional d'Art de Catalunya, Barcelona; l'Hotel de Sully, Paris; Musée de l'Elysée, Lausanne; Die Neue Sammlung – Staatliches Museum für angewandte Kunst, München; Galeric hlavního města Prahy – Dům U Kamenného zvonu, Praha

1999   *Český piktorialismus 1895–1928*, České centrum fotografie, Praha

2000   *Tschechische Avantgarde Fotografie der zwanziger und dreissiger Jahre aus der Sammlung des Kunstgewerbemuseums in Prag*, Tschechisches Zentrum, Berlin

2000   *Csek Avantgárd Fotográfia 1918–1939*, Hungarian House of Photography, Budapest

2000–01   *The Nude in Czech Photography / Akt v české fotografii*, Císařská konírna, Praha; Muzeum umění, Olomouc

2000–01   *Laterna Magica. Einblicke in eine Tschechische Fotografie der Zwischenkriegszeit*, Rupertinum, Salzburg; Museum Abteiberg, Mönchengladbach

2002   *!AVANTGARDEN! in mitteleuropa 1910–1930*, Haus der Kunst, München

2003–04   *Look Light / Ejhle světlo*, Moravská galerie, Brno

2004   *Czech Photography 1840–1950. A Story of a Modern Medium / Česká fotografie 1840–1950. Příběh moderního média*, Galerie Rudolfinum, Praha

2005   *Czech Photography of the 20th Century / Česká fotografie 20. století*, Uměleckoprůmyslové museum v Praze, Galerie hlavního města Prahy – Dům U Kamenného zvonu, Praha

2005   *The Birth of a Muse / Zrození Múzy*, Galerie 4, Cheb
2006   *Anna Fárová & fotografie / Photography*, Langhans Galerie Praha – PRO Langhans, Praha
2006   *In Morbid Colours: Art and the Idea of Decadence in the Bohemian Lands 1880–1914 / V barvách
        chorobných: Idea dekadence a umění v českých zemích 1880–1914*, Obecní dům, Praha

Represented in Galleries / Zastoupení ve sbírkách

Bibliothèque nationale de France, Paris
Dayton Art Institute, Dayton
Fotografie Forum, Frankfurt am Main
Galerie Františka Drtikola, Příbram
Galerie hlavního města Prahy, Praha
Instituto Valenciano de Arte Moderno, Valencia
International Museum of Photography, George Eastman House, Rochester
Moravská galerie, Brno
Münchener Stadtmuseum, München
Musée d'Orsay, Paris
Musée national d'Art moderne, Centre Georges Pompidou, Paris
Museum Folkwang, Essen
Museum Ludwig, Köln
Muzeum umění, Olomouc
Národní archiv, Praha
Národní galerie, Praha
Národní muzeum, Praha
Okresní muzeum, Příbram
Památník národního písemnictví, Praha
PPF Art, a. s., Praha
Sammlung Fotografis – Österreichische Länderbank, Wien
San Francisco Museum of Modern Art, San Francisco
Société française de photographie, Paris
Stedelijk Museum, Amsterdam
The Art Institute of Chicago, Chicago
The J. Paul Getty Museum, Los Angeles
The Museum of Fine Arts, Houston
The Museum of Modern Art, New York
The Royal Photographic Society, Bath
The Tokyo Metropolitan Museum of Photography, Tokyo
Uměleckoprůmyslové museum, Praha
University of New Mexico, Albuquerque
Victoria and Albert Museum, London

Bibliography / Literatura

Portfolios / Portfolia

Drtikol, František & Škarda, Augustin: *Z dvorů a dvorečků staré Prahy. Půl sta olejotisků*, Praha, Artěl 1911.

Drtikol, František: *J. S. Machar*, Praha, Drtikol a spol. 1914.

Drtikol, František: *Dorostenky, rytmický tělocvik ve volné přírodě*, Praha, Sokol v Žižkově 1914.

Drtikol, František: *Portréty presidenta republiky T. G. Masaryka*, Praha, Emporion 1923.

de Santeul, Claude: *Les nus de Drtikol*, Paris, Librairie des Arts décoratifs 1929.

Kainar, Josef: *Fotografie 1928–1958*, Praha, SNKLHU 1959.

Dvořák, Karel: *Akt v české fotografii*, Praha, Orbis 1967.

Klaricová, Kateřina: *František Drtikol*, Praha, Pressfoto 1981.

Pastor, Suzanne: *František Drtikol*, Praha, Prague House of Photography & Odephil Editions 1996.

František Drtikol Portfolio, Brno, Galerie AmbrosianA 1998.

František Drtikol 1883–1961, Praha, Uměleckoprůmyslové museum v Praze & Trico 2000.

Mlčoch, Jan: *František Drtikol*, Praha, České centrum fotografie 2002.

Dobra, Rifo: *František Drtikol*, Praha, Dobra fotogalerie 2003.

Birgus, Vladimír: *František Drtikol – 10 Modernist Nudes*, Praha, Vladimír Birgus 2004.

Books / Knihy

Formes nues, Paris, Editions d` Art Graphique et Photographique 1935.

Drtikol, František: *Žena ve světle*, text by Josef Richard Marek, Praha, Eduard Beaufort 1938.

Jeníček, Jiří: *Fotografie jako zření světa a života*, Praha, Československé filmové nakladatelství 1947.

Gruber, Renate & Fritz: *Das imaginäre Photo-Museum. Meisterwerke aus 140 Jahren Photographie*, Köln, DuMont Buchverlag 1981.

Fárová, Anna: *Frantisek Drtikol. Photograph des Art Deco*, München, Schirmer / Mosel 1986; 1993.

Birgus, Vladimír & Braný, Antonín: *František Drtikol*, Praha, Odeon 1988; 1989.

Klaricová, Kateřina: *František Drtikol. Výběr fotografií z celoživotního díla*, Praha, Panorama 1989.

Faber, Monika & Kroutvor, Josef: *Photographie der Moderne in Prag 1900–1925*, Schaffhausen, Edition Stemmle 1991.

Štekl, Evžen: *Síla moudrosti. Interpretace učení Fráni Drtikola*, Praha, DharmaGaia 1992.

Funk, Karel: *Mystik a učitel František Drtikol*, Praha, GEMMA 89 1993.

Birgus, Vladimír: *Fotograf František Drtikol*, Prostor, Praha 1994.

Birgus, Vladimír: *František Drtikol – Modernist Nudes*, San Francisco, Robert Koch Gallery 1997.

Doležal, Stanislav & Fárová, Anna & Nedoma, Petr: *František Drtikol photographe, peintre, mystique*, Praha, Galerie Rudolfinum 1998.

Doležal, Stanislav & Fárová, Anna & Nedoma, Petr: *František Drtikol fotograf, malíř, mystik*, Praha, Galerie Rudolfinum 1998.

Kolektiv: *Dějiny českého výtvarného umění 1890 / 1938*, Academia, Praha 1998.

Horneková, Jana (ed.): *České art deco 1918–1938*, Praha, Obecní dům 1998.

Mlčoch, Jan: *František Drtikol. Photographs from the period between 1901–1914 and the album From Large and Little Courtyards of Old Prague. Fotografie z let 1901–1914 a album Z dvorů a dvorečků staré Prahy.* Praha, Uměleckoprůmyslové museum v Praze & Kant 1999.

Birgus, Vladimír (ed.), *Česká fotografická avantgarda 1918–1948*, Praha, Kant 1999.

Birgus, Vladimír (ed.), *Tschechische Avantgarde-Fotografie 1918–1948*, Stuttgart, Arnoldsche 1999.

Birgus, Vladimír: *František Drtikol*, Praha, Kant 2000.

Funk, Karel: *Mystik a učitel František Drtikol*, Olomouc, Fontána 2001.

Drtikol, František: *Deníky a dopisy z let 1914–1918 věnované Elišce Janské*, Praha, Svět 2001.

Scheufler, Pavel: *Galerie c. k. fotografů*, Praha, Grada Publishing 2001.

Vladimír Birgus (ed.), *Czech Photographic Avant-Garde 1918–1948*, Cambridge & London, The MIT Press 2002.

Drtikol, František: *Duchovní cesta*, Praha, Svět 2004.

Drtikol, František: *Workbook of Photographs / Pracovní kniha fotografií*, Praha, Svět 2006.

Film / Film

Fotograf František Drtikol, režie Jiří Holna, 2001

Exhibition Catalogues / Katalogy výstav

Jiřík, F. X.:*Výstava fotografií*, Praha, Umělecko-průmyslové museum Obchodní a živnostenské komory v Praze 1914.

Siblík, Emanuel: *Tanec v čsl. umění výtvarném a ve fotografii*, Praha, Československý svaz Tanec–rytmika–gymnastika 1936.

Wirth, Zdeněk (ed.): *Sto let české fotografie 1839–1939*, Praha, Umělecko-průmyslové museum Obchodní a živnostenské komory v Praze 1939.

Teige, Karel: *Das moderne Lichtbild in der Čechoslovakei*, Praha, Orbis 1947.

Skopec, Rudolf: *Československá fotografie mezi dvěma světovými válkami*, Praha, Galerie hlavního města Prahy 1967.

Fárová, Anna: *Fotograf František Drtikol. Tvorba z let 1903–35*, Praha, Uměleckoprůmyslové museum 1972.

Fárová, Anna: *František Drtikol dalla collezione del museo d'Arti decorative di Praga*, Milano, Sicof 1973.

Fárová, Anna: *Osobnosti české fotografie I*, Roudnice nad Labem, Oblastní galerie výtvarného umění 1973.

Fárová, Anna: *Osobnosti české fotografie I*, Praha, Uměleckoprůmyslové museum 1974.

Dufek, Antonín: *Česká medzivojnová fotografia (zo sbierok Moravskej galérie v Brne)*, Bratislava, Mestský dom kultúry a osvety 1977.

Fárová, Anna & Mrázková, Daniela: *Drtikol*, Köln, Rudolf Kicken Galerie 1983.

Hlaváč, Ľudovít: *František Drtikol. Fotografie z mladosti 1901–1912*, Bratislava, Komorná galéria fotografie Profil 1974.

168

Fárová, Anna: *František Drtikol 1883–1961*, Bruxelles, Photographies Galerie Houyoux, Bibliothèque Royale 1976.

Weiermair, Peter: *Photographie als Kunst 1879–1979*, Innsbruck, Allerheiligenpress 1980.

Dufek, Antonín & Anděl, Jaroslav & Šmejkal, František: *Česká fotografie 1918–1938*, Brno, Moravská galerie 1981.

Dufek, Antonín & Kirschner, Zdeněk & Klaricová, Kateřina & Sayag, Alain: *Photographes tchèques 1920–1950*, Paris, Centre Georges Pompidou, Musée national d'Art moderne 1983.

Dufek, Antonín & Eskildsen, Ute: *Tschechische Fotografie 1918–1938*, Essen, Museum Folkwang 1984.

Dufek, Antonín & Czartoryska, Urszula: *Czeska fotografia 1918–1938*, Łódź, Museum Sztuki 1985.

Fárová, Anna: *Ursprung und Gegenwart tschechoslowakischer Fotografie*, Frankfurt am Main, Album 3 / 1985.

Rousová, Hana (ed.): *Linie / Barva / Tvar*, Praha, Galerie hlavního města Prahy 1988.

Andel, Jaroslav & Tucker, Anne W. (eds.): *Czech Modernism: 1900–1945*, Houston, The Houston Museum of fine Arts – Bulfinch Press (USA) 1989; Little, Brown & Company (Canada) 1989.

Mrázková, Daniela (ed.): *What is Photography. 150 Years of Photography / Co je fotografie. 150 let fotografie*, Praha, Videopress & Credit Praha 1989.

Scheufler, Pavel & Klaricová, Kateřina & Moucha, Josef: *Proměny české dokumentární fotografie (1839–1989)*, Cheb, Galerie 4 1989.

Kroutvor, Josef & Kirschner, Zdeněk: *Česká fotografická moderna (V. J. Bufka, F. Drtikol, K. Novák, J. A. Trčka)*, Praha, Uměleckoprůmyslové museum v Praze 1989.

Kroutvor, Josef: *Fotografija Česke moderne 1908–1926*, Ljubljana, Cankarjev Dom & Zagreb, Muzej suvremene umjetnosti, CEFFT 1990.

Fárová, Anna: *František Drtikol 1883–1961*, Toulouse, Galerie municipale du Château d'Eau 1990.

Primus, Zdenek & Philippot, Claude: *Photographie Progressive en Tchécoslovaquie 1920–1990*, Vandoeuvre-lès-Nancy, Centre Culturel André Malraux 1990.

Birgus, Vladimír & Kirschner, Zdeněk: *The Other Side of František Drtikol*, Chicago, Jacques Baruch Gallery 1991.

Anděl, Jaroslav (ed.): *The Art of the Avant-garde in Czechoslovakia 1918–1938 / El Arte de la Vanguardia en Checoslovaquia 1918–1938*, Valencia, IVAM, Centre Julio González 1993.

Anděl, Jaroslav (ed.): *Umění pro všechny smysly. Meziválečná avantgarda v Československu*, Praha, Národní galerie 1993.

Vlnas, Vít: *Za zrcadlem. Čeští sochaři ve fotografiích a dokumentech*, Praha, Národní galerie 1993.

Stanislawski, Ryszard & Brockhaus, Christoph (ed.): *Europa, Europa. Das Jahrhundert der Avant-garde in Mittel- und Osteuropa*, Bonn, Kunst- und Ausstellunsghalle der Bundesrepublik Deutschland 1994.

Anděl, Jaroslav & Starcky Emmanuel (ed.): *Prague 1900–1938. Capitale secrète des avant-gardes*, Dijon, Musée des Beaux-Arts de Dijon 1997.

Birgus, Vladimír & Bonhomme, Pierre: *Beauté moderne. Les avant-gardes photographiques tchèques 1918–1948*, Paris, Mission du Patrimoine photographique & Praha, Kant 1998.

Birgus, Vladimír & Bonhomme, Pierre: *Modern Beauty: Czech Photographic Avant-garde 1918–1948 / Moderní krása. Česká fotografická avantgarda 1918–1948*, Praha, Kant 1999.

Birgus, Vladimír & Mlčoch, Jan: *The Nude in Czech Photography / Akt v české fotografii*, Praha, Kant 2000.

Zuckriegl, Margit (ed.): *Laterna Magica. Einblicke in eine tschechische Fotografie der Zwischenkriegszeit*, Salzburg, Rupertinum 2000.

Birgus, Vladimír & Zuckriegl, Margit: *Maestri della fotografia dell' avanguardia ceca negli anni Venti e Trenta*, Milano, Silvana Editoriale 2001.

Mlčoch, Jan: *František Drtikol. Fotografie z let 1901–1914 a album Z dvorů a dvorečků staré Prahy*, Praha, Uměleckoprůmyslové museum v Praze & Kant 2000.

Zemánek, Jiří: *Look Light / Ejhle světlo*, Praha, Kant & Brno, Moravská galerie 2003.

Mlčoch, Jan: *František Drtikol. Photographs from the Years 1918–1935*, Moscow, The Moscow House of Photography 2003.

Mlčoch, Jan: *František Drtikol. Photographs from the Years 1918–1935 in the Collections of the Museum of Decorative Arts in Prague / Fotografie z let 1918–1935 ze sbírek Uměleckoprůmyslového musea v Praze*, Praha, Uměleckoprůmyslové museum v Praze 2004.

Anděl, Jaroslav: *Czech Photography 1840–1950. A Story of a Modern Medium / Česká fotografie 1840–1950. Příběh moderního média*, Praha, Kant 2004.

Birgus, Vladimír & Mlčoch, Jan: *Czech Photography of the 20th Century. A Guide*, Praha, Kant 2005.

Birgus, Vladimír & Mlčoch, Jan: *Česká fotografie 20. století. Průvodce*, Praha, Kant 2005.

Moucha, Josef: *Gallery 4 Retrospective / Retrospektiva Galerie 4*, Cheb, Galerie 4 2005.

Meisnerová Wismer, Zuzana (ed.): *Anna Fárová & fotografie / Photography*, Praha, Langhans Galerie Praha – PRO Langhans 2006.

Moucha, Josef & Musilová, Helena: *The Photogeny of Identity. The Memory of Czech Photography / Fotogenie identity. Paměť české fotografie*, Praha, Kant & Pražský dům fotografie – Prague House of Photography 2006.

Urban, Otto M. (ed.): *In Morbid Colours: Art and the Idea of Decadence in the Bohemian Lands 1880–1914 / V barvách chorobných: Idea dekadence a umění v českých zemích 1880–1914*, Praha, Obecní dům & Arbor vitae 2006.

Articles / Články

K. A. [Karel Anderle]: Klub návštěvou v atelieru Drtikolově, *Fotografický obzor* 20, 1912, č. 3, s. 71–72.

Drtikol, František: Muž u fotografa, *Gentleman* 1, 1924, č. 12, s. 14–15.

P. A.: František Drtikol. K padesátinám umělcovým 3. března 1933, *Světozor* 33, 1933, č. 9.

ef: K obrazům, *Fotografický obzor* 48, 1940, č. 3, s. 28–29.

Teige, Karel: Cesty československé fotografie, *Blok* 2, 1948, č. 6, příloha P, s. 77–82.

Jeníček, Jiří: Na besedě u Františka Drtikola, *Československá fotografie* 6, 1955, č. 2, s. 16–18.

Boček, Jaroslav: Drtikol a jeho akty, *Československá fotografie* 15, 1964, č. 9, s. 302–305.

Skopec, Rudolf: Fotografický akt včera a dnes, *Fotografie* 9, 1967, č. 2, s. 66–68.

Skopec, Rudolf: František Drtikol, *Creative Camera*, 1972, No 93, s. 518–525.

Fárová, Anna: Ze sbírek fotografií UPM v Praze XII – František Drtikol, *Československá fotografie* 23, 1972, č. 12, s. 548–549.

Fárová, Anna: František Drtikol (1883–1961), *Revue Fotografie* 16, 1974, č. 1, s. 10–23.

Hejdová, Eva: Portrét slavného fotografa, *Mladá fronta – Víkend* 39, 19. 3. 1983, č. 11, s. 4–5.

František Drtikol, *Camera International*, 1984, No 1, s. 22–31.

Fárová, Anna: František Drtikol – mysticisme et sexualité, *Clichés*, 1986, č. 26, s. 48–51.

Nikolaus, Frank: Der nackte Körper als „Kleid der Seele", *Art*, 1986, č. 12, s. 60–65.

Doležal, Stanislav: František Drtikol, *Post, příloha časopisu Kavárna AFFA*, únor 1989, nestr.

Kroutvor, Josef: Tanec jako inspirace Františka Drtikola, *Československá fotografie* 41, 1990, č. 10, s. 444–446.

Sayag, Alain: Saudek – Drtikol, *Camera International*, Summer 1990, No 26, s. 56–65.

Kroutvor, Josef: Česká fotografická moderna, *Revue Fotografie* 34, 1990, č. 3, s. 68–73.

Fárová, Anna: František Drtikol. Magie imaginativního plození, *Výtvarné umění*, 1992, č. 2, s. 20–38.

Drtikol, František: Muž u fotografa, *Bulletin MG*, 1992, č. 48, s. 95–96.

Dufek, Antonín: Drtikolův neznámý text, *Bulletin MG*, 1992, č. 48, s. 95.

Dufek, Antonín: Drtikol's Unknown Text, *Bulletin MG*, 1992, č. 48, s. 96.

Birgus, Vladimír: Druhá strana Františka Drtikola, *Ateliér* 5, 1992, č. 8, s. 3.

Birgus, Vladimír: František Drtikol, nejdražší český fotograf, *Starožitnosti a užité umění*, 1995, č. 2, s. 9–11.

Moucha, Josef: Výprodej idejí, *Audio Video Revue* 5, 1996, č. 1, s. 34–35.

Zinke, Petr: Úvaha o tvorbě a religiózních tendencích s přihlédnutím k životnímu příkladu Františka Drtikola, *Závěrečná teoretická bakalářská práce*, Praha, FAMU 1996.

Moucha, Josef: Dvě otázky pro Annu Fárovou, *Ateliér* 10, 1997, č. 24, s. 3.

Moucha, Josef: Drtikol jako dobrodružství objevu, *Xantypa* 4, 1998, č. 2, s. 68–73.

Šmejkalová, Jana: Hamletovský odkaz Františka Drtikola, *Antique* 5, 1998, č. 5, s. 44.

Wittlich, Petr: Drtikolova mystika, *Ateliér* 11, 1998, č. 9, s. 16.

Chuchma, Josef: Portréty, které přežily, *Magazín Dnes* 7, 1999, č. 19, s. 12–17.

Moucha, Josef: Vydrží stálá expozice reprodukcí? *MF Dnes* 11, 8. 8. 2000, č. 183, s. 18.

Scheufler, Pavel: Radikál František aneb Drtikol neznámý, *Foto Video*, 2000, květen, s. 22–24.

Doležal, Stanislav: Cesta k Poznání – F. Drtikol, *Dotek* 9, 2000, č. 5, s. 14–17.

Moucha, Josef: Dvě drtikolovské otázky pro Annu Fárovou, *Ateliér* 14, 2001, č. 12, s. 7.

Moucha, Josef: Drtikolovo milostné romaneto, *Ateliér* 14, 2001, č. 12, s. 7.

Fárová, Anna: Právě vychází kniha Deníky a dopisy z let 1914–1918 věnované Elišce Janské. František Drtikol, *Dotek* 10, 2001, č. 6, s. 18–19.

Moucha, Josef: Fixed Light, *Fotograf* 2, 2003, č. 3, s. 90–95.

31   Hana Benešová (1885–1974), wife of Edvard Beneš; 1929 (NA 55214)

32   Karel Engliš (1880–1961), economist and six times Minister of Finance; Vice-Chancellor of the University of Brno and Prague; Governor of the Czechoslovak National Bank; c. 1920 (NA 56384)

33   Antonín Švehla (1873–1933), three times Czechoslovak Prime Minister, head of the Agrarian Party; c. 1920 (NA 56377)

34   František Topič (1858–1941), publisher and bookseller; c. 1930 (NA 56039)

35   Alois Rašín (1867–1923), economist and first Minister of Finance, assassinated; c. 1921 (NA 56432)

36   Jiří Kroha (1893–1974), architect, artist, teacher; c. 1925 (NA 56277)

37   Marie Calma (1883–1966), real name Marie Veselá (née Hurychová), writer, translator, journalist, singer; 1922 (NA 56894)

38   Jan Šrámek (1870–1956), Roman Catholic priest, founder and Chairman of the Czechoslovak People's Party, 1921–39, was a minister in every government; c. 1925 (NA 56444)

39   Milan Hodža (1878–1944), Slovak journalist and commentator, five times minister and, 1935–38, Czechoslovak Prime Minister; c. 1928 (NA 56369)

40   Ferdinand Josef Lobkowicz (1885–1953), Bohemian nobleman and lawyer, with his wife, born Clotilde Leopoldine Volková (1888–1970); c. 1921 (NA 56740)

41   Maximilian Lobkowicz (1888–1967), Bohemian nobleman and Czechoslovak diplomat; 1925 (NA 55737)

42   Max Švabinský (1873–1962), painter and print-maker; 1922 (NA 56915)

43   Rudolf A. Dvorský (1899–1966), real name Rudolf Antonín; singer, pianist, composer, pianist, dance-band leader; 1919 (NA 55926)

44   Václav Vilém Štech (1885–1974), art historian; c. 1914 (NA 56129)

45   Jaroslav Horejc (1886–1983), sculptor and art glass designer; c. 1918 (NA 55297)

46   Paul Valéry (1871–1945), French poet, essayist, philosopher; c. 1920 (NA 56159)

47   Jelizaveta Nikolská (1904–1955), Russian-born dancer and choreographer; c. 1924 (NA 55096)

48   Jan Vávra (1861–1932), actor; c. 1919 (NA 55549)

49   Rabindranath Tagore (1861–1941), Bengali poet, fiction writer, philosopher, recipient of the 1913 Nobel Prize for literature; 1921 (NA 56118)

50   Jan Laichter (1858–1946), publisher and fiction writer; c. 1922 (NA 55916)

51   Vítězslav Novák (1870–1949), composer, pianist, and teacher; 1920 (NA 55940)

52   Karel Hašler (1879–1941), songwriter, actor, dramatist, director, writer, translator; c. 1925 (NA 55927)

53   Leoš Janáček (1854–1928), composer, known particularly for his operas; c. 1920 (NA 55948)

54   Radola Gajda (1892–1948), born Rudolf Geidl; officer of the Czecho-Slovak Legion, General in the Czechoslovak Army, head of the National League of Fascists, forced to retire; c. 1925 (NA 56914)

55   František Hrabčík (1894–1967), army general; c. 1932 (NA 56029)

56   Josef Svatopluk Machar (1864–1942), poet, essayist, co-author of the "Czech Modern" manifesto (1895), politician, Inspector General of the Czechoslovak Army at the time of this portrait; 1921 (NA 57099/a)

57   Otakar Ostrčil (1879–1935), composer, conductor, teacher; 1924 (NA 56392)

58   Jan Kotěra (1871–1923), first modern Czech architect, as well as a painter and architectural theorist; c. 1921 (NA 57101)

59   Josef Scheiner (1861–1932), lawyer, politician, head of the Czechoslovak Sokol movement,
      Inspector General of the Czechoslovak Army; c. 1920, (NA 55054)
60   Josef Čapek (1887–1945), painter, graphic artist, and writer; 1922 (NA 55539)
61   Marie Grossová (1902–1972), stage and film actress; c. 1925 (NA 56196)
62   Vratislav Nechleba (1885–1965), portraitist, teacher at the Academy of Fine Art, Prague; c. 1930
      (NA 56927)
63   Josef Suk (1874–1935), composer and violinist; c. 1926 (NA 55844)
64   Ervina Kupferová (1899–1978), dancer, dance teacher, first wife of František Drtikol; 1921 (NA 57112)
65   Emanuel z Lešehradu (1877–1955), born Josef Maria Emanuel Lešetický; bank archivist, writer,
      greatly interested in mysticism and the occult, collector; 1921 (NA 55495)
66   Enrique Stanko Vráz (1860–1932), traveller, photographer, writer; c. 1933 (NA 56478)
67   Kitty Červenková, violinist (1904–?); c. 1925 (NA 55822)
68   Jelena Ježićová-Hanáková (1894–1934), born in Mostar; opera singer and journalist; worked
      at the National Theatre, Brno, and the Slovak National Theatre, Bratislava; c. 1925 (NA 55403)
69   Václav Talich (1883–1961), conductor; c. 1926 (NA 55907)
70   Jarmila Kronbauerová (1893–1968), actress; 1922 (NA 56597)
71   Jarmila Kronbauerová, 1922 (NA 55463)
72   Lída Klímová-Grossmannová (1901–1984), singer, dancer, actress; c. 1922 (NA 55511)
73   Míla Mellanová (1901–1964); born Miloslava Mrázková, actress, director, dramatist, translator;
      c. 1925 (NA 55447)
74   Helena Friedlová (1889–1966), actress; c. 1925 (NA 56212)
75   Jarmila Horáková (1904–1928), actress; c. 1925 (NA 55391)
76   Anny Ondra (1902–1987), born Anny Ondráková; actress, singer, wife of the world heavyweight
      champion Max Schmeling; c. 1925 (NA 56992)
77   Vlasta Burian (1891–1962), born Josef Vlastimil Burian, and his wife Nina (1893–1962), born
      Františka Červenková; comic actor of stage and screen, theatre director, soccer player in his
      youth; c. 1933 (NA 56210)
78   Maria Molinari, wife of the conductor Bernardino Molinari; c. 1923 (NA 56003)
79   Bernardino Molinari (1880–1952), Italian conductor; c. 1923 (NA 56001)
80   Arnold Jirásek (1887–1960), physician, surgeon, professor, pioneer of neurosurgery; c. 1934
      (NA 55988)
81   Karel Weinfurter (1867–1942), writer, occultist, mystic; c. 1929 (NA 56468)
82   Karel Hugo Hilar (1885–1935), born Karel Hugo Bakule; theatre director, poet, and dramatist;
      c. 1930 (NA 56175)
83   Zuzka Zguriška (1900–1984), born Ľudmila Šimonovičová-Dvořáková; Slovak writer; c. 1925
      (NA 55622)
84   Alphonse Mucha (1860–1939), painter, print-maker, illustrator and stage designer; 1927 (NA 55879)
85   Jan Konůpek (1883–1950), painter, print-maker, illustrator; 1928 (NA 55889)
86   Heinrich Mann (1871–1950), German writer, refugee from Nazism, granted Czechoslovak
      citizenship; 1934 (NA 56512)
87   Alois Musil (1868–1944), explorer, orientalist, co-founder of the Czechoslovak Oriental Institute;
      c. 1930 (NA 55617)

88   Karel Dostal (1884–1966), actor, director; c. 1931 (NA 55636)

89   Oldřich Nový (1899–1983), film star; c. 1929 (NA 55806)

90   Káďa Pešek (1895–1970), born Karel Pešek; soccer and hockey player, later received a degree in
        natural sciences and became a bureaucrat at the Ministry of Health; 1923 (NA 56043)

Soupis publikovaných fotografií

s. 2   Autoportrét, 1913 (olejotisk, GF UPM 43.183)

1   Jakub Obrovský (1882–1949), malíř, sochař, spisovatel, profesor Akademie výtvarných umění
        v Praze; 1913 (NA 57070)

2   Anna Sedláčková (1887–1969), herečka; 1912 (NA 56322)

3   Anna Sedláčková, 1912 (NA 56664)

4   Jarmila Bechyňová (1906–1992), herečka; c. 1925 (NA 55450)

5   Marie Majerová (1882–1967), rozená Marie Bartošová; spisovatelka; c. 1913 (NA 56907)

6   Jaroslav Kocian (1883–1950), houslista, skladatel; 1913 (NA 56861)

7   Eduard Vojan (1853–1920), herec; 1913 (NA 56882)

8   Ema Destinnová (1878–1930), vl. jm. Emilie Pavlína Věnceslava Kittlová; operní pěvkyně
        mezinárodního věhlasu; 1914 (NA 55900/2)

9   Ladislav Šaloun (1870–1946), sochař; c. 1914 (NA 57085)

10   Vlastislav Hofman (1884–1964), architekt, výtvarník, designér, scénograf; c. 1919 (NA 55913)

11   Josef Váchal (1884–1969), malíř, grafik, spisovatel; 1913 (NA 56925)

12   Jan Zrzavý (1890–1977), malíř, grafik, ilustrátor, scénograf; 1919 (NA 55029)

13   Lydie Kamenská (? – ?), vl. jm. Lída Pecánková; šansoniérka, herečka divadla Rokoko v období
        1915–35 za ředitelského působení Karla Hašlera; 1919 (NA 56655)

14   Duška Vronská (1885–1939), vl. jm. Ludmila Šmatláková; členka zpěvohry pražského Vinohradské-
        ho divadla v období 1907–16; c. 1925 (NA 55390)

15   Jan Štursa (1880–1925), sochař, od roku 1917 profesor Akademie výtvarných umění v Praze; c. 1912
        (NA 55319)

16   Jan Štursa, 1924 (NA 55317)

17   Josef Mařatka (1874–1937), sochař; c. 1912 (NA 57090)

18   Leopolda Dostalová (1879–1972), herečka; c. 1914 (NA 55342)

19   Růžena Nasková (1884–1960), herečka; c. 1920 (NA 55363)

20   Jarmila Novotná (1907–1994), operní pěvkyně mezinárodního věhlasu, filmová herečka; 1928 (NA
        55006)

21   Jakub Deml (1878–1961), spisovatel, římskokatolický kněz; c. 1914 (NA 55542)

22   Antonín Sova (1864–1928), spisovatel; c. 1920 (NA 56146)

23   Ignát Herrmann (1854–1935), spisovatel, novinář; 1918 (NA 55486)

24   Marie Hübnerová (1865–1931), herečka; c. 1925 (NA 55376)

25   Jiří Steimar (1887–1968), herec; c. 1922 (NA 55571)

26   Vojtěch Mastný (1874–1954), právník, diplomat; 1921 (NA 56363)

27   Alois Jirásek (1851–1930), romanopisec, dramatik; 1919 (NA 56935)

28   Tomáš Garrigue Masaryk (1850–1937), filozof, sociolog, politik, první československý prezident; 1919 (NA 55158)

29   Alice Masaryková (1879–1966), dcera prezidenta, zakladatelka a první předsedkyně Československého Červeného kříže; 1919 (NA 55165)

30   Edvard Beneš (1884–1948), politik, druhý československý prezident; 1921 (NA 57103)

31   Hana Benešová (1885–1974), choť Edvarda Beneše; 1929 (NA 55214)

32   Karel Engliš (1880–1961), ekonom, šestinásobný ministr financí, guvernér Československé národní banky, vysokoškolský pedagog; c. 1920 (NA 56384)

33   Antonín Švehla (1873–1933), trojnásobný československý premiér, předseda agrární strany; c. 1920 (NA 56377)

34   František Topič (1858–1941), nakladatel, knihkupec; c. 1930 (NA 56039)

35   Alois Rašín (1867–1923), ekonom, první československý ministr financí, oběť atentátu; c. 1921 (NA 56432)

36   Jiří Kroha (1893–1974), architekt, výtvarník, pedagog; c. 1925 (NA 56277)

37   Marie Calma (1883–1966), vl. jm. Marie Veselá, rozená Hurychová; spisovatelka, překladatelka, novinářka, koncertní pěvkyně; 1922 (NA 56894)

38   Jan Šrámek (1870–1956), římskokatolický kněz, spoluzakladatel a předseda Československé strany lidové (1919–30), vládní činitel (1921–39); c. 1925 (NA 56444)

39   Milan Hodža (1878–1944), slovenský novinář, pětinásobný ministr, československý premiér (1935–38); c. 1928 (NA 56369)

40   Ferdinand Josef Lobkowicz (1885–1953), český šlechtic a právník s chotí, za svobodna Klotyldou Leopoldinou Volkovou (1888–1970); c. 1921 (NA 56740)

41   Maxmilián Ervín Lobkowicz (1888–1967), český šlechtic, diplomat; 1925 (NA 55737)

42   Max Švabinský (1873–1962), malíř, grafik; 1922 (NA 56915)

43   Rudolf A. Dvorský (1899–1966), vl. jm. Rudolf Antonín; zpěvák, skladatel, klavírista, kapelník; 1919 (NA 55926)

44   Václav Vilém Štech (1885–1974), historik umění; c. 1914 (NA 56129)

45   Jaroslav Horejc (1886–1983), sochař, umělecký sklář; c. 1918 (NA 55297)

46   Paul Valéry (1871–1945), francouzský básník, esejista, filozof; c. 1920 (NA 56159)

47   Jelizaveta Nikolská (1904–1955), tanečnice a choreografka ruského původu; c. 1924 (NA 55096)

48   Jan Vávra (1861–1932), herec; c. 1919 (NA 55549)

49   Rabíndranáth Thákur (1861–1941), bengálský básník, prozaik, filozof, od roku 1913 nositel Nobelovy ceny za literaturu; 1921 (NA 56118)

50   Jan Laichter (1858–1946), nakladatel, prozaik; c. 1922 (NA 55916)

51   Vítězslav Novák (1870–1949), hudební skladatel, pianista, pedagog; 1920 (NA 55940)

52   Karel Hašler (1879–1941), písničkář, herec, scénárista, režisér, spisovatel, překladatel; c. 1925 (NA 55927)

53   Leoš Janáček (1854–1928), hudební skladatel; c. 1920 (NA 55948)

54   Radola Gajda (1892–1948), vl. jm. Rudolf Geidl; generálmajor čs. legií v Rusku, generál Čs. armády (1926 degradován a propuštěn do civilu); vůdce Národní obce fašistické (1931 uvězněn); c. 1925 (NA 56914)

55   František Hrabčík (1894–1967), divizní generál; c. 1932 (NA 56029)

56   Josef Svatopluk Machar (1864–1942), básník, publicista, spoluautor manifestu České moderny (1895), politik; fotografován jako generální inspektor Československé armády; 1921 (NA 57099/a)

57   Otakar Ostrčil (1879–1935), hudební skladatel, dirigent, pedagog; 1924 (NA 56392)

58   Jan Kotěra (1871–1923), architekt, malíř, teoretik moderní architektury; c. 1921 (NA 57101)

59   Josef Scheiner (1861–1932), právník, politický činitel, starosta Československé obce sokolské, generální inspektor Československé armády; c. 1920 (NA 55054)

60   Josef Čapek (1887–1945), malíř, spisovatel; 1922 (NA 55539)

61   Marie Grossová (1902–1972), filmová a divadelní herečka; c. 1925 (NA 56196)

62   Vratislav Nechleba (1885–1965), portétista, profesor malby na Akademii výtvarných umění v Praze; c. 1930 (NA 56927)

63   Josef Suk (1874–1935), hudební skladatel, houslista; c. 1926 (NA 55844)

64   Ervina Kupferová (1899–1978), tanečnice, taneční pedagožka, první Drtikolova žena; 1921 (NA 57112)

65   Emanuel z Lešehradu (1877–1955), vl. jm. Josef Maria Emanuel Lešetický; archivář Zemské banky, spisovatel s okultistickými zájmy, překladatel, sběratel, zakladatel literárněhistorického archivu Lešehradeum; 1921 (NA 55495)

66   Enrique Stanko Vráz (1860–1932), cestovatel, fotograf, spisovatel; c. 1933 (NA 56478)

67   Kitty Červenková (1904–?), houslistka; c. 1925 (NA 55822)

68   Jelena Ježićová-Hanáková (1894–1934), původem z Mostaru; operní pěvkyně, publicistka; působila v Národním divadle v Brně a ve Slovenském Národním divadle v Bratislavě; c. 1925 (NA 55403)

69   Václav Talich (1883–1961), dirigent; c. 1926 (NA 55907)

70   Jarmila Kronbauerová (1893–1968), herečka; 1922 (NA 56597)

71   Jarmila Kronbauerová, 1922 (NA 55463)

72   Lída Klímová-Grossmannová (1901–1984), operetní zpěvačka, tanečnice, divadelní a televizní herečka; c. 1922 (NA 55511)

73   Míla Mellanová (1901–1964), rozená Miloslava Mrázková; herečka, režisérka, dramatička, překladatelka; c. 1925 (NA 55447)

74   Helena Friedlová (1889–1966), herečka; 1925 (NA 56212)

75   Jarmila Horáková (1904–1928), herečka; c. 1925 (NA 55391)

76   Anny Ondráková (1902–1987), herečka, zpěvačka, žena mistra světa v boxu Maxe Schmelinga; c. 1925 (NA 56992)

77   Vlasta Burian (1891–1962), vl. jm. Josef Vlastimil Burian, s chotí Ninou (1893–1962), za svobodna Františkou Červenkovou; divadelní a filmový komik, divadelní ředitel, v mládí fotbalista; c. 1933 (NA 56210)

78   Maria Molinari, choť dirigenta Bernardina Molinariho; c. 1923 (NA 56003)

79   Bernardino Molinari (1880–1952), dirigent italského původu; c. 1923 (NA 56001)

80   Arnold Jirásek (1887–1960), profesor lékařství, průkopník neurochirurgie; c. 1934 (NA 55988)

81   Karel Weinfurter (1867–1942), spisovatel, okultista, mystik; c. 1929 (NA 56468)

82   Karel Hugo Hilar (1885–1935), rozený Karel Hugo Bakule; režisér, básník, dramatik; c. 1930
      (NA 56175)
83   Zuzka Zguriška (1900–1984), vl. jm. Ľudmila Šimonovičová-Dvořáková, slovenská spisovatelka;
      c. 1925 (NA 55622)
84   Alfons Mucha (1860–1939), malíř, grafik, ilustrátor, scénograf; 1927 (NA 55879)
85   Jan Konůpek (1883–1950), malíř, grafik, ilustrátor; 1928 (NA 55889)
86   Heinrich Mann (1871–1950), německý spisovatel, exulant z nacistického Německa, československý
      občan; 1934 (NA 56512)
87   Alois Musil (1868–1944), orientalista, spoluzakladatel Československého orientálního ústavu;
      c. 1930 (NA 55617)
88   Karel Dostal (1884–1966), herec, režisér, recitátor; c. 1931 (NA 55636)
89   Oldřich Nový (1899–1983), filmový herec; c. 1929 (NA 55806)
90   Káďa Pešek (1895–1970), vl. jm. Karel Pešek; doktor přírodních věd, fotbalista, hokejista,
      ministerský úředník; 1923 (NA 56043)

Digitization of the Drtikol Negatives

The portraits in this book have been made from large-format glass negatives deposited in the National Archives, Prague. Since the plates are so large, the digitization methods normally used there could not be employed, but the National Archives was willing to allow in help from the outside. The condition for that, however, was that digitization take place right in the Archives, since glass negatives are fragile and can be damaged by handling and transport. A special light box (to provide uniform light) was taken into the Archives, and on a stand over a table I placed a Hasselblad D2 with an Imacon digital back with 22 million pixels. Exposure quality was controlled on a notebook computer. The negative was thus photographed, which is, I believe, the method of digitization that causes less wear and tear on the negative than using a flatbed scanner, and it is also saves time. The resulting 16-bit RGB per channel image had 130 MB. For the Fototorst publication it was then transferred to a 16-bit gray-scale image.

Digitization was only the first stage. Most of the negatives had been greatly damaged by handling and bad storage in the past. By being left to rub against each other the plates had become scratched. Many were covered with tiny spots and tarnish caused by various things, from organic dry spots left by mould to stains caused by having been insufficiently fixed during developing. Judging from some of his own prints, we can safely say that Drtikol would probably never have shown damaged work. These portraits therefore also have a right to their former glory. This approach is also emphasized, for example, by advocates of cleaning the *Mona Lisa* (whereas their opponents point to pictures that look artificial after restoration, like something out of, say, a pseudo-historical epic film by Cecil B. DeMille).

How far to go in restoring historical photographs is always a thorny question. To be sure, works of studio photographers of the nineteenth and early twentieth centuries were, in comparison to today's, more brilliant, more luminous, richer in tone, and sometimes even more in focus. Seeing that the photographs are in bad shape, the only thing to do now is to store them in a way that minimizes further deterioration. The most responsible approach to publishing a photograph in a book is to show it in its present condition, not trying to "improve" the photographic image, despite the temptations presented by superb image-processing software. Adjustments are usually made to photographs for printing reasons, particularly in view of the raster graphics, the type, and the quality and surface of the paper, and they are then wholly justified. Things get even more complicated if negatives (or new prints from historic negatives) constitute the basis of what is to be printed; an interpretation of the original work can involve considerable debate.

I prefer to present historical photographs in their present condition (including damaged emulsion, cracked glass, and deterioration of the edges of the photo). Only in exceptional, justifiable cases can one consider reconstructing an original photograph. The digital method is then highly effective, and, disregarding special work with ultraviolet, x-ray, or infrared radiation, it is also the only method possible. Three basic approaches are used for reconstruction of this sort. The first is restricted to removing flaws that are clearly the result of damage after the photo was made (for example, spots and stains). In expert work with graphics software, the second approach, involving a debatable manipulation of the photo, can make faded parts visible and also adjust tonality here and there. The third approach, which is highly moot, can in some parts complete an image presumed to have once been there (but now gone, owing, for example, to a spot worn through, a broken-off corner, emulsion that has peeled off). With Drtikol's negatives the first approach was used, whereby some photos required three to five hours each to be cleaned digitally. Work with curves was done in a way that got the maximum information out of the photograph while corresponding to what was assumed to have been Drtikol's ideas about photography. In this case manipulation is also highly debatable. A photograph printed in a book is of course always an interpretation and, owing to the nature of printing, is different from the original.

Digitally removing obviously later accretions from photographs is a sign of respect to the photographer, who would not have shown his or her work with scratches or cracks. Retouching was an integral part of the craft. Employing it with sensitivity is a duty, as is the proper storage of the photograph in a clean environment with the proper temperature and humidity. Meeting the highest international standards, this work is now being done for Drtikol's negatives.

Pavel Scheufler

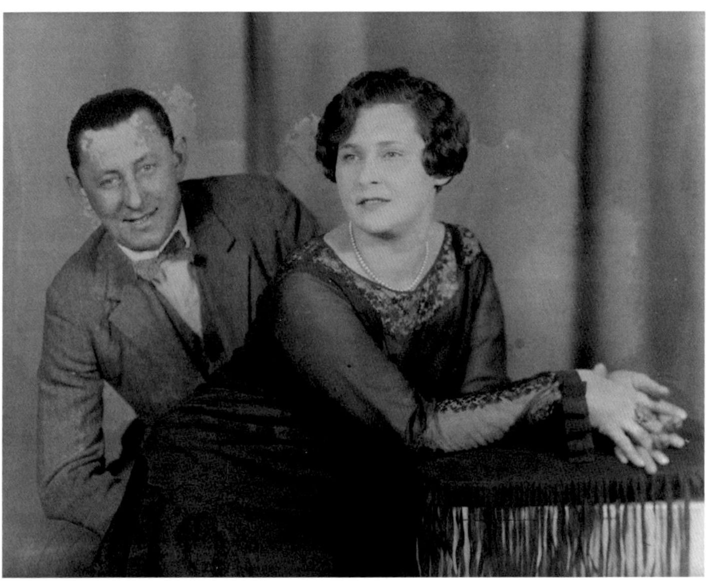

Vlasta Burian with his wife Nina – un-retouched photograph / neretušovaná fotografie

Digitalizace negativů Františka Drtikola

Podkladem vyobrazení v přítomné knize jsou skleněné velkoformátové negativy uložené v Národním archivu v Praze. Vzhledem k velikosti desek nebylo možno využít digitalizačních metod tam užívaných a bylo přistoupeno k externí spolupráci. Podmínkou bylo, že digitalizace se musí provádět přímo v archivu. Jakákoli manipulace a zejména pak transport skleněné negativy ohrožuje. Přivezl jsem speciální prosvětlovací pult s rovnoměrným osvětlením a nad pult na stojan umístil fotoaparát Hasselblad D2 s digitální zadní stěnou Imacon s 22 miliony pixelů. Kvalita expozice se řídila a kontrolovala na notebooku. Negativ byl tedy ofotografován, což považuji za vůči negativu šetrnější a také časově úspornější metodu digitalizace než skenování skleněného negativu na plošném skeneru. Výsledný RGB snímek při 16 bitech na kanál měl 130 MB, pro účely publikace byl posléze převeden do šestnáctibitové šedé škály.

Vlastní digitalizace byla jen první etapou práce. Negativy byly většinou nesmírně poškozené manipulacemi a nevhodným uložením v minulosti. Byly poškrábané, jak se o sebe třely, na mnohých byly drobné tečky a povlaky vzniklé z různých příčin, od organických typu zaschlých skvrn po plísních k zplodinám vzniklých vlivem nedostatečného ustálení. Je zřejmé, a bylo to možné v některých případech srovnat s autorskými pozitivy, že autor by

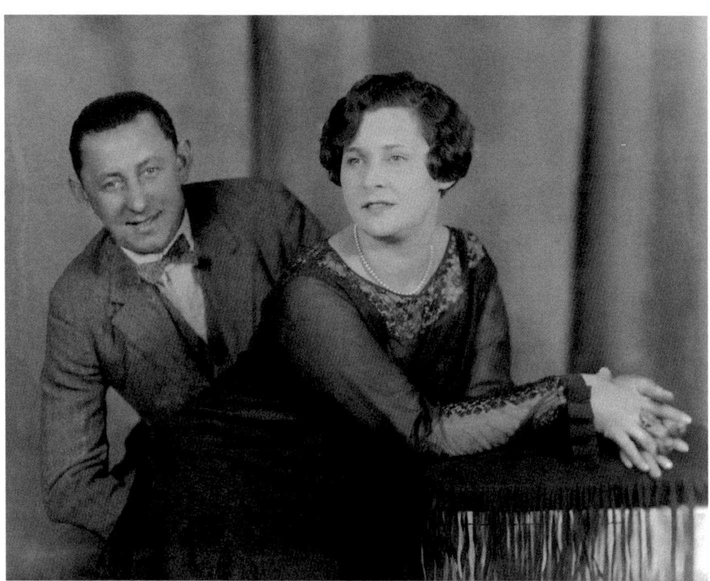

Vlasta Burian s chotí Ninou – retušovaná fotografie / retouched photograph

takto poškozená díla nikdy neprezentoval. V tomto případě tvrdím, že obrazy mají právo na svůj bývalý lesk, což zdůrazňují například i stoupenci očištění Mony Lisy (zatímco odpůrci poukazují na obrazy, které po vyčištění vypadají uměle, třeba jako produkty Cecil B. DeMille, který vytvářel pseudohistorické velkofilmy).

Míra zásahů do historických snímků je vždy problematická. Je jisté, že fotografie, které vzešly z ateliérů fotografů 19. a počátku 20. století, měly ve srovnání s dnešním stavem větší brilanci, jasnost, sytost, některé i ostrost. Fakt degradace je třeba vzít v úvahu, ale nelze s ním dělat nic jiného než snímek uložit tak, aby nepokračovala. Při prezentaci snímku v knize je nejodpovědnější ukázat současný stav a nepokoušet se o „vylepšení" fotografického obrazu, i když k tomu dokonalost některých programů pro zpracování fotografií svádí. Úpravy pro tisk se na fotografiích zpravidla provádějí z polygrafických důvodů, zejména vzhledem k tiskovému rastru, typu, jakosti a povrchu papíru a v tomto vztahu mají své plné opodstatnění. Pokud jsou podkladem pro tisk negativy (nebo nové kopie z historických negativů), je situace ještě o něco komplikovanější, protože interpretace původního díla pro tisk může být předmětem větší diskuse.

V zásadě preferuji prezentaci historického fotografického záznamu v podobě, v jaké se zachoval (tedy včetně poškozené emulze, prasklého skla, náletů na okrajích snímku). Jen ve výjimečných zdůvodnitelných případech lze přistoupit k rekonstrukci původního snímku. Samozřejmě, že digitální způsob je v tomto případě velmi efektivní a pomineme-li speciální fotografickou práci v UV záření, RTG záření či s využitím IR záření, také v zásadě jedině možný. Taková rekonstrukce může mít tři základní podoby, přičemž v té první se pouze odstraňují vady vzniklé evidentním poškozením po vzniku snímku (například se vymažou výše zmíněné druhotné skvrny a potřísnění). Ta druhá, která už je diskutabilním zásahem do snímku, může zkušenou prací v grafickém editoru zviditelňovat zašlé partie i třeba lokálně upravit tonalitu. Třetí, která je velmi diskutabilní, může v některých částech doplňovat předpokládaný obraz (u prodření, ulomení rohu, odlouplé emulze…). V případě Drtikolových negativů se prováděl v zásadě onen první stupeň, přičemž u některých snímků jejich digitální vyčištění zabralo 3–5 hodin práce. Práce s křivkami se prováděla takovým způsobem, aby ze snímku bylo zřejmé maximum informací a aby odpovídalo tomu, co můžeme charakterizovat jako autorův názor na fotografii v době vzniku snímku. V tomto případě jde rovněž o velmi diskutabilní zásah, zobrazení fotografie v knize je ovšem vždy její interpretací a z podstaty tisku má jinou povahu než samotný originál.

Digitální čištění fotografií od prokazatelně druhotných nánosů je podle mého názoru projevem úcty vůči fotografovi, který by přece také neprezentoval své dílo se škrábanci a prasklinami. Retuš byla nedílnou součástí řemesla. Její citlivé provedení můžeme chápat i jako svou povinnost, stejně jako uchování snímku v čistotě a v řádných úložných podmínkách. V případě Drtikolových negativů se tak nyní děje na světové úrovni.

Pavel Scheufler

František Drtikol

by Josef Moucha
Photo selection: Josef Moucha
Translation: Derek & Marzia Paton
Graphic concept: Studio Najbrt, Prague
Graphic design: Pavel Lev & Klára Stíbalová, Studio Najbrt
Lithography: Art D, Prague
Digitization: Pavel Scheufler
Printed by Trico, Prague
Copy editors: Jan Šulc, Lenka Urbanová, and Derek Paton
Published by TORST with the National Archives, Prague
Address: Opatovická 24, Prague 1
CZ-110 00, Czech Republic
foto@torst.cz
First edition, 2007

Also available through D. A. P./Distributed Art Publishers
155 Sixth Avenue, 2nd Floor, New York, N.Y. 10013, USA
Tel: ++1 (212) 627-1999 Fax: ++1 (212) 627-9484